PARTY SCHOOL

THE NORTHEASTERN SERIES
ON GENDER, CRIME, AND LAW

Editor: Claire Renzetti

For a complete list of books available in this series, please visit www.upne.com

Karen G. Weiss, *Party School: Crime, Campus, and Community*

Claire M. Renzetti and Sandra Yocum, editors, *Clergy Sexual Abuse: Social Science Perspectives*

Taryn Lindhorst and Jeffrey L. Edleson, *Battered Women, Their Children, and International Law: The Unintended Consequences of the Hague Child Abduction Convention*

Edward W. Gondolf, *The Future of Batterer Programs: Reassessing Evidence-Based Practice*

Jessica P. Hodge, *Gendered Hate: Exploring Gender in Hate Crime Law*

Molly Dragiewicz, *Equality with a Vengeance: Men's Rights Groups, Battered Women, and Antifeminist Backlash*

Mary Lay Schuster and Amy D. Propen, *Victim Advocacy in the Courtroom: Persuasive Practices in Domestic Violence and Child Protection Cases*

Jana L. Jasinski, Jennifer K. Wesely, James D. Wright, and Elizabeth E. Mustaine, *Hard Lives, Mean Streets: Violence in the Lives of Homeless Women*

Merry Morash, *Women on Probation and Parole: A Feminist Critique of Community Programs and Services*

Drew Humphries, *Women, Violence, and the Media: Readings in Feminist Criminology*

Gail A. Caputo, *Out in the Storm: Drug-Addicted Women Living as Shoplifters and Sex Workers*

Michael P. Johnson, *A Typology of Domestic Violence: Intimate Terrorism, Violent Resistance, and Situational Couple Violence*

Susan L. Miller, editor, *Criminal Justice Research and Practice: Diverse Voices from the Field*

Jody Raphael, *Freeing Tammy: Women, Drugs, and Incarceration*

Kathleen J. Ferraro, *Neither Angels nor Demons: Women, Crime, and Victimization*

Michelle L. Meloy, *Sex Offenses and the Men Who Commit Them: An Assessment of Sex Offenders on Probation*

Amy Neustein and Michael Lesher, *From Madness to Mutiny: Why Mothers Are Running from the Family Courts — and What Can Be Done about It*

Jody Raphael, *Listening to Olivia: Violence, Poverty, and Prostitution*

Cynthia Siemsen, *Emotional Trials: Moral Dilemmas of Women Criminal Defense Attorneys*

Lori B. Girshick, *Woman-to-Woman Sexual Violence: Stories of Women in Prison*

KAREN G. WEISS

PARTY

Crime,
Campus,
and
Community

Northeastern University Press Boston

Northeastern University Press
An imprint of University Press of New England
www.upne.com
© 2013 Northeastern University
All rights reserved
Manufactured in the United States of America
Designed by Mindy Basinger Hill
Typeset in Minion Pro by Walton Harris

University Press of New England is a member
of the Green Press Initiative. The paper used
in this book meets their minimum requirement
for recycled paper.

For permission to reproduce any of the material
in this book, contact Permissions, University Press
of New England, One Court Street, Suite 250,
Lebanon NH 03766; or visit www.upne.com

Library of Congress Cataloging-in-Publication Data

Weiss, Karen G.
Party school : crime, campus, and community / Karen G. Weiss.
pages cm — (The Northeastern series on gender, crime, and law)
Includes bibliographical references and index.
ISBN 978-1-55553-795-1 (cloth : alk. paper) —
ISBN 978-1-55553-819-4 (pbk. : alk. paper) —
ISBN 978-1-55553-820-0 (ebook)
1. College students—Alcohol use—United States. 2. College students—
Drug use—United States. 3. College students—United States—
Social conditions. 4. College environment—United States. I. Title.
LA229.W425 2013
378.1'980973—dc23   2012047685

5   4   3   2   1

Contents

Preface ix

Acknowledgments xi

Introduction: Welcome to the Party School xiii

OVERVIEW
1. Situating the Party School 3
2. Contextualizing the Party Lifestyle 14

PARTY UNIVERSITY: A CASE STUDY
3. Introducing Party University 27
4. Playing Hard: Students' Drinking and Drug Routines 38
5. Getting Wasted: Extreme Party Rituals and Risks 54
6. Flirting with Danger: Criminal Consequences
   of the Party Subculture 73
7. Party Disturbances: Secondhand Harms
   to Campus and Community 99
8. Rationales in Defense of the Party Subculture 115

Conclusion: Sobering Reflections of the Party School 132

Appendix A. Research Methods 151
Appendix B. Data Tables 161
Appendix C. Student Conduct Code and Regulations 181
Appendix D. Official Crime Statistics for Party University
and Ptown 195

Notes 201
Works Cited 211
Index 221

Preface

When I first arrived to teach at a so-called party school, I experienced a bit of culture-shock. Having previously taught at urban commuter colleges, I was unprepared for life at a large residential university located in an isolated college town. But as unnerved as I was on a personal level, as a sociologist and criminologist I was captivated by the unique student culture at my new school. I was especially awed by students' almost cult-like worship of alcohol, the unfathomable amounts of liquor that they claim to drink, their unrelenting passion for getting wasted, and their overwhelming pride toward such "accomplishments." The larger-than-life stories that students gleefully share with one another seemed so out of sync with my own undergraduate experiences, that I couldn't help but be fascinated, if not a bit skeptical. After all, how is it possible that students drink as much as they say they do and still pass their classes? How is it possible that they witness so many fights, fires, and other criminal activities at a school that, officially, has a rather low crime rate? And why do they seem so unconcerned about the negative effects of such extreme partying on their academics and health?

Although the research project presented in this book began as a study of campus crime, by the time I began collecting my data in 2009, it had become clear to me that an investigation of crime at a party school required an in-depth investigation of students' drinking, drug use, and overall "partying," or what I refer to in the book as the party subculture. This student-regulated subculture, existing mostly at night, is an alternative world where otherwise respectful and well-behaved students are encouraged and rewarded for risk-taking, recklessness, and, above all, extreme intoxication. Within the context of a party subculture, failed classes, injuries, and even crime victimization are just "stuff that happens." Meanwhile, students seldom express regret or embarrassment for their own bad behaviors while intoxicated; getting wasted seems to excuse it all. From the outside looking in, the party world seems quite disruptive and even dangerous, but from the perspective of students who participate, it is all rather ordinary. In fact, extreme partying has become so ordinary where I teach that it is easy to lose sight of just how extraordinary it really is in terms of its excesses, its recklessness, and the many problems it causes. Thus, the party school is a unique social environment for a study of crime and deviance, not just because certain violations of law and behavioral norms occur so frequently, but because when violations do occur, they seem so normal to many of the students who attend these schools.

The research presented in this book is my attempt to make sense of the "normativity" of crime and other reckless behaviors within the social milieu of a party school. It is also an attempt to measure empirically the phenomenon of partying, to capture the extremities of the party lifestyle, and to understand its impact on crime, disorder, and life more broadly on campus and in the surrounding communities. It does so by allowing students to describe for themselves their experiences and perceptions of their lives at the party school. I leave it up to readers to make their own judgments as to the normativity of it all.

Acknowledgments

This book could not have been written without the cooperation and assistance of numerous students over the years, all of whom have provided me with invaluable insight and a much greater understanding of their lives outside of the classroom. Therefore, I would like to express my gratitude to all of the students who have shared quite candidly their anecdotal experiences, excuses, and exploits related to their participation in the party subculture. Such stories have both inspired and guided the research utilized in this book.

I would especially like to thank my undergraduate research assistants Kayla Carter, Chris Peterson, Anthony Zungri, and Lynsie Doty, whose hard work and insights were particularly helpful in shaping this project. I am also grateful for my sociology and anthropology colleagues, whose encouragement of this endeavor and shared anecdotes of their experiences working at a party school further shaped and motivated my work. I also thank Bonnie Fisher and John Foubert for their very helpful reviews of the book, and Phyllis Deutsch, my conscientious editor at UPNE, for patiently guiding me through the process of writing my first book. And, finally, I would like to thank the host University — the school that I refer to in this book by the pseudonym Party University (PU) — for providing the resources and granting me access to a truly unique real-life laboratory for collecting my data.

Introduction

WELCOME TO THE
PARTY SCHOOL

Each year millions of young Americans head off to college with varying aspirations and expectations. For some students, going to college is about learning new ideas; for others it is about training for a specific career; and for some it is a symbolic first step toward achieving the American dream of economic success. But for many students today, going to college is simply what young people do. With no particular ambition or plan of study, college is where many young people go after high school to postpone adult responsibility and "party" for four years. For these students, going to college is as much about "partying" as it is about studying, learning or training for future success.

This book is about partying, the nonacademic hallmark of modern college life, and the crimes and other problems associated with it. Though students party (i.e., drink alcohol and use drugs) to some degree at most residential universities and colleges today, nowhere is the student partier as well represented as at the so-called party school. The party school, the American university most emblematic of a party lifestyle, has captivated the public imagination in recent decades due, in part, to the "party school" lists published every year (most famously by Princeton Review), and the corresponding media images that convey students at these schools as largely drunk, out-of-control and behaving badly. The party school has also captured attention over the years due to the extensive research conducted since the 1980s that has highlighted the problems of binge drinking on the college campus. In contrast to an earlier view of the American university as a safe, idyllic retreat from the vice and grit of the "real" world, the image of student life at the party school, as well as at many large residential universities and colleges in the United States today, is often about vice, victimization, and a much "darker side of the ivory tower" (Sloan and Fisher 2011, p. 31).

The reality of life at the party school lies somewhere in between these divergent images of college as a sheltered oasis or hedonistic hot spot for decadence and crime. The good news is that most colleges today, including the party school, are rather safe in terms of serious crime. Yet there are a disproportionate number of minor crimes and other nuisance problems that occur at the party school, and they can be attributed to its "party subculture," a student-regulated cultural presence at such schools characterized by extreme drinking, drug use, and risk taking. *Party School: Crime, Campus and Community* provides a comprehensive investigation of this party subculture, its linkages to crime and disorder at the party school, and the rationales that defend it all.

This introduction begins the investigation with a brief description of party schools, and "Party University" (PU) in particular, the school that serves as a case study for an in-depth exploration of students' party routines, rituals, and risks at a party school. Also included is an overview of three sociological and criminological theories most relevant to a study of crime and deviance at the party school: routine activities, social learning, and subcultural theory. A fourth theoretical perspective — a situated theory of normativity — is presented as a conceptual framework to help explain the "ordinariness" of students' extreme party behaviors, crime, and misconduct within the context of the party situation. Making sense of the normativity of excessive drinking and risk-taking behavior at the party school is a core objective of this book. The book's other two objectives — to describe the routines and rituals of the party subculture and to identify the risks associated with extreme partying — are also outlined in this chapter, followed by an overview of the research methods used to collect and analyze the data presented in the book. The chapter concludes with a brief summary of each of the book's remaining chapters.

DEFINING THE PARTY SCHOOL

In today's consumer-based marketplace, there is a college for everyone ranging from small religious institutions, specialist colleges, and even virtual (online) schools to large sprawling residential universities. With literally thousands of educational institutions to choose from, selecting the "right" university or college can be an arduous task for prospective students. Helping applicants (and their parents) sort through the myriad options available to them are several published lists that rate schools' academic programs (e.g., "best colleges" from *US News and World Report*) and rank the various dimensions of student life, including a college's overall "party" scene, as captured by "party school" lists, most famously compiled by Princeton Review (a test preparation company) but also published annually by *Newsweek*, *Playboy*, and the *Daily Beast*.

Even though there are at least some students who party (i.e., drink alcohol and use drugs) at most every university and college across the nation, what distinguishes the party school from other colleges is the disproportionate number of students eager to boast of their party-related "accomplishments" in surveys (and beyond). Rankings of party schools are determined primarily by students' own perceptions of how much they and their peers drink alcohol and smoke pot while at college. For instance, the criteria for Princeton Review's popular list of top twenty party schools contrasts students' combined scores for "lots of beer," "lots of hard liquor," "reefer madness" (a measure of how much marijuana is available), and "popularity of fraternities and sororities," to a score for "amount of time students study" (Princeton Review n.d.). A party school label suggests an environment where students party lots and study rarely. And though such labels can be an embarrassment to college administrators, faculty, and some of the students at these so-called party schools, making the party school list is also seen as an achievement by many students at these schools, validating their purpose at college and identities as "partiers." For some students, making it onto a party school list is a self-fulfilling prophecy (i.e., a catalyst for shaping future behaviors based on the expectations associated with a label). Once a college has been labeled a party school, students will try very hard to live up to the image and sustain its legacy as the ultimate school to party.

Although the specific universities and colleges on these party school lists vary from year to year, the types of schools that appear most consistently on them have several things in common. First, most party schools are public or state universities with large undergraduate populations of more than 10,000. Second, these schools tend to be situated on large residential campuses where the majority of undergraduate students live on campus or just off-campus in geographically isolated "college towns." With little else to do in these isolated college towns, and with easy access to countless bars and liquor stores near campus, drinking has become the primary extracurricular activity for many students living at these schools (Sperber 2000; Wechsler and Wuethrich 2002).

A third characteristic of party schools is that a large percentage of the undergraduates at these schools are "traditional students," aged eighteen to twenty-four. Traditional students are primarily full-time students who live at college during the academic year and tend to have fewer financial obligations than older and "nontraditional" college students, as they are more likely to be supported financially by parents who pay for at least part of their tuition and living expenses. Although many traditional students work at jobs during their semesters, few work more than twenty hours a week (Seaman 2005). Therefore, traditional students generally have more time and opportunity to party while at college.

A fourth characteristic of party schools is that a sizeable percentage of students at such schools (10–20 percent) are involved in Greek life, an association that is itself linked to greater amounts of partying (Hickson and Roebuck 2009; Tewksbury and Mustaine 2003). A final characteristic of party schools is their sports orientation. A large proportion of students at almost all party schools are avid sports fans and exhibit an exceptionally strong pride toward their school's sports teams. In fact, many students choose party schools for their nationally recognized, if not nationally ranked, football and basketball teams. And like the association between Greek life and partying, there is a well-documented connection between sports and excessive drinking at college. Studies have found that students at schools where sports are a central component of student life tend to drink alcohol more frequently and have higher rates of binge drinking than students at other types of schools (Nelson and Wechsler 2003; Sperber 2000; Wechsler and Wuethrich 2002). In fact, drinking at sports-oriented colleges is so common that students who abstain are often marginalized. In Sperber's *Beer and Circus*, a book about the connections between alcohol and sports on the college campus, there is a quote from a university official who jokingly suggests that at his sports-oriented school it is easier for students to come out as gay than as nondrinkers (165). With drinking at these schools seen as the norm, abstinence becomes an alternative lifestyle choice.

INTRODUCING PARTY UNIVERSITY

This book takes readers inside the world of the party school by exploring one such school, Party University (PU), a pseudonym used to maintain the anonymity of the university, its students, and the surrounding community. PU is a real school and bona fide party school, having earned a top spot on Princeton Review's party school list for several years in a row. PU is also an exemplary case study for an examination of the party school, as it encompasses each of the structural and cultural elements that comprise the typical party school, including size, geography, proportion of traditional students, visible Greek presence, sports orientation, and a resounding pride for both sports and the party lifestyle. Though no two schools are exactly alike, findings from PU are generalizable to other party schools, and allow for a meaningful and much broader investigation of life at the American party school.

THEORETICAL OVERVIEW

Before delineating the theoretical perspectives used in this book to contextualize the party lifestyle and explain its linkages to crime, it is necessary to first state the obvious: students party at college because it is fun. There is a pleasure element involved in getting wasted (Riemer 1981). Intoxication offers drinkers an escape from reality and gives them permission to be free spirited, adventurous, unpredictable, and unencumbered by many of the rules by which they are expected to abide while sober. Since "intoxicated selves" care less about what others think, drinking alcohol also frees students to take more social risks with less inhibition or remorse (Vander Ven 2011, p. 66). In this manner, partying at college is a simple rational choice by which students weigh the reward of partying (i.e., it is fun) to potential risks that they most likely assume to be rather low.

But even while acknowledging that alcohol and drug use can be fun (and well worth the risks), this simple truism cannot explain the variations among students' partying routines or the different rates of harms experienced by students while partying. Nor does a "drinking is fun" mantra explain why students may continue to party long after experiencing negative consequences (i.e., it is no longer fun). These are the questions that require theoretical explanations that take into consideration the important social forces that may influence participation in a party subculture and its risks.

This book incorporates three broad theories from sociology and criminology — routine activities, social learning, subcultural theory — that best address why students party at college to the extent that they place themselves and others at risk of harm. A fourth more interpretive perspective — a situated theory of normativity — is also used in this book to help explain the normativity of extreme drinking, risk-taking behavior, and "intoxicated crime" at the party school. Each of these theoretical perspectives is examined below.

Routine Activities Theory

Routine activities theory, a popular theory for explaining victimization risk, suggests that what people do and how they spend their time affects their chances of becoming victims (Cohen and Felson 1979; Fisher, Daigle, and Cullen 2010; Miethe and Meier 1990). More specifically, the theory argues that certain routines, lifestyles, and environments provide greater opportunities for crime to occur based on the convergence of motivated offenders, attractive targets (i.e., potential victims) and an absence of capable guardians such as police and witnesses (Fisher and Wilkes 2003; Kuehnle and Sullivan 2001).

Applying the concepts of a routine activities theory to the college environment suggests that students will be at greater risk of crime based on how they spend their time. One particular way in which students spend their time at the party school — "getting wasted" — may especially increase student risk for campus crime. For instance, research has shown that a large proportion of college crime takes place when offender, victim, or both participants have been drinking alcohol (Mustaine and Tewksbury 2007; Sloan, Fisher, and Cullen 1997; Tewksbury and Mustaine 2003). From a routine activities perspective, these "intoxication crimes" can be explained in the following ways. First, alcohol dulls awareness of dangerous situations and slows reaction time, meaning that persons who are inebriated are more vulnerable to attacks and unable to resist them once underway (Dowdall 2007; Mustaine and Tewksbury 2007; Tewksbury and Pedro 2003). Second, persons who consume alcohol tend to be more careless, reckless, impulsive, and aggressive, which collectively makes intoxicated persons more likely to cause and get into trouble. By increasing excitability, and reducing a person's ability to reason or interpret others' actions calmly and rationally, alcohol is a common factor leading to physical altercations (i.e., fights) (Harford, Wechsler, and Muthen 2003).

Third, intoxication makes persons less effective witnesses or capable guardians during and after crime. For instance, when persons are drunk, they are less able to intervene in a positive manner to stop crime or to get help for persons in need. Intoxicated persons may also have poor recall of important details about crime incidents afterward, reducing their potential to help police in identifying offenders or solving crimes. And, of course, persons who drink under the legal age of twenty-one or use illicit drugs may refuse to cooperate with the police in order to avoid getting into trouble themselves.

Finally, persons who drink alcohol or use drugs tend to do so in environments that place them within close proximity to motivated offenders (often intoxicated themselves). Such crime-prone environments, commonly referred to as "hot spots," also tend to have insufficient regulation or social control that increases the potential for intoxication crimes (Robinson and Roh 2007). For instance, college students who spend a lot of time at party-related hot spots such as bars, clubs, or house parties, or live near such hot spots, are at greater risk of crime victimization (Brower and Carroll 2007; Mustaine and Tewksbury 2007; Robinson and Roh 2007). Taken together, "routine" intoxication, the time spent with others who routinely get wasted, and the time spent in party hot spots, will increase risks of crime victimization at the party school.

Social Learning Theory

A second theoretical perspective that helps to explain the empirical linkages between students' party behaviors and crime victimization risk is based broadly on social learning theories that focus on socialization and how people learn appropriate behavior for different situations. Concepts based on Sutherlands's classic theory of differential association (1939) and the ideas of differential reinforcement (Burgess and Akers 1966) are especially relevant for explaining how persons "learn" behaviors that violate laws and other conduct codes. Differential association suggests that persons learn the techniques and attitudes favorable for committing crime from the persons with whom they associate most frequently (Shinew and Parry 2005). Differential reinforcement emphasizes the importance of receiving reward or positive sanctions from the persons who are most significant in their lives (e.g., parents, intimate partners, peers). Taken together, differential association and reinforcement suggest that crime and recklessness (including binge drinking and drug use) are learned behaviors that are positively encouraged by close and significant associates (especially peers) even as they may be discouraged by the larger society.

Within a college setting, endorsement of extreme partying by one's peer group is an especially important socializing influence and a primary predictor of binge drinking. For instance, in their study of college drinking, Durkin, Wolfe, and Clark (2005) argue that students are more likely to binge drink when they have friends who also binge drink. Mustaine and Tewksbury (2007) found that belonging to close-knit peer groups such as fraternities or athletic groups increases binge drinking based on the encouragement and positive reinforcement of such behavior by group members. Moreover, drinking and drug use become primary group activities that bond group members together via highly ritualized and shared intoxication experiences.

Peer groups are also responsible for indoctrinating new students at college into the party lifestyle. This indoctrination includes techniques for how to drink "successfully (e.g., how to drink mid-week and still do well in class, where to buy alcohol when underage, how to avoid underage drinking citations) and how to minimize risks and the negative effects of extreme intoxication. Drawing upon Howard Becker's classic study of marijuana smoking as a learned process, Vander Ven (2011, p. 7) argues that binge drinkers at college learn techniques for extreme drinking that include how to "manage" intoxication by reframing some of the unpleasant aspects of intoxication, such as hangovers and nausea, in more favorable ways. Part of this reframing process involves learning appropriate rationales that students can use to neutralize the harms they experience ("it was no big deal"; "stuff happens") and excuse bad behaviors while intoxicated. From a social learning perspective, getting wasted at college is a collaborative process that is shaped, regulated, managed, neutralized, and reinterpreted as a harmless, mostly pleasurable, and rather normal activity.

Subcultural Theory

A third theoretical perspective — subcultural theory — is particularly helpful for understanding students' varied participation in the party subculture and corresponding risks associated with membership. Within sociology, subcultures are seen as groups with their own distinct customs, values, norms, and language (Thompson and Hickey 1999, pp. 83–85). Subcultural groups provide members with a sense of identity and bond them together by shared beliefs, values and interests. While most of these groups are rather conventional (e.g., boy scouts, work-related associations, fraternal groups such as the Elks), others may be considered much more "deviant" (e.g., gangs, religious cults) with members exhibiting behaviors that reject or contradict the values and norms of conventional society. But participation in these so-called deviant groups is rarely a complete rejection of dominant culture. Rather, commitment and involvement in subcultures are generally part-time and temporary, with most participants drifting back and forth between the subculture and dominant (conventional) culture (Bynum and Thompson 2005; Fox 1987). Members decide for themselves just how much time to devote to the subculture and how much time to engage in more conventional activities and pursuits.

Subcultures — both conventional and deviant — can be found in all facets of American society, and researchers have long recognized their presence on the college campus (Clark and Trow 1966; Sperber 2000, Vander Ven 2011). One of the most enduring typologies of undergraduate subcultures at college by Clark and Trow (1966), identifies four coexisting groups: *academics*, who emphasize serious academic effort, hard work, and getting good grades; *vocationals*, whose off-campus family or work responsibilities prevent them from actively participating in either an academic or social life on campus; *rebels*, made up of nonconformists detached from college life and searching for identities beyond their student roles; and *collegiates*, who prioritize social activities over academic endeavors. Clark and Trow describe the collegiate subculture as "a world of football, fraternities and sororities, dates, drinking and campus fun" (as cited in Sperber 2000, p. 3). They further distinguish the groups by suggesting that academics, above all, seek knowledge; vocationals seek a diploma; rebels pursue an identity; and collegiates pursue fun (as cited in Sperber 2000, p. 11).

Though all of these groups exist at the party school, the two most prominent groups by far are the academics, who comprise the conventional student culture focused on educational pursuits, and the collegiates, who participate most enthusiastically in what is referred to in the present book as the *party subculture*. At the party school, students navigate between these two worlds, striking a balance that works best for their own priorities. While more academically focused students will apportion only a small amount of time to the party subculture, more party-centric students will devote a much greater amount of time to a "partier" role. For the most extreme or hardcore devotees of the party subculture, studying and classes may become almost optional activities, as partying can consume almost all of their attentions. For these partiers, membership in the party subculture may provide them with a sense of identity and purpose for being at college. These are also the partiers who are the most stalwart defenders of the party school; they proselytize on its behalf and, like most zealots committed to a cause, are often unaware (or unconcerned) of how their extreme party behaviors impact the college or community.

Examining students at a party school in terms of their commitment to the party subculture allows for a more comprehensive investigation of the variations in students' party routines, rituals, and risks of crime victimization and other harms. It also allows for a comparison of partier types by student characteristics, experiences and perceptions of life at the party school. Finally, it allows for an examination of how students negotiate between their academic and partier roles, and how they determine for themselves when it is time to disassociate all together from the party subculture.

A Situated Theory of Normativity

Even as the three theoretical perspectives outlined above are helpful for elucidating students' party routines and their impact on victimization risk, they can not adequately explain why excessive drinking, drug use and party-related crime have become such a normative part of college life. Understanding the centrality of the party subculture at a party school requires a more interpretive approach that emphasizes the situational mutability of definitions of crime and criminal misconduct. An interpretive or situational perspective, most common among social constructionists (Best 1990; 1999; Reinarman2006) and symbolic interactionists (Blumer 1969; Hewitt 1988; O'Brien 2006), emphasizes the fluidity of definition and suggests that what is considered normal or normative is often relative. In other words, behavior can be condemned, tolerated or even admired, all dependent upon a specific situation and the expectations of the audience.

An investigation of students' behaviors at a party school requires such a perspective. For instance, by day, even the most hardcore partiers are expected to attend classes (at least occasionally), take tests, write assignments, and meet with professors as necessary — all norms of the conventional academic culture. Few students would think it appropriate to show up for class drunk or high on drugs, be disrespectful to professors, vandalize school property, or get into fights with their classmates in the middle of the day. But at night, particularly during weekends, these same bad behaviors are reinterpreted as much more acceptable and even normal, at least among partying students and their peers.

The importance of situation in determining normativity of behavior is not just applicable on the individual level but also on the institutional level. For instance, a party subculture that celebrates excessive drinking and risk-taking behaviors may be considered much more acceptable at a party school than at an academically rigorous or religious-oriented school. This is not to say that everyone at a party school embraces the values or norms of a party subculture. In fact, there are many non-partiers at these schools who neither party nor approve of excessive partying by their peers. However, even as not all students participate in the party subculture, there is generally an acceptance or at least tolerance of partying behavior at these schools (i.e., as just what college students do). Moreover, at a party school, it is typically the non-partiers who are marginalized and who must rearrange their lives in order to avoid or accommodate the party subculture. By making such accommodations, the party subculture is inadvertently perpetuated as the dominant culture, with nonparticipants seen as engaging in deviant or alternative lifestyles.

THE BOOK'S OBJECTIVES

Party School: Crime, Campus, and Community has three primary objectives. First, it describes students' drinking, drug routines, and other party rituals by identifying the types of partiers at the party school. Not all students at a party school "party," and not all students who party do so to such extremes. Instead, many students party moderately and many students participate only temporarily, "aging out" or reducing their involvement in the party subculture for other reasons. This book explores the variations of partying behaviors among students and compares partier types by students' characteristics, associations, and routines. A second objective of this book is to look at victimization risks and other harms associated with the party lifestyle, including injuries, illnesses, and criminal consequences experienced by students who party and *caused* by them. A third objective of this book is to examine students' perceptions of the party subculture and their rationales in defense of it. As students minimize the negative consequences related to the party lifestyle and excuse the reckless and sometimes criminal conduct of their intoxicated peers, they perpetuate the normativity of extreme drinking, drug use and the problems these behaviors often cause for the campus and community.

RESEARCH METHODS

The data used in this book draw primarily from the Campus Crime Victimization Survey (CCVS), a survey distributed to a random sample of undergraduate students at Party University (PU) in Spring 2009. Additional data for the book were collected in Spring 2011 based on a revised CCVS (CCVSr) and semistructured interviews using convenience samples of undergraduate PU students. Each of these three research methods are described briefly below, starting with the original CCVS. (See appendix A for more detail on each method.)

Campus Crime Victimization Survey (CCVS)

The CCVS is a self-administered survey implemented in spring 2009 at Party University (PU), a large public university with an undergraduate population of approximately twenty-two thousand. The overall objective of the survey was to investigate crime victimization on campus, especially as it relates to students' drinking and drug use. Drawing from a random sample of five thousand undergraduate students, the CCVS measured crime victimization on and near the college campus, and gathered details on the context and consequences of these crimes. The survey also gathered information on students' drinking, drug routines, and various consequences (e.g., health, criminal, and legal) that students attributed to intoxication.

Students participated in the CCVS via an invitation by e-mail that provided them with a link connecting them to the survey questionnaire in SurveyMonkey, a user-friendly Web-based survey program that allows respondents to navigate easily through a series of questions. The final survey instrument, launched in late April 2009, consisted of approximately three hundred closed-ended questions with predetermined response categories. Some of the closed-ended questions required respondents to choose only one answer, while others allowed them to "click all that apply." There were also two open-ended questions at the end of the survey that allowed students to respond in their own words. One question asked respondents to add any additional comments regarding their experiences with crime while at college that had not already been covered in the survey. A second question asked respondents to comment on their perceptions of police and overall campus safety.

The final CCVS sample used for analysis in this book consists of 787 undergraduate students, aged eighteen to twenty-four. This sample was filtered to exclude students older than twenty-four in order to focus on traditional students, who are most likely to participate in the party subculture. The mean age of the filtered sample is 20.63. Sixty-three percent of the sample are females and 37 percent are males. Moreover, 93 percent of the sample are white, only 4 percent are Latino, and almost all (99 percent) are U.S. citizens. (See appendix A for more information on sampling, and see appendix B, table 1 for sample descriptives.)

Revised Campus Crime Victimization Survey (CCVSr)

In spring 2011, the original CCVS was revised by adding an additional thirty open-ended questions related to party rituals and related consequences. The revised survey was distributed to a smaller convenience sample of mostly upper-division sociology and criminology students ($n = 97$). Findings from this study were used primarily as descriptive anecdotes to illustrate the quantitative findings from the original CCVS. Like the original CCVS, students received an invitation to participate in the revised survey via an e-mail with a link that connected them to the survey questionnaire in SurveyMonkey. Though not a random sample, the students who participated in this revised survey adequately represent PU's traditional undergraduate population in regard to sex, race, and other basic demographic variables.

Interviews

In addition to the survey responses from the CCVS and CCVSr, data used in this book also come from semistructured student interviews conducted in late spring 2011 and based on a small snowball sample of twenty students (half were self-identified partiers and half were non-partiers). The overall objective of these interviews was to investigate more thoroughly students' drinking rituals (e.g., pregaming, tailgating) and their perceptions of the party subculture, both good and bad. It also examined students' assessments of the risks and consequences of their participation in the party subculture. These interviews were tape recorded, transcribed, and analyzed according to predetermined themes (e.g., perceptions of safety, party identity). Excerpts from these interviews (cleaned up) are used in the book to provide richer descriptions of students' party experiences, perceptions, and rationales in defense of the party subculture.

A second but related interview project (for use primarily in a future project on neighborhood conflict and disorder) was conducted via a focus group of five nonstudent residents of "Ptown," the town that hosts PU. The objective of this focus group was to learn more about the impact of the party subculture on the surrounding neighborhoods near PU, and to explore the social interactions and conflicts between students and nonstudent residents. A small portion of the dialogue from these nonstudent residents is included in chapters 7 and 8 of this book.

Limitations of the Research

Two potential limitations of the data used in this book should be noted. (See appendix A for a much more detailed elaboration of sample biases and other possible research limitations.) First, crime frequencies drawn from CCVS findings should be read with caution due to the possibility that students who had experienced crime during their time at PU may have been more motivated to respond to a crime survey, thereby resulting in an overrepresentation of crime victims in the final sample.

Second, as all survey and interview data is dependent upon respondents' accuracy and honesty, it is possible that the frequencies of routines and crimes reported in the book reflect either an underreporting of certain behaviors that respondents may not have been comfortable talking about (e.g., sexual victimization, drug use), or an overreporting of behavior that they may be particularly eager to boast about (e.g., drinking routines and rituals). Furthermore, it is possible that the incidents that students describe in vivid detail in many of their open-ended responses are merely exaggerations of how partiers are expected to behave at a party school. However, since it is mostly students' hyperbole that sustains PU's reputation as a party school, it seemed appropriate to let their sometimes larger-than-life responses represent and even allegorize life at a party school, regardless of whether these responses accurately reflect "reality."

ORGANIZATION OF THE BOOK

The remainder of this book is organized into three parts, beginning with an overview in chapters 1 and 2 of the structural and cultural characteristics of American universities and colleges in order to better situate the party school among the thousands of institutions of higher learning in the United States. More specifically, chapter 1, "Situating the Party School," looks at the spatial and structural characteristics of college campuses and college towns, and delineates what is currently known about crime at U.S. universities and colleges based on official crime statistics (i.e., Clery Statistics). Chapter 2,

"Contextualizing the Party Lifestyle," provides an overview of the cultural climate at residential universities and colleges, specifically exploring what is currently known about students' drinking and drug routines from prior research studies. The chapter also provides an overview of crime and secondhand harms related to the party lifestyle at these colleges.

Chapters 3 through 8 comprise the second and primary section of the book, and provide an in-depth exploration of life at the party school. Chapter 3, "Introducing Party University," introduces the case study — Party University (PU) — that represents the "typical" party school. The chapter provides an overview of PU, its campus, community, conduct codes, and official crime statistics. Chapter 4, "Playing Hard: Students' Drinking and Drug Routines," provides a closer look at students' party routines at the party school, drawing its data from the Campus Crime Victimization Survey (CCVS) and interviews with PU students. Based on students' own responses, the chapter delineates four distinct types of partiers and investigates how students negotiate between their roles as partiers and conventional students. Chapter 5, "Getting Wasted: Extreme Party Rituals and Risks," looks more closely at students' party rituals, including pregaming, party pranks, and couch burning. The chapter also explores some of the harms (e.g., injuries, illnesses) that accompany such extreme rituals. Chapter 6, "Flirting with Danger: Criminal Consequences of the Party Subculture," looks more specifically at students' risks of crime victimization (including property crime, physical attacks/fights and sexual violence) and their increased potential of committing crimes themselves while intoxicated. Chapter 7, "Party Disturbances: Secondhand Harms to Campus and Community," looks at the ways in which students' reckless behaviors while intoxicated negatively affect others, including non-partiers, residents, and the entire campus and community. Finally, chapter 8, "Rationales in Defense of the Party Subculture," examines students' largely ambivalent responses to party-related crimes and secondhand harms. More specifically, the chapter looks at the reasons why students do not report intoxicated crime to police and delineates the rationales they use to minimize harms, excuse their peers' misconduct while intoxicated, condemn students who complain, and more generally defend the party subculture.

The concluding chapter, "Sobering Reflections of the Party School," sums up the core findings from the Campus Crime Victimization Survey (CCVS) and reiterates the theoretical explanations for students' party-related routines, rituals, and consequences at the party school. The chapter also explores the ways in which schools have responded to drinking-related problems and secondhand harms on their respective campuses. The chapter concludes with some suggestions for how to encourage a cultural shift toward more responsible partying. Foremost, it suggests that little will change at today's party school until extreme drinking rituals and risks are no longer encouraged, rewarded, accommodated, and rationalized as a normal part of college life.

OVERVIEW

1

Situating the Party School

Today in the United States there are almost three thousand four-year post-secondary institutions of higher education, enrolling over nine million undergraduate students pursuing bachelor degrees, and more than two million graduate students.[1] American universities and colleges range in size from fewer than a thousand students to over fifty thousand students enrolled at any given time. Some of these schools are public or state-funded, and some are private.[2] Some have sprawling residential campuses, and some are small commuter schools with no on-campus housing. Whatever students' preferences, there is surely a college to fit their needs, from small, private, liberal arts colleges to large, public, sports-oriented "party schools."

This chapter provides an overview of the variations of geography and infrastructure at today's American universities and colleges, and highlights the traits most typical of the American party school. Recall from the introduction that the typical party school (like most of the schools on Princeton Review's list of top twenty party schools) are large four-year public universities with vast residential campuses located in geographically isolated "college towns." The purpose of this chapter is to distinguish the party school from among the thousands of other American universities and colleges. It does so by identifying the structural traits that characterize the type of campus and community most welcoming to a party lifestyle. The chapter concludes by delineating what is currently known about crime at U.S. universities and colleges based on official crime statistics, and explains why these numbers provide only a limited scope of a much larger and mostly "hidden" problem.

THE AMERICAN COLLEGE AND CAMPUS

American universities and colleges are diverse and vary according to many structural aspects, including size of school and enrollment, type of campus (e.g., residential or commuter), location, and whether they are public or private. Today's four-year institutions of higher education range in size from admitting fewer than one thousand students to more than fifty thousand, with schools that enroll ten thousand students or more accounting for well over half of total college enrollment (Knapp et al. 2011). Most large universities with enrollments over ten thousand consist of several colleges, usually distinguished by their academic emphasis (e.g., law, engineering, arts and sciences), and are typically spread out upon one or more sprawling campuses. The campuses of these large universities are often open to the general public, and many are integrated into the surrounding communities with no clear boundaries separating university property from the bordering neighborhoods. In contrast, smaller colleges are often situated on more compact campuses, are much more restrictive about access, and usually have clear signage identifying the boundaries of the campus and separating college-owned roads and facilities from public streets (Bromley 2007).

U.S. universities and colleges also vary greatly in terms of geographic location, with some schools located in or near densely populated urban or suburban areas, whereas other schools are tucked away in much more remote or rural areas far away from major cities and other large towns.[3] Geography tends to influence whether or not students will commute to school (i.e., travel back and forth to campus for classes) or live on or near campus during the academic year. Geography also influences how often students who live on campus travel home on weekends. For instance, at universities and colleges located farthest away from nearby cities, the majority of students will stay on or near campus during a good part of the academic year. It is at these residential schools, often located in isolated college towns, where students tend to party most and where many of today's party schools are found.

In addition to size and geography, another distinction among American universities and colleges is whether they are public or private. According to the Department of Education's 2010–2011 statistics, just under seven hundred of the three thousand four-year institutions are public institutions, which include research-intensive facilities, land-grant universities (whose primary mission is to serve the state), and regional state universities that focus more on teaching (Gumprecht 2008). Public universities are partially supported by appropriations from the state. And though all public universities were originally established to provide a low-cost education for its own state's residents, many of these public schools now enroll a sizable proportion of students from outside of their home states. In fact, as schools have begun to receive much less of their overall budgets from their respective states, many public universities are beginning to take on much more of an entrepreneurial character that includes a dependence on more external resources such as tuition from out-of-state "consumers."[4] Marketing and promotion of these schools often include heavy recruitment of non-state residents to increase student enrollments and revenues (as they pay higher tuition), and a stepped-up fundraising campaign to solicit money from alumni and other potential donors.

As part of their promotional strategies to attract more students and alumni donations, sports programs have become an especially popular draw for many public universities. Football and basketball games are huge events at many large public universities, financed in part by student fees and gate receipts, and driven by the millions of dollars that schools can collect from television deals to broadcast the games and merchandizing partnerships with companies that produce sports apparel and other collegiate items for sale (Sperber 2000). A high-profile athletic program can help raise the profile of the university, which, in turn, stimulates enrollment, increases alumni donations, and often benefits local neighborhoods by providing taxes and increasing business revenues for local shops. Moreover, athletics can serve to unify the student population and community by providing a common source of pride and identity.

Despite the benefits of college athletic programs, critics have argued that sports have become too big and too important at many universities with little payoff for students (Sperber 2000). For instance, less than a quarter of college sports programs at public universities are profitable after expenses (Wieberg, Upton, and Berkowitz 2012).[5] Moreover, the lure of big money increases the potential of exploitations within college sports programs and the abuses of power, as seen most recently in the Pennsylvania State University sexual abuse scandal where top officials in 2011 were accused of ignoring or covering up incidents of sexual assault by assistant football coach Jerry Sandusky. Though the case is still unfolding, critics allege that the head coach and top administrators failed to report the suspected sexual abuse to police in order to avoid bad press for their football program (Rohan 2012).

Big-budget college sports programs can also cause resentments within the institutions, as top athletic personnel are often paid more than faculty, and head coaches can even earn salaries that exceed what university presidents earn. Moreover, student athletes are often treated as celebrities and given special treatment on campus and in many aspects of their student lives, including "help" to ensure that they pass all their classes (Sperber 2000). Meanwhile, sports events at many schools can dictate the academic calendar, with classes cancelled and campus facilities shut down to accommodate home games and sport-related activities.

Home football games at most sports-oriented universities are spectacular events, drawing thousands of spectators into town to cheer on their teams. Keeping all these fans safe during sports events and directing the traffic flow of these thousands of fans travelling in and out of town to attend these games is no small task and requires a large-scale effort coordinated by university police (Bromley and Territo 1990). Making sure fans are safe and traffic flows smoothly on game days are just a couple of the many functions of the university or campus police.[6] Foremost, the university police are the public face of safety on the college campus. They are responsible for protecting students, faculty, and staff of the university and enforcing laws and university conduct codes.

Depending on the school's size and location, the configuration and extent of the police force on college campuses vary. For instance, most large universities employ an independent police force that provides many of the same services rendered by local police departments in similar sized municipalities. This means that many campus law enforcement officers have the authority to make arrests and carry weapons (Bromley and Territo 1990). According to a special report on campus law enforcement published by the Bureau of Justice Statistics (BJS), almost three-fourth of law enforcement agencies serving four-year colleges with at least twenty-five hundred students have sworn law enforcement personnel that have arrest privileges, and nearly nine in ten agencies with sworn officers use armed patrol officers (see Flowers 2009, p. 59). When comparing public and private schools, these numbers become more pronounced. For instance, nearly all public campuses (93 percent) employ sworn officers, compared to less than half of private campuses (42 percent) (Reaves 2008).[7] Most campus police agencies also have working relationships with local law enforcement in the surrounding communities, with clearly defined mutual aid agreements that ensure cooperation in critical situations (Bromley and Territo 1990; Reaves 2008). Such cooperation is especially important for "porous" campuses where up to 85 percent of students live off campus in surrounding neighborhoods, or "college towns."

Just as college campuses vary considerably, so do the communities that host them. One of the most apparent differences in regard to college communities is the relationship between the college and its immediate neighborhoods. Whereas some colleges are located in cities or towns that barely acknowledge their presence, other schools are a much more integral part of the community. "College towns," where many of America's largest public universities (and most party schools) are located, are communities that would probably not exist without the presence of the university. In most college towns, there is a symbiotic relationship between the university and town, with both highly dependent upon college students for their survival.

According to Gumprecht in his comprehensive book *The American College Town* (2008), college towns are often ranked high on lists of "best places to live" for reasons that include access to cultural amenities reminiscent of small cities; a heterogeneous population in regard to race and ethnicity; and a healthy, youthful, and environmentally conscious population (Gumprecht 2008, p. 13).[8] And with so many of the town's full-time labor force working at the university, college towns are among the most educated places in the United States, with residents twice as likely to possess a college degree than the average American, and six times more likely to have a PhD (Gumprecht 2008). Grumprecht also points out that college towns have relatively low unemployment, due to the university as the single largest employer in town. With so many of its residents dependent upon the college as their primary economic resource, college towns often resemble "company towns," where a large proportion of adults work for a single employer. Working for a solvent university may also explain why college towns are economically stable and insulated from economic downturns. Even in the recent economic recession, most state universities and their college towns held up rather well, some even growing in size and revenue.[9]

Perhaps the most indisputable fact about college towns is that they are exceptionally transient places as compared to most American towns and cities. Students, often comprising from one-third to almost half of the town's population during the academic school year, tend to move frequently during their undergraduate years, and most of them leave the area permanently upon graduation (Gumprecht 2008). Aside from a four- to five-year graduation-based turnover, college town populations ebb and flow according to the academic calendar. For instance, most college towns experience rather sleepy summers as students empty out by mid-May to return to their parents' homes for June, July, and part of August, followed by an influx of students returning back to town in late August for the start of the fall semester. During the course of the academic calendar, there are also two shorter periods of mass student exodus: the first during the winter holiday, and the second during spring break.

To accommodate its student demographics and transience, college towns, especially those that are geographically isolated, tend to have a disproportionate number of rental units. With little choice but to live in town (if not on campus) while attending school, students are a captive clientele for the town's rental industry. And, based on simple supply and demand economics, rental units in college towns can be extremely overpriced. Students often complain that there are not enough "good" rental properties (e.g., clean, safe, walking distance to campus) that are affordable. The high costs and lack of available units force students to double- or triple-up (or worse) in whatever rental properties are available. In fact, residents of college towns are three times more likely than persons in the general U.S. population to share their homes with unrelated roommates (Gumprecht 2008).

Moreover, as enrollments at many public universities continue to increase and exceed the supply of student housing available on and off campus, students are beginning to "invade" formerly designated nonstudent neighborhoods, including the once-exclusive "faculty enclaves" near campus. According to Gumprecht, college towns have historically been segregated, with some of the nicer neighborhoods close to campus reserved for faculty, high-ranking administrators, and wealthier long-term residents. In contrast to faculty enclaves with large, single-family houses and manicured lawns, most student neighborhoods, or "student ghettoes," are dominated by large apartment complexes and older homes carved into multiple rental units. These neighborhoods also tend to have a much more "blighted" physical appearance (Gumprecht 2008). As Gumprecht describes it, student ghettos are characterized by cheaply constructed or dilapidated housing, litter, graffiti, and artifacts of students' unique lifestyle, such as beat-up couches and beer pong tables on front porches, windows covered with newspapers and bedsheets rather than curtains, and empty beer bottles decorating window sills and porch railings (87).[10]

The migration (or invasion) of students into faculty enclaves has been increasing in recent years due, in part, to a trend whereby landlords buy up single-family homes in residential neighborhoods and resection them as multiunit rentals (Gumprecht 2008). For instance, Gumbrecht describes a six-fold increase in rental properties in Newark, home to the University of Delaware where many large homes have been converted into rental units, transforming owner-based neighborhoods into areas of concentrated student rentals with four or five students often sharing a single house (Gumprecht 2008; Wechsler and Wuethrich 2002). Meanwhile, as demand exceeds supply, landlords have fewer incentives for improving their properties to attract or keep renters. Ambivalent landlords who fail to maintain or renovate their properties, coupled with lenient code enforcement from town officials, have contributed to an expansion of blighted neighborhoods in many college towns.

Concerns from property owners about their home values and quality of life in these formerly quiet and family-based neighborhoods are causing resentment and exacerbating conflicts in some neighborhoods between students and nonstudent residents. Though conflict between students and nonstudents in college towns is not new, this most recent "town-gown conflict" is accelerated within a climate of limited resources, with both groups trying to stake a proprietary claim to these neighborhoods. Residents complain that neither landlords nor student renters seem to care about their properties. Moreover, they suggest that there is seldom enough oversight from the city governance to enforce property cleanup or to prevent the ever-growing incidents of disorderly conduct (Gumprecht 2008). For instance, residents living in these newly "mixed" college neighborhoods complain that they are confronted almost daily by noise, litter, and a variety of other disturbances that can range from minor vandalism to arson or parties turned riotous (Seaman 2005; Sperber 2000; Wechsler and Wuethrich 2002). In their book *Dying to Drink*, Wechsler and Wuethrich describe the increase in crime and disorder in a "once-stately neighborhood" near a university in Nevada shortly after its conversion into a mixed neighborhood. According to nonstudent residents living there, students and their parties have become wilder with each passing year, and neighbors who complain to police sometimes find their car windows broken and beer bottles thrown at their houses. Some residents complain of students urinating in their yards. And one neighbor complained that she sometimes finds underwear (e.g., panties, bras, men's shorts) in her yard the morning after all-night student parties (183–84).

With their frustrations mounting, residents in many college towns are beginning to fight back to reclaim their neighborhoods, with some residents seeking legal solutions (e.g., holding landlords accountable for their renters' misconduct) and some adopting more grassroots solutions such as canvassing their neighborhoods and distributing flyers to student residents about "safe and responsible drinking" that summarizes alcohol laws and provides a list of alcohol-free social events (Gumprecht 2008, p. 308). Some residents are working with university administrators and local police to crack down on "house parties." For instance, at Frostburg State University in Maryland, the president has made it a top priority to crack down on boisterous off-campus parties, reaching out to the police to step up patrols (Wilson 2008).

Perhaps the toughest ordinances implemented in some college towns, commonly known as "Animal House Laws," require landlords to begin eviction proceedings against tenants who repeatedly violate "quality-of-life" laws (US State News 2007). Moreover, in Tucson, home to the University of Arizona, tags can be posted on houses where there are frequently loud parties, indicating an "unruly gathering" (Wilkins 2012). A similar ordinance has been passed in communities near the University of Rhode Island, which has also experienced chronic loud parties from college students moving into the area (Tucker 2009). The ordinance in Rhode Island allows police to place a ten-by-fourteen-inch orange sticker on homes where parties of five or more people are creating substantial disturbances (e.g., loud noise, public drunkenness, illegal parking). Stickers that label the house as a nuisance or "locale of unruly gathering" remain up for the duration of the school year. Since 2005, the police have cited more than three hundred homes under the town law aimed at curbing disorderly gatherings (Tucker 2009). Finally, at the University of Delaware (UD) in collaboration with its host town, Newark, residents are now required to obtain a permit for large parties. In addition to the permit, the town has doubled its fines for noise violations, and has amended its housing code to require the eviction of tenants after two disorderly conduct violations (Gumprecht 2008, p. 306). Despite these efforts, students continue to party at UD, and continue to cause disruption and disorder in the neighborhoods.

CRIME AT THE AMERICAN COLLEGE

By most accounts, the American college campus and college town are safe places to live, at least in terms of serious crime. According to prior research, college students experience far fewer serious crimes than other persons of comparable ages (Baum and Klaus 2005; Flowers. 2009). For instance, college students aged eighteen to twenty-four experience a rate of violence at 61 per 100,000 as compared to 75 per 100,000 for nonstudents in the same age group (Baum and Klaus 2005). Additionally, crime on campus, like all crime nationally, has been stable or decreasing slightly over the past decade (Flowers 2009). And though there have been some exceptional cases of violence at postsecondary schools over the years (e.g., Virginia Tech and Northern Illinois shootings, Kent State riots), murders and serious violent crime are anomalies and not reflective of the typical crimes that take place at college (Fisher, Daigle, Cullen, and Turner 2003).[11]

Of course, crime prevalence at universities and colleges vary according to certain structural factors related to campus and community. First, crime rates tend to be higher at schools located in or close to urban environments that themselves have high crime rates. Second, college campuses that are more integrated into the surrounding community and open to the public tend to provide easier access to buildings and cars for motivated thieves (Bromley and Territo 1990; Flowers 2009). Third, and according to a statistical analysis by the National Center for Education Statistics on campus crime, residential four-year institutions report higher rates of both violent and property crimes than other institutions (Lewis, Farris, and Green 1997). For instance, residential college campuses (with 25 percent or more students living in campus housing) report more fights, sexual assaults, larceny theft, and burglary.

The higher rates of crime at residential colleges can be largely explained by students' routines and lifestyles at such schools. For instance, at residential colleges there are a steady flow of young people walking about at night, often drunk, making them more convenient and vulnerable targets for both violent and property crime (Bromley and Territo 1990). Students who spend more time together on campus, living and "playing" together, are also more susceptible to sexual assault and fights, two types of crime most prevalent among persons aged eighteen to twenty-four and typically perpetrated by acquaintances (Fisher et al. 2010). Also, in college towns, there is a mass exodus of students during semester breaks and holidays, which leaves many homes unoccupied and vulnerable to burglary. And, of course, much of the crime at large residential universities can be explained by students' drinking and drug routines that make them more vulnerable to victimization, as well as more responsible for certain types of crimes such as assault, rape, and vandalism. Many of these "intoxication crimes," offenses that occur when victim, offender, or both participants are intoxicated, are "hidden" crimes that are not typically included in official college crime data, such as Clery statistics.

Indeed, much of what is known today about college crime is based on data collected as part of the 1990 Clery Act, also known as the Student Right-to-Know and Campus Security Act. Named after Jeanne Clery, a freshman who was raped and murdered in her dorm room at Lehigh University in 1986, the act requires all colleges that participate in (Title IV) federal aid programs to disclose to the public serious crime that occurs on or near campus (Flowers 2009; Sloan and Fisher 2011; Fisher et al. 2003).[12] More specifically, colleges are required to publish crime statistics for the previous three years, publish policies related to campus security, and disclose criminal activity on campus through public crime logs made available to the public for seven years. Under the act, colleges are also required to disseminate timely warnings about crimes that pose threats to the campus community.[13] Finally, the act requires a disclosure of arrests for violations of liquor, drug, and weapon laws and disciplinary actions taken by the university or college in regard to these student violations.[14] Schools failing to comply with any of the act's mandates risk fines of up to $27,500 per infraction or loss of eligibility to receive federal funds (Flowers 2009).

Though the Clery Act ensures that serious crime that occurs at college is disclosed to the public, there is a lot of crime that takes place at college that remains "hidden" from public scrutiny for the following reasons. First, Clery statistics are limited in regard to the types of crimes it reports. For instance, it includes criminal homicide, rape, robbery, aggravated assault, burglary, motor vehicle theft, and arson, most of the index crimes collected by the FBI's Uniform Crime Reports (UCR). But it does not include larceny, vandalism, or simple assaults, three of the crimes most likely to occur at college (although some colleges voluntarily disclose these numbers on their police websites).

Second, Clery numbers represent only crimes that occur on campus. Many, if not most, of the offenses that take place at college occur off campus in the surrounding communities. According to one study, 93 percent of violent victimization occurs off campus (Baum and Klaus 2005). Although colleges are supposed to include crimes that occur in public areas that "immediately border" and are accessible or "reasonably contiguous" to campus (based on information shared from local police in the surrounding community), it is unclear whether they actually do so (see U.S. Dept. of Education 2011, p. 19).[15]

Finally, like all official crime statistics, Clery data include only incidents known to police. With less than half of crime reported to police in general (Hart and Rennison 2003), official statistics present a rather limited purview of crime. The limitations of official crime numbers may be especially evident in the college setting, where many of the crimes that take place are minor offenses, or misdemeanors that are less likely to be reported to authorities. Moreover, most college crimes are peer-perpetrated, and occur when victim, offender or both participants are intoxicated, circumstances that further complicate students' willingness to report to police. Within the context of the party school, these types of offenses are less likely to be seen as serious, or "real" crimes worth reporting.[16]

SUMMING UP

With thousands of universities and colleges in the United States to choose from, prospective students (and their parents) must consider many factors when choosing the right college for them, including size and location of the school, whether there is an active sports program, and whether they will be able to live on campus or in the surrounding community (often a college town). Another factor that students (or at least their parents) might consider is crime risk. A safe campus and college community provides some peace of mind to both students and parents.

According to official crime data, such as Clery statistics, serious crime at U.S. universities and colleges is rare. However, such statistics provide a rather limited scope of overall crime incidence at college, as they include only certain types of crimes and only incidents known to the police. As will be discussed in the following chapters, most of the criminal incidents that take place at residential universities, and especially at party schools, are offenses that occur within the context of a party situation. Only a small proportion of these student-perpetrated and alcohol-infused offenses (e.g., vandalism, fights, and sexual assaults) are captured in official crime statistics, or for that matter, recognized by students as real or reportable crime. Instead, intoxication crimes are often seen as a rather normal part of life at the party school.

Contextualizing the Party Lifestyle

As described in the previous chapter, American universities and colleges are vastly diverse in terms of size, location, on-campus student housing, sports orientation, and even crime prevalence. Though serious crime is infrequent at most U.S. universities and colleges, minor crime related to alcohol and drug consumption can be rather common at residential universities, especially at schools located in remote and isolated college towns. It is within these encapsulated environments where party schools, characterized by a distinct student lifestyle of heavy drinking, drug use, and reckless behaviors, are most often found.

This chapter looks more closely at the party lifestyle so common among students at four-year residential universities and colleges, and especially emblematic of life at the party school. The chapter begins with an overview of prior research on college students' alcohol and drug consumption and then looks more specifically at the risks of excessive drinking at college, including injuries, illnesses, crime victimization, and arrests. The chapter concludes with an introduction to the concepts of secondhand harms and the negative impact that students' party lifestyle can have on an entire campus and community.

ALCOHOL AND DRUGS: AN OVERVIEW OF PRIOR RESEARCH

Despite students' varied interests and leisure activities while at college (e.g., intramural sports, music, art, theater), the most popular extracurricular activity at most residential universities, and at all party schools, is the consumption of alcohol and experimentation with other drugs. Of course, neither drinking nor drug use at college are modern activities. Research (Seaman

2005; Sloan and Fisher 2011; Sperber 2000; Vander Ven 2011) suggests that alcohol has been part of the college landscape dating back to the origins of the American university in the eighteenth century when "the sons of the rich came to college for four years of pleasure and social contacts" (Sperber 2000, p. 4). Though college drinking is no longer limited to elite male collegians, drinking remains a favorite leisure activity among students who go away to college.

Surely, not all students drink alcohol while at college. Many students abstain from alcohol because they are not yet twenty-one (the minimum legal age to purchase and publicly consume alcohol in all states today).[1] And many students choose not to drink due to personal responsibilities (e.g., jobs, children, or other dependents) or commitments to academic or religious organizations (Vander Ven 2011). Moreover, many students who do use alcohol at college do so in moderation. Still, the majority of traditional college students at most residential universities drink alcohol, and as many as 40 to 60 percent of these students drink frequently and extensively (Wechsler and Nelson 2008). Recall from the introduction that a large percentage of undergraduate students at party schools are "traditional students" aged eighteen to twenty-four who are full-time students living on or near the college campus. Traditional students tend to work fewer hours at jobs and have fewer financial obligations, leaving them more time and inclination to devote to an active party lifestyle centered around beer, harder liquor, and occasional drugs (Sperber 2000; Wechsler and Wuethrich 2002; Wilson 2008). The following section reviews what is currently known about alcohol consumption at college, followed by what is known about drug use, another common albeit much less popular pastime among college students today.

Alcohol Consumption

Studies comparing college students to their non-college peers find that students at college drink more often and in greater quantities than nonstudents (Neal and Fromme 2007; Chen, Dufour, and Yi 2004). National surveys on alcohol and drug use, such as Monitoring the Future (Johnson, O'Malley, Bachman, and Schulenberg 2005), the Core Institute's Alcohol and Drug Survey (Presley and Meilman 1994), the National College Health Risk Behavior Survey (CDC 1997) and the Harvard School of Public Health's College Alcohol Study (CAS) (Wechsler and Wuethrich 2002) show that approximately 80 percent of college students drink alcohol. These and other studies also find that a sizable proportion of students drink with the clear intention of getting drunk (O'Grady, Arria, Fritzelle, and Wish 2008; Neal and Fromme 2007; Tewksbury and Pedro 2003). For instance, according to CAS, two out of five students who drink alcohol at four-year colleges binge drink, which the researchers define as drinking more than five drinks per occasion for men and more than four drinks per occasion for women (Wechsler and Nelson 2008).

Researchers have also found rather consistent patterns regarding the types of students who are most likely to binge drink while at college. For instance, male students tend to drink more frequently and consume greater quantities of alcohol than female students (Wechsler and Wuethrich 2002; Johnson et al. 2005). First-year students have been found to binge drink more than advanced students, due, in part, to their newfound freedom away from parents (Harford, Wechsler, and Seibring 2002). And a few studies have suggested that white and U.S.-born students are more likely to binge drink than nonwhite and international students (Wechsler and Nelson 2008). Age, however, does not seem to matter much in terms of alcohol consumption, despite laws that prohibit persons under twenty-one from buying alcohol. This can be explained by how seemingly easy it is for students under twenty-one to obtain alcohol at most colleges simply by using fake identification, asking older students to purchase liquor for them, or going to parties where alcohol is readily available to anyone willing to pay a small admission fee (Fabian, Tommey, Lenk, and Erickson 2008; Vander Ven 2011).

In addition to demographic variables, there are several behavioral predictors of binge drinking at college that include students' routines and associations. For instance, binge drinking is less prevalent among students who are involved in academic activities outside the classroom and who participate in scholastic organizations and honor societies (e.g., Phi Beta Kappa, Phi Kappa Phi) (Brenner, Metz, and Brenner 2009). Contrarily, binge drinking is more likely among students who live off campus, who go out more frequently to bars and parties, and who associate with groups heavily involved in drinking activities, such as fraternities (Tewksbury, Higgins, and Mustaine 2008). In fact, members of fraternities and sororities have especially high rates of binge drinking as compared to their non-Greek counterparts (Durkin et al. 2005; Mustaine and Tewksbury 2004; Hickson and Roebuck 2009; Wechsler and Wuethrich 2002). These group differences can be explained, in part, by the drinking rituals embedded within the subculture of Greek life, including recruitment and initiation (Kimmel 2008).

Many Greeks also live in fraternity or sorority housing that increases the opportunity to drink with minimal supervision, at least relative to on-campus housing (Scott-Cheldon, Carey, and Carey 2008). Fraternity house parties have become a primary locale for binge drinking on campus for both Greeks and non-Greeks, even though "open parties" that allow anyone access are now prohibited at some colleges (Gumprecht 2008; Sperber 2000). However, most fraternity members consider such regulations a nuisance, not a deterrent (Gumprecht 2008).[2] Wechsler, a prominent researcher on college binge drinking, suggests that college administrators may look the other way in regard to these parties because they don't want to alienate the Greek alumni donors who fondly remember their own years of college partying (cited in Sperber 2000, p. 160).[3]

College athletes are another group that drinks more heavily and frequently as compared to other students, although drinking patterns are moderated by type of sport and season, with drinking much higher during the off-season for an athlete's respective sport (Brenner et al. 2009; Meilman, Leichliter, and Presley 1999; Simons et al. 2005; Sperber 2000). The relationship between athletics and binge drinking may at first seem counterintuitive, considering the intense training involved in most competitive sports. In fact, social bond theory (Barkan 2012; Hirshi 1969) would suggest that exposure to conventional activities such as sports should *reduce* involvement in risky behavior such as binge drinking, as athletes should be too busy and committed to their sports to participate in activities that could jeopardize athletic performance. However, the connection between athletic participation and alcohol consumption can be explained by a social learning perspective. At college, athletes and their teammates form close-knit groups similar to fraternities, where drinking becomes a significant team "bonding" activity and substantial part of many rituals off the field, such as celebrating wins, initiating new teammates, and even recruitment of new athletes (Brenner et al. 2009). With the encouragement of their peers and their competitive drive, drinking can become its own extreme sport among athletes, as well as among many other peer groups on the college campus.

Drug Use

Illicit drug use is another common leisure activity among college students today, though not nearly as popular as alcohol consumption. While four out of five students use alcohol, approximately one in five students use illicit drugs, with most of their drug usage limited to marijuana. Studies estimate that anywhere from 20–30 percent of college undergraduates use marijuana and from 5 to 14 percent use other drugs, such as cocaine, hallucinogens, amphetamines, and ecstasy (Seaman 2005; Mohler-Kuo, Lee and Wechsler 2003; Mustaine and Tewksbury 2004; CORE Institute 2010). While some research indicates that drug prevalence at college has dropped slightly since its peak in the 1980s (Flowers 2009), other research indicates that marijuana use among college students has been gradually increasing in recent years, due largely to the decriminalization of possessing small amounts of the drug, and changing perceptions of its harms, reinforced by the recent legalization of marijuana for medical uses in several states (Mustaine and Tewksbury 2004; O'Grady et al. 2008).

Like alcohol, research suggests that the heaviest drug users at college are men, freshman, and students who are least committed to academic pursuits (Mustaine and Tewksbury 2004). Students who live off campus are also more likely to use drugs than their on-campus counterparts, most likely because there are more opportunities to buy and use drugs off campus (Mustaine and Tewksbury 2004; Scott-Cheldon et al. 2008).[4] And like alcohol, students' routines and associations play a large role in whether or not they use drugs. For instance, involvement in Greek life increases the potential of drug use (Scott-Cheldon et al. 2008; Grossbard, Hummer, LaBried, Pederson, and Neighbors 2009). Findings from one study show that 57 percent of members of fraternities or sororities had used pot within the past thirty days, as compared to 36 percent of non-Greeks. Moreover, 34 percent of Greeks had used some other illicit drug, as compared to 17 percent of non-Greeks (Scott-Cheldon et al. 2008). Though it is unclear whether these differences are due to their memberships as Greeks or because of housing arrangements that provide greater opportunity to use drugs in a "protective" environment with minimal social control, differences in drug use hold true for both sorority women compared to non-Greek women, and fraternity men compared to their non-Greek counterparts (Scott-Cheldon et al. 2008).

Student athletes are also more likely to use drugs than nonathletes, especially marijuana, despite the negative consequences of drug use on athletic performance and eligibility (i.e., athletes will be disqualified from competitions if caught with drugs in their systems) (CORE 2001; Grossbard et al. 2009). But like Greek members, athletes spend a lot of time with peers who encourage and even reinforce risk-taking behaviors such as drug use.

Drugs, like alcohol become part of team bonding rituals (Simons et al. 2005). Moreover, at many schools student athletes are treated as celebrities, given special treatment, and excused for all types of bad behavior, including drug use (Sperber 2001). At these schools, athletes may internalize a sense of invincibility, or at least entitlement to indulge in drugs with little or no concern about potential consequences.[5]

Finally, it is important to note that almost all drug users at college drink alcohol. In fact, drug users are more likely to binge drink than non–drug users, and binge drinkers are more likely to use drugs than light drinkers (Buddie and Parks 2003; Mustaine and Tewksbury 2004). When light drinkers use drugs, it is usually only marijuana and only on rare occasions (Mustaine and Tewksbury 2004). Perhaps these results are not surprising considering that both binge drinking and drug use are considered risk-taking behaviors. Students willing to drink recklessly are more willing to use drugs, and are also more willing to brush aside the occasional harms that can occur while partying.

ALCOHOL-RELATED HARMS: AN OVERVIEW OF PRIOR RESEARCH

Researchers have documented a vast laundry list of problems associated with binge drinking and drug use while at college, including poor academic performance, injuries, accidents, crime victimization, and legal troubles (Dowdall 2007; Tewksbury and Pedro 2003, Mustaine and Tewksbury 2007; Seaman 2005; Wechsler and Wuethrich 2002). Much more than marijuana and other illicit drugs, alcohol, or more specifically the excessive amount of alcohol that students drink, has been found to contribute to most of the problems at college. For instance, binge drinking students are more likely to miss classes, fail, or do poorly in their courses. These students are also more likely to have lower overall grade point averages (GPAs) than nondrinkers or students who drink in moderation (Wechsler and Wuethrich 2002). In fact, a significant number of binge-drinking first- and second-year students have abbreviated college careers as a result of poor or failing grades caused by excessive drinking and its health consequences.[6] Many of these students are placed on academic probation and are never able to catch up.

Research has also linked binge drinking to a wide array of physical harms, ranging from cuts and scrapes to alcohol poisoning and drunk driving fatalities (NIAAA 2002; Wechsler and Wuethrich 2002). According to a report from the National Institute on Alcohol Abuse and Alcoholism (NIAAA), an estimated seventeen hundred students, ages eighteen to twenty-four, are killed each year as a result of alcohol consumption, and more than half a million college students suffer from some type of alcohol-related injury (NIAAA 2007; Flowers 2009; Hingson, Heeren, Winter, and Wechsler 2005).[7] Emergency rooms in hospitals located near residential universities and colleges treat students every weekend for injuries, illnesses, and accidents caused by excessive drinking (Seaman 2005; Wechsler and Nelson 2008; Wechsler and Wuethrich 2002). For example, Seaman reports in his book *Binge* that in 2003 Dartmouth College, with four thousand four hundred undergraduates, admitted two hundred alcohol-related emergencies to its campus heath center, and Middlebury College with two thousand one hundred students admitted one hundred students to area hospitals for alcohol related problems (p. 109).[8]

Intoxication Crimes

In addition to injuries and health problems caused by heavy consumption of alcohol, research shows that binge drinking increases risks for crime victimization, including theft, vandalism, physical attack, rape, and unwanted sexual advances (Fisher and Wilkes 2003; Fisher, Sloan, Cullen, and Lu 1998; Harford, Wechsler, and Muthen 2003; Mustaine and Tewksbury 2007; Novik, Howard, and Boekeloo 2011; Neal and Fromme 2007; Tewksbury et al. 2008; Wechsler and Wuethrich 2002). Studies suggest that half to three-fourths of victims who experience violent crime while at college are intoxicated at the time of their victimization (Flowers 2009; Mohler-Kuo, Dowdall, Koss, and Wechsler 2004; Presley and Meilman 1992).

Not only are binge drinking students at higher risks of crime victimization, they are also more likely to participate themselves in criminal offenses while drunk, including fighting, property destruction, and sexual assault (Harford et al. 2003; Tewksbury and Pedro 2003; Wechsler and Wuethrich 2002). According to findings from the National Crime Victimization Survey (NCVS), each year almost seven hundred thousand students between the ages of eighteen and twenty-four are physically assaulted by other students who were drinking at the time of an incident, and over ninety-seven thousand students are sexually assaulted by intoxicated students (Flowers 2009, p. 13). Other studies have found that students are more likely to coerce sex and exhibit sexual aggression when they are drunk (Tewksbury and Pedro

2003; Wechsler and Wuethrich 2002). Also, according to Flowers (2009), one out of every ten students who drinks alcohol admits to damaging property while intoxicated (Flowers 2009).

Considering the increased potential to criminally offend when drunk, it is not surprising that students who binge drink are also more likely to get into trouble with the law. Nationwide, it is estimated that a hundred thousand college students aged eighteen to twenty-four are arrested each year for alcohol-related offenses, including driving drunk, public drunkenness, and underage drinking violations (Flowers 2009, p. 13). Like college crime rates discussed in the previous chapter, the numbers of student arrests and disciplinary actions for liquor law and drug violations vary by type of institution.[9] According to a report by the National Center for Education Statistics, rates for on-campus arrests for liquor law and drug violations on college campuses are highest at large public four-year residential universities (enrolling ten thousand or more students) than for other types of schools (Lewis et al. 1997).[10] Of course, these numbers may reflect greater enforcement of alcohol and drug policy at these schools. After all, these are schools with large campus police departments, and with more agents available to make arrests and issue citations. Also, at residential schools, students are more likely to live on or near campus and will, therefore, be more visible to various social control agents when they are drinking and using drugs.

Still, despite the rather high numbers of arrests and disciplinary actions for alcohol and drug violations at many large universities, these official numbers may reflect only a small fraction of students' drinking and drug use, as they represent only incidents known to police and other authorities. Similarly, official data can provide only a glimmer of the overall problems caused by students' reckless partying on the college campus and in the local communities surrounding it.

Secondhand Harms

Similar to the concept of secondhand smoke and the problems it causes for nonsmokers, secondhand harms caused by binge drinking pose many potential health risks and other problems for students who come into regular contact with heavy "partiers" (e.g., binge drinkers, drug users). Secondhand harms from binge drinking (e.g., property disruption, noise, litter, and verbal harassment) can negatively impact the quality of life for an entire college neighborhood (Brower and Carroll 2007; Dowdall 2007; Durkin, Wolfe, and May 2007; Presley and Meilman 1992; Tewksbury and Pedro 2003; Wechsler and Wuethrich 2002; Wechsler and Nelson 2008). For instance, in a documentary on the public radio series *This American Life*, entitled #1 Party school, (Glass and WBEZ 2009), the producers showcase some of the secondhand effects of drunk and rowdy students at the Pennsylvania State University, the top-rated party school in 2009. During the course of a few hours one night (sometime after midnight), the producers witness or are informed about a cacophony of alcohol-related incidents including drunk students tossing garbage cans, taking down street signs, urinating in residential backyards, vomiting on sidewalks, fighting in the street, setting furniture on fire, and the "drunk kid in the house" (i.e., an intoxicated student who wanders into and passes out in someone else's home).

Even as some of the behaviors highlighted in this documentary may seem extraordinary or outrageous to people listening to the program, for many of the students who live at these party schools, this behavior is rather typical of a Friday or Saturday night. Indeed, the most intriguing part of this documentary isn't that college students engage in such deviant behaviors while drunk, but that many of the students at these schools see this conduct as rather ordinary. For many students at the party school, blackouts and occasional injuries fail to elicit more than a shrug (Wechsler and Wuethrich 2002, p. 178). Meanwhile, bad behavior while intoxicated seldom evokes shame or regret. Instead, most binge drinking students appear rather indifferent or unsympathetic toward the problems that their excessive behaviors may cause to their peers, campus and community. Students' ambivalence toward the risks and consequences to themselves and others from their binge drinking and drug use stands in stark contrast to the alarms often sounded by researchers, who view these student behaviors as a serious health or crime problem. For many students at the party school, binge drinking, drug use, and some occasional disruptions to the community are just a normal part of college life.

SUMMING UP

Prior studies have shown that four out of five college students consume alcohol while at college and over half of student drinkers do so in a manner that is excessive, or commonly referred to as binge drinking. Studies also show that one in five college students use illicit drugs, most commonly marijuana. "Partying" (i.e., drinking and drug use) has become the primary leisure activity for many students at residential universities. Students party because it is fun, because they can, and because there is little else to do. But mostly they party because it is just what students do at college, or at least at the party school.

But partying is not always harmless fun; it can come at a cost. Prior studies have shown that a sizable number of college students who binge drink and use drugs experience injuries, illness, and crime victimization due to their intoxication. In fact, research on students' party behaviors at college portrays this lifestyle as rather dangerous and disruptive for both students who party and for many others in the community (i.e., secondhand harms). Yet students who party while at the party school, rarely see their behaviors as problems, but rather as a normal part of college life. The remaining chapters of this book explore student life at the party school, illuminating the routines, rituals, and risks that characterize a party subculture, as well as the rationales that defend it all.

PARTY UNIVERSITY

A Case Study

3

Introducing Party University

Amid the thousands of universities and colleges in the United States today sits Party University (PU), a so-called party school recognized as much for its active party scene as for its academic programs. As described in previous chapters, the party school is typically a large public university with a sprawling residential campus, and is typically located in a geographically isolated college town. The party school has a vibrant Greek life and active sports program. Students at the party school take great pride in their sports, and an even greater pride in their alcohol consumption.

This chapter begins an in-depth exploration of the party school. Though no two schools are exactly alike, PU represents the ideal party school in terms of its campus and community structure, security and conduct policies, student lifestyle, and incidence of intoxication crime and disorder on campus and in the surrounding college community. The primary purpose of this chapter is to provide sufficient background information about PU and "Ptown," the college town where PU is located, and to help contextualize the research findings on students' party routines and risks that will be presented in the remaining chapters. This chapter starts with an overview of PU's campus structure and conduct codes, and then provides a similar overview for Ptown, and finishes with a brief discussion of official crime statistics at PU and in Ptown.

OVERVIEW OF PARTY UNIVERSITY (PU)

Just over twenty-nine thousand students attend Party University's main campus each year, approximately twenty-two thousand undergraduates and seven thousand graduate and professional students.[1] According to PU's Web-based student profile from 2009, 51 percent of PU undergraduates are male, 93 percent are white (with 4 percent African American and 3 percent other races), and 2 percent are international students. The average age of undergraduate students is twenty-one, with only 7 percent of these students older than twenty-five. Approximately 25 percent of undergraduates (primarily freshmen) reside in university housing, with the remainder of these students living mostly in the surrounding neighborhoods within walking distance or a short drive from campus.

PU is a public land-grant university founded over 125 years ago. Like most U.S. land-grant institutions, PU's original mission was to deliver a high-quality education to benefit the residents and communities within the state. Today, PU is part of the North Central Association of Colleges and Universities and is classified by the Carnegie Foundation as a research I institution. Just about half of PU undergraduates are in-state students, with most of its out-of-state students from neighboring states in the north eastern and central regions of the United States.

PU consists of thirteen colleges that together offer 191 bachelor's, master's, doctoral, and professional degree programs in arts and sciences, business and economics, creative arts, engineering, education, journalism, law, agriculture and natural resources, medicine, dentistry, nursing, and sport sciences. The university awarded over six thousand degrees in 2009, with 65 percent at the undergraduate level. It employs roughly sixteen hundred full-time faculty, six hundred part-time faculty and approximately three thousand staff. PU has grown rapidly over the last ten years, increasing its enrollment by more than 20 percent since 2000, largely by actively recruiting more out-of-state students.

PU's academic colleges, residence halls, and two large sports arenas are located on three separate campuses that together comprise almost eleven hundred acres of land. The health sciences facilities, law school, and engineering departments are located on two campuses on one side of town, whereas social sciences, life sciences, and miscellaneous programs of study are located on the downtown campus, the university's original campus. It is also on the downtown campus where the student activities center and main library are located. Downtown PU is also where Fraternity Row is located, as well as most of the student-oriented bars, clubs, and house parties.

PU and its students take its sports very seriously. As a member of the National Collegiate Athletic Association (NCAA), PU participates in one of the Division I conferences, and competes in seventeen intercollegiate varsity sports. Two major sports at the university, football and basketball, are aired on ESPN and local networks. Home games attract thousands of fans to PU's stadiums from all over the area. The games and tailgating parties beforehand are massive events, suspending business as usual and engulfing the campus and community in a carnival-like frenzy of school spirit. Home football games require a massive coordinated effort on the parts of both campus and local police who oversee and implement security measures during games, and divert and keep traffic moving before and after games.

Aside from keeping students and other fans safe on game days, PU's police department provides twenty-four-hour protection on campus to PU students, faculty, employees, and visitors. Comprised of approximately twenty-five officers with full arrest powers, PU's police department is one of the larger police departments in the state, according to its own website. Its formal mission, as stated on the website, is "preventing crime, preserving the peace and protecting lives and property by enforcing the laws of our state in a just, impartial, and equitable manner." The PU police department is responsible for processing all student conduct violations that occur on campus, as well as collecting and reporting crime statistics in compliance with the Clery Act (see chapter 1).

PU's Student Conduct Code

The PU Student Conduct Code (see appendix C) requires that PU students and student organizations engage in "responsible social conduct that reflects credit upon the University community." Every student is expected to share PU's commitment to honesty; integrity; and respect for self, others, and property, even when off campus. Violations of the Student Conduct Code include plagiarism and cheating; breach of peace at university functions; and violations of all federal, state, and local laws. The University cooperates fully with local police in the enforcement of criminal law.[2] In addition, hazing, defined as the reckless or intentional endangerment of another person as a condition for continued membership in a team, group, or student organization, is a violation of PU's conduct code, as well as a violation of state law (see appendix C, Anti-hazing laws). It is also a violation of the student conduct code to refuse to comply with directions from university officials or law enforcement officers acting in performance of their duties. Any student suspected of violating any of these conduct codes is subject to disciplinary action by a university judicial board comprised of faculty and student representatives. Sanctions range from probation with mandatory counseling or community service to suspension or even expulsion.

In addition to PU's Student Conduct Code, there are also specific rules and regulations for students who live in campus residence halls, including several codes pertaining to alcohol and drugs (See appendix C). For instance, alcohol is not allowed in any residence hall even if students are over twenty-one years of age. A first violation can result in parental notification and ten to fifteen hours of community service, whereas a third violation can result in the student's removal from the residence hall. Students are also prohibited from possessing, using, or distributing controlled substances or any prescribed drug in a manner inconsistent with a prescription. Minimum sanctions for possessing small quantities of marijuana (under 15 grams) or prescription drugs without valid prescriptions can include parental notification, counseling sessions, or ten to fifteen hours of community service. Possession of larger amounts of marijuana or any illicit drug, including narcotics, depressants, stimulants, or hallucinogens, may result in a student's removal from the residence hall and a referral to the University's Student Conduct Office for additional disciplinary action.[3]

Aside from prohibition of alcohol and drug consumption in campus residence halls, PU prohibits illicit drug use anywhere on campus and alcohol consumption by students under twenty-one, in adherence with minimum drinking age laws. PU also enforces sanctions against violators for other alcohol-related misconduct. A flier recently distributed to PU students highlights some of the most common alcohol-related violations at PU and reminds students: "You have choices, know the consequences." A few of the reminders pertaining to alcohol violations on and off campus include:

- Underage possession of alcohol (open container) carries a mandatory six hours of community service, attendance at approved alcohol awareness classes, and a fine of up to $500.
- Using a fake driver's license to get into bars could result in the loss of your real license and $500 in fines. The citation will remain on your record for seven years.
- Lending a drivers license to underage persons to purchase alcohol or gain admission into a bar can mean a fine of $500 and having your license suspended for ninety days.
- Driving under the influence will result in jail time and revocation of driving privileges. If an accident occurs, further criminal charges and civil action may be added.
- Having an open container of alcohol within city limits is a violation and carries a fine from $100 to $500 regardless of age.

- Charging entry into a party is considered operating a business without a license. You can be fined $500 for charging admission or selling cups. If underage students are found drinking alcohol at a house party, the party host will be fined $500.

The flyer also urges students to celebrate their schools' athletic events with good sportsmanship and to "represent [the] town, players, coaches, university and state with class." This message is particularly relevant for PU students, as bad sportsmanship and bad behavior more generally have become rather common occurrences at PU sports events. These instances are often televised for all the world to see, embarrassing to the administration but emblematic of PU's reputation as a party school.

OVERVIEW OF PARTY TOWN (PTOWN)

"Party town," (henceforth known as Ptown) the city-town that hosts PU, is located in a geographic area that is approximately eleven square miles and has a population officially listed at just over thirty thousand full-time residents, according to the U.S. Census Bureau (2012). However, Ptown's official population does not include the thousands of part-year student residents who live in Ptown during the academic year (e.g., fall and spring semesters) but do not declare it as their primary domicile. The population in Ptown nearly doubles from late August until early May with the influx of these part-year undergraduate students.

Ptown is located in a mostly rural county in a north central state of the United States. Despite its classification by residents as a city, Ptown maintains much of its rural origins. For instance, Ptown is accessible by mainly rural roads and is surrounded by farmland and sparsely populated towns. There are only two major highways connecting Ptown to its closet major cities, and only a couple of main roads leading in and out of town. Ptown provides minimal options for mass transit as compared to most urban environments and larger towns. Ptown has a tiny airport with three scheduled flights per day, all heading to the same destination. The closest major airport is a two-hour drive.

In many ways, Ptown is similar to other college towns that host land-grant institutions. As argued by Gumprecht (2008), college towns hosting land-grant universities tend to be much more reflective of their rural orientations, demographics, and economics of their home state, in contrast to the diversity and broader economic opportunities of college towns with wealthier flagship research universities. For instance, in terms of demographics, Ptown, like the state where it is located, is rather racially homogenous, with 90 percent of its residents identifying as white (and only 4 percent African American, 3 percent Asian, and 3 percent of Latino origin). And though Ptown is relatively affluent compared to many parts of its state, as a college town it is rather economically depressed, with a reported median household (2006–2012) income of only $25,495 and with 37 percent of residents living under poverty level.[4] These numbers are not merely reflective of the full-time student population living there (particularly graduate students who claim Ptown as a primary domicile), but the large proportion of working poor in the economically depressed county where Ptown is located. Ptown's economic profile may also reflect the lack of progressive businesses and employment options beyond the university itself, which pays much lower salaries than most of its wealthier peer institutions.[5]

Still, Ptown has experienced steady population growth during the past twenty years and is located in one of the fastest growing counties in the state, primarily due to a rapid increase in undergraduate student enrollments at PU. This is not necessarily good news for residents, as the town's infrastructure is currently stretched beyond what it can bear. There is simply not enough housing and parking available to accommodate the accelerated influx of PU students (as well as new faculty and staff). Traffic on the main roads between campuses is gridlocked several times a day. Downtown Ptown is especially affected by both the heavy traffic and the "invasion" of student rentals into what were once quiet family-oriented neighborhoods. The demographic shift from owner-occupied houses to rental-based units has increased noise and other disorder within these neighborhoods. Residents unaccustomed to frequent loud music at night or parties that last until the early morning complain of disrupted sleep from the noise and other unruly behaviors from their new student neighbors. Yet, from the students' perspective, they are doing nothing wrong. In fact, they see Ptown residents who complain about noise as uptight and overreacting to nothing. Some students even accuse them of being "anti-student." After all, this is a party school; it is what students do here. And with easy access to alcohol — there are more than fifty bars, clubs and liquor stores in Ptown (twenty within walking distance to the downtown campus) — it certainly is what most students do while at PU.

PU AND PTOWN OFFICIAL CRIME STATISTICS

No university campus or college town is free from crime all together, and over the past few years PU and Ptown have had their fair share of crime, including some serious crimes such as armed robberies, aggravated assaults, and at least one homicide in each of the past few years. According to Clery statistics, in 2009 there were nine aggravated assaults on campus, twenty-one burglaries, five robberies, and four rapes (See appendix D, Table 1). PU's overall crime rate at 15.28 per 10,000 is comparable to many large residential schools located in isolated college towns (i.e., party schools) (see ope.ed.gov).[6]

As for Ptown, Uniform Crime Report (UCR) statistics show that in 2009, there was one murder, ninety-six aggravated assaults, 196 burglaries, twenty-three robberies, and ten rapes (see appendix D, Table 2). As a comparison to major U.S. cities, Ptown's overall violent crime rate of 43 per 10,000 and property crime rate of 274 per 10,000 are rather low. However, compared to other college towns, such as Ann Arbor, Michigan, at 23 and 255 respectively, and Newark, Delaware, at 42 and 320 respectively, they are somewhat comparable.[7]

Most of the violent crime that takes place at PU and in Ptown can be attributed to students' active party lifestyle. In fact, almost all of the serious violence perpetrated by students against other students within the past five years at PU have been "intoxication crimes," where victim, offender, or both participants were drunk at the time of the incident. For example, in 2006 a twenty-three-year-old male student was stabbed and fatally wounded by another student around 2 AM while he and his friends were walking home from a bar near the downtown campus. The fight, purportedly started after a snowball was thrown at one of the students, quickly escalated into a fist fight and then to a deadly stabbing. In 2007, the jury found one student guilty of involuntary manslaughter and sentenced him to less than a year in jail, a rather lenient penalty due, in part, to the large amounts of alcohol that all parties involved had consumed that night, and the conflicting eyewitness accounts of what happened (Offredo 2007a, 2007b).

In 2009, an eerily similar incident occurred in Ptown, purported to have originated as an argument over baseball. A physical altercation ensued among three students late one night, all of whom were intoxicated. The fight ended with two of the men kicking the third student in the head while he was lying on the ground, resulting in the student ending up in a coma-like state in which he remains today. Both of the other students involved were convicted of crimes, one for malicious assault, and the other for battery (DA Staff 2009; Harki 2010; WBOY News 2010).

Most recently in 2011, a PU student was taken to the hospital after yet another argument turned violent. At 3 AM, a group of drunk students — both men and women — were in the downtown PU parking garage when a debate began over whose hometown was better. It quickly escalated into a violent fight among several of the students. One of the students was charged with malicious wounding in connection with the altercation (Crum 2011).

Another 2011 incident at PU that involved serious violence and intoxication occurred after the loss of a football game. Four fans of the rival team were allegedly assaulted by drunk PU fans (students who were angry at their team's loss) as they were getting in to their vehicle to head home. One of the passengers was hit by a rock thrown at his car and suffered a broken nose and crushed eye socket. Another passenger who was twenty-two weeks pregnant and had rushed out of the car to help her husband, was knocked down, suffering bruises on her arms, legs, and shoulders (Zack 2011; Associated Press 2011). At the time of this writing, charges were still pending.

Though this previous case is extreme, PU sports fans are no strangers to violent outbursts, as both students and nonstudent fans have exhibited more than their share of bad sportsmanship over the years. In one such example, dating back to 2003, PU fans rushed the football field and tore down the goal posts following their team's victory over a rival school. The fans, mostly students who were drunk and emboldened by the win, then took their "celebration" into the streets, uprooting street signs and igniting a series of property fires (e.g., couches, mattresses, trash bins, dumpsters) (Teed et al. 2010).

Of course, setting property on fire, especially couches, is not necessarily seen as bad sportsmanship by many PU students, but rather a tradition of sorts. PU students often burn property as a means to celebrate sports victories or other events.[8] In fact, the tradition of setting couches on fire at PU is commemorated on T-shirts and other merchandise (e.g., magnets, bumper stickers, candles) that can be purchased online and in local stores, and features artwork of a flaming couch and a slogan that reads, "Where Greatness is Learned and Couches are Burned." Fire officials suggest that the ritual of burning couches dates back to about the 1970s, but peaked between 1997 and 2003 when PU's football team had a multiyear winning streak. During that time there were more than four hundred street fires reported, costing more than $280,000 worth of property damage, and garnering PU its reputation as the couch-burning capital of college football (Nuzum 2011; Teed et al. 2010).

For several years now, town officials have been stepping up their efforts to put an end to this potentially dangerous tradition. For instance, in 2011, Ptown enforced a temporary removal of furniture from front porches in preparation for a big rivalry football game. Although the furniture ban was temporary, Ptown has begun to enforce more serious penalties for the malicious burning of property. Previously, burning private property was considered a misdemeanor and prosecuted under local ordinances, with sanctions of no more than a $1,000 fine. Now, it is charged as a felony arson charge, which carries the possibility of up to three years in prison. In addition to enforcing these more serious charges, city and private property owners have collaborated to promote public awareness that includes passing out "Learn Not to Burn" stickers and flyers around campus. The university also now includes an anti-burning segment in freshman orientation classes, and prior to this past football season, all PU students received an e-mail warning them about the dangers and consequences of setting fires.

Only time will tell if such efforts are effective. But as of now, purposefully set fires continue to occur rather regularly at PU. In fact, burning couches has been so normalized at PU that most students defend the practice and see the new penalties as punitive and "anti-student." A criminology student likened the anti-burning campaign, with its new felony charges and harsher penalties, to a moral panic, an exaggeration of a minor problem or harmless behavior (see Weiss and Colyer 2010). This perspective, echoed by many other PU students, suggests that the fire marshals and law makers are making way too much of the dangers of a perfectly normal activity, and scapegoating students in the process.

The perspective that students are being persecuted by unfair policies and laws may help to explain the rather large numbers of students who violate many of PU's student conduct codes quite regularly. If students do not believe in the validity of the rules and laws they are expected to obey, they are unlikely to conform to them. For instance, few PU students appear to be deterred by the potential of fines or disciplinary actions imposed by the school for violations of liquor or drug laws. Despite PU's seemingly strict formal conduct codes and policies that prohibit underage drinking and drug use, students frequently drink under the age of twenty-one, use drugs, and frequently get in trouble for using these substances. According to the Clery statistics, in 2009, 428 PU students were arrested for liquor law violations, and another 1,231 were disciplined through the university. An additional 121 students were arrested for drug violations, and another 98 received disciplinary actions from the university. With a rate of 576 per 10,000 for alcohol violations (combined arrests and disciplinary actions) and 76 per 10,000 for drug violations (combined arrests and disciplinary actions), PU rates are rather high, even compared to other party schools such as Penn State, with 270 alcohol violations and 39 drug law violations, respectively.

A quick look at PU's campus crime logs (i.e., summary incidents mandated by the Clery Act) further substantiates the frequency of alcohol and drug violations at PU (see appendix D, table 3). In accordance with the Clery Act, these logs reflect daily police activity on campus and are available through the university's police website. According to the crime logs, on any given weekend night, police will issue upwards of ten citations for underage alcohol consumption and will make about five arrests for public intoxication. Drug arrests and disciplinary actions primarily for marijuana (less than fifteen grams), are also frequent, with about three per weekend night. In addition to alcohol and drug violations, police commonly respond to a number of fights, property destruction incidents, and thefts during a typical weekend night. Many (if not most) of these incidents are intoxication crimes.

Clearly, alcohol, drug, and other violations keep the police very busy at PU and in Ptown. Yet, neither the threat of sanctions or the laws themselves seem to be very effective deterrents in slowing down the party lifestyle at PU. Instead, drinking, drug use, and the reckless behaviors that often accompany extreme intoxication have simply become a way of life for both students and police at the party school.

SUMMING UP

Party University (PU), a large public residential and sports-oriented university, is representative of the typical party school in many ways, including its students' preoccupation with alcohol. Meanwhile, Ptown, the college town that hosts PU is representative of the typical college town where most party schools are located — geographically isolated towns with easy access to alcohol. Students' active party lifestyle at PU keeps both the university and local police very busy. In fact, an inspection of official crime statistics on and near campus shows that much of the crimes that take place at PU can be attributed to students' excessive drinking and drug use.

Yet, the frequency of intoxication crimes and sanctions issued for alcohol and drug violations, as reflected in the Clery statistics and PU crime logs, stand in stark contrast to the formal laws and student conduct codes implemented by the university. Clearly, students are not deterred by the laws or polices that prohibit alcohol and drugs on campus. Despite occasional legal consequences, partying seems to be well worth the risks for many students. Just how much some students are willing to risk for the sake of the party is the subject of the following chapters.

Playing Hard

STUDENTS' DRINKING
AND DRUG ROUTINES

Although students party (i.e., drink and use drugs) to some degree at almost all residential universities and colleges, nowhere do as many students party, and to such extremes, as at so-called party schools. Students party more at these schools due, in part, to their location in an isolated college town with easy access to alcohol and little else to do. Students also party more at these schools because a much larger proportion of them are "traditional" students who have fewer financial obligations and more time on their hands for such leisure activities. But students also party more at these schools due to a prominent party subculture that encourages playing hard, often to the detriment of studying. Recall from the introduction that subcultures consist of identifiable norms and rituals that bond members together and provide them with a sense of identity. Students who participate in a party subculture engage in unique drinking and drug routines that become an integral part of their shared experiences at college and often a large part of their identities as students at a party school.

Using sample data from the Campus Crime Victimization Survey (CCVS), a self-report survey distributed to undergraduate students ages eighteen to twenty-four, this chapter examines students' party routines at PU. More specifically, the chapter provides a descriptive account of students who party at the party school and how they party. It does so by delineating four distinct types of partiers at PU ranging from non-partiers to students who participate most extensively in the party subculture. The chapter concludes with a look at how students conceptualize a "partier" identity and party school label.

DESCRIBING PU STUDENTS
AND THEIR PARTY ROUTINES

Based on data from the Campus Crime Victimization Survey (CCVS), the clear majority of traditional PU students are full-time (97 percent), single (98 percent), and have no children (99 percent) (See appendix B, table 1). One-fifth of PU students live on campus in residence halls or fraternity/sorority housing, with most students (80 percent) living off campus. A third of PU students participate in some type of campus organization, including varsity sports (4 percent), marching band (4 percent), and club or intramural sports (26 percent). Fifteen percent of PU students belong to either a fraternity (6 percent) or Sorority (9 percent). Students in the sample represent a broad range of majors, with 32 percent of the students majoring in a discipline within the social sciences, 9 percent in health sciences, 16 percent in engineering and physical sciences and the remainder (42 percent) in assorted majors (e.g., journalism, creative arts, business). PU students self-report a relatively high grade point average (GPA). For instance, 39 percent of students surveyed claim to have a GPA above 3.5, and just 1 percent claim a GPA under 2.0.[1]

Approximately 18 percent of traditional PU students work at jobs for more than twenty hours per week, and 51 percent do not work at all. Only 20 percent of students are financially responsible for their own tuition, and 46 percent pay their own rents. One in seven students claim no personal obligation to pay any expenses while at college (including tuition, rent, gas, and utilities). Based on these numbers, there are clearly many students at PU with enough time on their hands and a lack of financial responsibility to indulge in lots of beer, hard liquor, and drugs — the relevant criteria (along with popularity of Greek life) for scoring high on party school lists, at least according to Princeton Review's methodology (see "Defining the Party School" in the introduction).

Lots of Beer and Hard Liquor

Like students at most residential universities and colleges, PU students consume large amounts of alcohol. CCVS data indicate that 79 percent of traditional students drink alcohol while at PU and 60 percent of students who drink alcohol typically consume five or more drinks on the occasions when they drink, the most common measure of "binge" drinking.[2] (See appendix B, table 2.) More specifically, 28 percent of PU students drink five to six drinks on average, 15 percent drink seven to eight drinks and 17 percent drink nine or more drinks. Not only do the majority of students who drink at PU binge drink, but according to a revised version of the CCVS, 39 percent of students believe that they could drink five or more drinks without getting drunk (with 26 percent of men claiming they can remain sober after seven to eight drinks). Moreover, 7 percent of students claim that they can consume five or more alcoholic drinks and still drive safely. Of course, as students point out, how much alcohol they consume and how drunk they get during any given occasion will depend on what type of alcohol they consume. For example, a male student suggests that he typically consumes twelve or thirteen beers to obtain "a good buzz" but only five or six glasses or shots of hard liquor for the same buzz.

Men drink more than women at PU (85 percent versus 75 percent) and men drink more extreme amounts of alcohol when they drink than women. For instance, when asked how much alcohol they consume in a typical night, 31 percent of men claim to drink more than nine drinks whereas only 7 percent of women drink such extreme amounts. However, in the five-to-eight-drink range, women drink more than men (i.e., 35 percent of women drink five to eight drinks as compared to 17 percent of men). Clearly, many women at PU are keeping up with the men in terms of binge drinking.

Another gender difference in regards to alcohol consumption is based on the number of days per week that students consume alcohol. More than half of all PU students who drink alcohol — both men and women — do so two or more days per week. Specifically, 41 percent of students report drinking alcohol once a week, 50 percent report drinking alcohol two to three days per week, and 9 percent report drinking alcohol more than four days in a typical week. When comparing men and women, the data show that men are almost twice as likely to drink four or more days per week than women (13 percent as compared to 7 percent).[3]

CCVS data also show a significant difference in terms of students' age and alcohol consumption. According to CCVS findings, 32 percent of PU students under twenty-one abstain from alcohol, as compared to only 11 percent of students twenty-one and older. Still, two-thirds of students under twenty-one drink alcohol while at PU, despite the minimum drinking age law that prohibits them from purchasing alcohol before the age of twenty-one. Age also factors into where students drink, but not as much as would be expected based on legal restrictions. While equal numbers of students in both age groups drink at parties (51 percent), 69 percent of students over twenty-one drink in bars as compared to 41 percent of students under twenty-one. The rather large number of underage students who are able to drink at bars in Ptown can be explained, in part, by the large number of students (33 percent) who admit that they have access to false IDs that enable them to drink at bars before twenty-one. Also, in Ptown, students who are eighteen and older are allowed admission into "eighteen-and-older" clubs, and once inside underage students will simply ask patrons over twenty-one to buy drinks for them. In fact, the majority of students (68 percent) say it is somewhat or very easy to consume alcohol at local bars while under twenty-one, the same percentage of students who agree that it is somewhat or very easy to purchase alcohol at liquor stores in town. As the saying goes, where there is a will there is a way, and apparently there is a very strong will among PU students under twenty-one to exert their "right" to party.

Reefer Madness and Beyond

According to the CCVS, 25 percent of traditional PU students use drugs (including marijuana, other illicit drugs such as cocaine and LSD, and pharmaceuticals without a valid prescription). Students who drink are more likely to use drugs (31 percent), and almost every drug user also drinks alcohol. In fact, many PU students use drugs only when drinking. Most students who use drugs while at PU are "experimental users" who use them less than a few times a year. However, marijuana is the exception. Almost 25 percent of marijuana users claim to use the drug daily, 20 percent once or a few times a week, 20 percent once or a few times a month and 34 percent a few times a year (see appendix B, tables 3 and 4).

Marijuana's popularity and frequent usage at PU and at many residential universities and colleges may be due, in part, to users' denials that it is a "real" drug. The distinction that students make between marijuana and other drugs is illustrated in the following interview responses from students asked about their drug usage at PU. Even as all three of the students deny "using drugs," they admit to using marijuana. Moreover, none of the students see "weed" as a real or serious drug.

> I don't use drugs, I mean, we all smoke weed, but I don't think that's the same as real drugs. (twenty-one-year-old male junior)

If someone is smoking a couple joints or taking a couple of pain pills, I don't think that is really "using drugs." (twenty-year-old female junior)

We don't use drugs, well maybe weed . . . but nothing serious like heroin or cocaine or anything. Pot isn't nearly the same. (nineteen-year-old male sophomore)

Irrespective of whether students use marijuana themselves, most PU students claim that the drug is somewhat or very easy to find on or near PU's campus. Students also suggest that other illicit drugs are fairly easy to find at PU, even though only a small percentage of students admit to using them (see appendix B, tables 3 and 4). For instance, according to the CCVS data, the three most commonly used drugs at PU (aside from marijuana) are cocaine (5 percent), ecstasy (3 percent) and psychedelics (6 percent). Moreover, the majority of students who use these drugs use them only occasionally. For instance, 73 percent of illicit drug users (not including marijuana) use drugs only a few times a year, 20 percent once or a few times a month, 5 percent once or a few times a week, and only 3 percent use them daily.

A final category of drugs, apparently also easy to find on or near the PU campus, are pharmaceutical drugs obtained without a prescription (See appendix B, tables 3 and 4). Thirteen percent of students claim to use pharmaceutical drugs, such as Ritalin (10 percent) and Adderall (11 percent). In terms of frequency, 45 percent of students who use pharmaceutical drugs use them only a few times a year, 41 percent once or a few times a month, 13 percent once or a few times a week, and only 1 percent use them daily.

Like alcohol, more men than women use illicit drugs while at PU, and more men then women use marijuana on a regular basis. For instance 30 percent of men use marijuana, 12 percent use other illicit drugs and 16 percent use pharmaceutical drugs without a prescription. In comparison, 21 percent of women use marijuana, 7 percent use other illicit drugs and 11 percent use pharmaceutical drugs without a prescription. Moreover, 44 percent of men who use marijuana do so more than once a week, as compared to 35 percent of women.

IDENTIFYING PARTIER TYPES

Despite PU's reputation as a party school, not all PU students drink or use drugs. As previously stated, 21 percent of traditional students do not drink alcohol while at PU, and 75 percent do not use marijuana or any illicit drug.

And among students who do drink or use drugs, there is a great variation in regard to overall frequency of usage and quantities used during any one occasion. Based on student responses to CCVS questions about drinking and drug use while at PU, students can be distinguished into four "partier" types: *non-partiers*, or students who do not drink or use drugs at all while at PU, and three partier categories — *light, heavy,* and *extreme* (see appendix B, tables 5, 6, and 7). More specifically, *light partiers* are defined as students who drink less than five drinks in a typical night of drinking, drink only one night in a typical week, were intoxicated no more than once in the past two weeks, and typically use no drugs. *Heavy partiers* are defined as students who drink five to eight drinks in a typical night of drinking, drink two to three nights in a typical week, were intoxicated more than once in the past two weeks, and typically use marijuana or other drugs less than a few times a month. Finally, *extreme partiers* are identified as students who drink nine or more drinks in a typical night of drinking, drink four or more nights in a typical week, were intoxicated more than twice in the last two weeks, and typically use marijuana or other drugs a few times a month or more.

Based on this operationalization, 21 percent of the sample of PU students were identified as non-partiers, 25 percent as light partiers, 40 percent as heavy partiers and 14 percent as extreme partiers. Predictably, more men than women meet the criteria to be defined as extreme partiers (24 percent as compared to 8 percent). However, there is only a slight difference between men and women in terms of heavy partying (43 percent as compared to 39 percent). There are also no statistically significant differences in terms of partying type by race or ethnicity. (See appendix B, table 8.)

In regards to party type by age and class rank, the findings were some-what unexpected based on previous literature and the stereotype of out-of-control young freshmen on their own for the first time and especially eager to party.[4] Findings from the CCVS show that older students twenty-one to twenty-four and more advanced students (i.e., juniors and seniors) appear slightly more committed to the party subculture at PU, when combining heavy and extreme partying routines. For instance, 46 percent of students under twenty-one party heavily or to an extreme (35 percent and 11 percent respectively) whereas 62 percent of students over twenty-one party heavily or to an extreme (46 percent and 16 percent respectively). Patterns based on class rank also reveal slightly more partying by upperclassmen, again when combining heavy and extreme partying. More specifically, 53 percent of freshmen are heavy or extreme partiers, 38 percent of sophomores, 57 percent of juniors and 61 percent of seniors.

However, it is important to note that Freshman are slightly more likely than upperclassmen to party in the extreme category. What is particularly striking in terms of the data are the especially low number of sophomores who party to an extreme — 8 percent — as compared to 18 percent of freshmen, 16 percent of juniors and 14 percent of seniors. These numbers may reflect returning sophomores who had partied a bit too much the prior year and spent their second year hunkering down in order to play catch up (e.g., repeating classes they failed, trying to raise their GPAs). The following excerpt from a sophomore reflecting back on his freshman year helps to explain his transition from extreme to light partier during his second year. The motivation for his transformation was apparently tied to a threat from his mother to cut him off financially if he did not improve his grades.

> Freshman year I used to go out 4 times a week, Tuesdays, Thursdays, Fridays and Saturdays. But after a year like that my grades and bank account really started to suffer so my mom said if I didn't improve my grades she would cut me off. So now I only go out on weekends. A lot of my friends still go out four days. But my roommate and I kind of help each other to avoid going out too often. (twenty-year-old male sophomore)

By their junior year, students who have been able to improve their grades during their probationary year may once again increase their partying routines, which may explain the larger number of students who party more heavily or extremely during their junior and senior years. Also at this point, students would have been adequately socialized into the party subculture, which would include learning how to successfully navigate between their academic obligations and their partier roles. The increased amount of partying in advanced years at PU can also be explained by the large numbers of transfer students who start at the school during their junior year and who, like freshmen, may be eager to take advantage of the vibrant party scene. One final reason why older students and upperclassmen may party more is that most traditional students turn twenty-one during their junior or senior year, making it easier to obtain alcohol legally. Thus, after twenty-one, students no longer have to be concerned about the risks of getting caught for underage drinking which may increase their consumption.

Irrespective of age or class rank, students who party most while at PU tend to study least. In fact, students at PU joke that they "work hard and play harder." Using GPA as a proxy for studying, CCVS results suggest that extreme partiers often play so hard that they hardly work. For instance, 25 percent of students with GPAs under 2.5 are identified as extreme partiers, whereas only 9 percent of students with GPAs over 3.5 party to such extremes. Looking at the relationship from the other direction, 13 percent of extreme partiers and 8 percent of heavy partiers have GPAs under 2.5 as compared to less than 5 percent of non- or light partiers. A greater devotion to partying rather than studying is also reflected in the numbers of missed and failed classes by partier type. For instance, 80 percent of extreme partiers and 63 percent of heavy partiers have missed class due to their alcohol or drug use, as compared to 20 percent of light partiers. Another 21 percent of extreme partiers have failed a class or did poorly as a result of their partying, as compared to 12 percent of heavy partiers, and less than 1 percent of light partiers. (See appendix B, table 9.)

CCVS findings also show a statistically significant difference in partier type by major, with students majoring in the social sciences much more committed to partying than students studying in the health science fields or engineering. More specifically, 16 percent of students in social science majors are extreme partiers, as compared to only 3 percent of health science majors and 5 percent of engineering majors. Perhaps this is not surprising considering that partying has an inverse affect on academic grades and, therefore, students in highly competitive fields will need to party less and study more in order to maintain higher GPAs and do well in their courses.

One final pattern regarding partier types pertains to students' involvement in jobs, school-based organizations, and scholarly associations. Social bond theory (Hirschi 1969) suggests that persons who are most committed to conventional activities and organizations will have less time and incentive to engage in deviant behavior. Drawing upon these theoretical concepts, it would be expected that college students who work at jobs or are engaged in challenging academic pursuits outside of the classroom would participate less in the party subculture. And participation in conventional activities does appear to curtail extreme partying at PU. For instance, only 8 percent of students who work at jobs more than twenty hours a week are extreme partiers as compared to 15 percent of students who do not work or work less than twenty hours a week.[5] Only 9 percent of students involved in academic organizations such as honors societies and 2 percent of students involved in religious groups party in the extreme category. Moreover, 10 percent of students with financial obligations (e.g., pay their own tuition or rent) party in the extreme category, as compared to 16 percent of students with fewer expenses.[6]

However, participation in two college-based activities — Greek life and sports — significantly increases rather than decreases the likelihood of extreme partying. For instance, 20 percent of Greek-affiliated students are identified as extreme partiers and 49 percent are heavy partiers, as compared to 12 percent of non-Greeks who are extreme partiers and 39 percent who are heavy partiers. And when looking at drug use, 37 percent of students involved in fraternities or sororities use illicit drugs as compared to 22 percent of non-Greeks. These numbers are consistent with prior research that suggests that students who participate in Greek life at college are more likely to binge drink and use drugs (Harford et al. 2002; Boswell and Spade 1996; Mustaine and Tewksbury 2007). Furthermore, and also consistent with prior research, there is a significant difference between college athletes and nonathletes in terms of how much they party. For instance, 64 percent of athletes (varsity or intramural sports) are extreme or heavy partiers as compared to 51 percent of nonathletes. For many PU athletes, partying appears to be as much of a competitive sport off the field as the sports they play on the field.

PARTYING AS TRANSITORY

Like students' commitments and involvement in conventional activities, participation in the party subculture is often transitory and can vary greatly by month, semester, or year based on personal circumstances and competing obligations. For instance, students may take a temporary hiatus from heavy or extreme partying during midterm or final exams and may even abandon the party subculture all together after some tangible crisis occurs, such as experiencing a serious accident, getting arrested for drunk driving, or being placed on academic probation. But even as a crisis can serve as a wake-up call for some students, for others, particularly those students whose participation in the party subculture provides them with a source of identity and purpose at college, a crisis may be merely an inconvenience that is minimized and brushed aside as inconsequential.

Students' commitment to the party subculture may also fluctuate over the years. According to students' own assessments of whether they party more or less since their freshman year, 50 percent of students say they party less, 34 percent party more, and 16 percent acknowledge no change.[7] For students who party less, it may be a matter of "aging out" or simply growing tired of the party scene. For many of these students, the proverbial light bulb ignites at some point during their junior or senior year as they realize that they are in college for a greater purpose than simply getting wasted. Practical concerns about getting a job after graduation may certainly sober students up as graduation approaches. Students may also begin to party less as they start to focus more on studying, increasing GPAs, or taking on internships, all to better position themselves for graduate school or for a competitive job market. Also, as advanced students begin to take more difficult courses in their respective fields (beyond general education courses commonly taken during the first two years of college), they will need to exert more effort toward studying, which may leave them with less time to party. Even the most extreme partiers may slow down during their senior year as commencement draws near, a pivotal event that signals the unofficial onset of adulthood with its corresponding grown-up responsibilities.[8] These themes are reflected in the following responses from seniors as they explain why they participate less in the party subculture than during their earlier years at PU.

I drink less now because I'm over it; it's not that exciting anymore and I don't have to drink to have fun. When I was a freshman and sophomore I always used to think that it was kind of cool to party all the time . . . but I'm starting to finally wind down because I'm getting serious about school work and finding a job, so I don't think it's really quite as cool as it used to be. (twenty-one-year-old male senior)

At twenty-two, I no longer get as crazy as I used to. I have a lot more responsibilities now. My class load is more demanding and stressful, and I work twenty hours a week. I just can't keep up with the kids; kind of lost my tolerance. (twenty-two-year-old male senior)

I love that our school is a party school, but now that I am a senior I am getting sick of getting wasted and living in run-down apartments where annoying drunk people yell and destroy my stuff. I am ready to move on. (twenty-one-year-old female senior)

In contrast to students whose partying has slowed down, many students suggest that their partying routines have actually increased since their freshman year. One reason for an acceleration of partying is that over the years students learn to more effectively balance partying and their school work. For some students, it was a matter of "turning legal," and no longer having to worry about getting citations for underage drinking. Similarly, for some students partying increased only after they moved out of the dorms where alcohol is prohibited and where there is a much greater risk of sanctions (i.e., disciplinary actions) from social control agents on the premises (e.g., residence advisors, security personnel). These themes are illustrated in the following responses from upperclassmen who claim to participate more in the party subculture now than during their earlier years at PU.

I party a lot more now that I can buy alcohol myself. After my twenty-first birthday I was able to purchase alcohol legally as well as enter and purchase drinks at bars/clubs without worrying about getting caught. So it's easier and more fun now to drink. (twenty-one-year-old male junior)

I was caught drinking several times while in the dorm. So when I moved into an apartment, and I could no longer get into trouble, I really started partying. This past year has probably been my craziest year by far. (twenty-one-year-old male junior)

It took me a while to figure out when I could party and when I needed to study. I was finally able to do both pretty successfully by the latter half of my sophomore year. By my junior year, and especially by the time I turned twenty-one, I had a pretty good handle on how to party and still do reasonably well in all of my classes. It is definitely a learning process. (twenty-two-year-old female senior)

Clearly, "successful" partying at PU is contingent upon students' abilities to keep up their grades and stay out of trouble. In fact, all successful partiers (i.e., those who pass classes and eventually graduate) understand that partying is a balancing act that requires that they determine for themselves just how much time to devote to the party subculture and how much time they must apportion to academics and other responsibilities. Successful partiers, from light to extreme, must find the proper balance if they hope to survive at the party school.

PARTIER IDENTITY

Just as participation in the party subculture is varied and transitory, the ways in which students identify with the party subculture and a party school label are also variable. For instance, while some students self-identify as "partiers" and see PU's reputation as a "party school" in a positive light, others see these labels as negative and even detrimental to their experiences at college. Variations of perception and identity can be seen in the very different ways in which students describe what partying means to them. For instance, in the following set of survey responses, students see partying as a substantial part of their student role and a positive aspect of college life.

> I wear the party label with pride. We party hard, but it's college and you are supposed to party hard. You are only young once, you have to enjoy it. (twenty-two-year-old male junior)

> I like to party. I go out like every night practically. It's nuts. Even when I don't want to go out, my friends convince me to. I am in the dorm now, but next year I plan to get a house near all the hot party spots. Why else come to a party school if not to party? (eighteen-year-old male freshman)

> I guess I could say I am a partier, at least right now. Especially right now . . . I don't have a lot of classes. I probably go out five nights a week. I know at least one bartender at every bar! (twenty-one-year-old female junior)

In contrast to these overtly proud partiers, many students at PU, including some students who do party on occasion, take a much more negative view of a partier label, and view students who party too hard as "sloppy drunks" who care little about their studies or the school's image. As illustrated in the following responses, the partier label signifies students who are irresponsible, lack ambition, and who, collectively, make the university look bad.

> To me a partier is someone who cares more about their social life than their education, or for that matter the school itself. (nineteen-year-old male sophomore)

> I think a partier is someone that goes out throughout the week and drinks, and they hardly ever make it to class. If they do make it to class, they're hung over, they don't do well, and they can't wait to go get drunk. They're not

worried about a job and they don't focus on their education. And they make the rest of us look bad. (twenty-three-year-old female senior)

A third perspective on partiers and partying at college, and one that is much less black and white, acknowledges that *how* students party matters in regards to perceptions. For instance, students who respond in this category tend to reserve a negative label for their peers who party recklessly and irresponsibly, and cause trouble while doing so. As articulated in the following responses, a partier who drinks in moderation and is quiet and responsible while doing so is a very different type of partier from the loud "idiot" drunk who starts fights and is much more "obnoxious."

A lot of students are idiots when they party. You have three kinds of drunks. You have the loud ones; you have the angry ones who want to start fights; and then you have the quiet ones, who don't cause trouble. (twenty-year-old female sophomore)

There's different classifications of partiers. Me, I'm the weekend partier or the special occasion partier. Then there are the partiers who go out probably every other day of the week — they even go out on a Monday. That is a little extreme and irresponsible. (twenty-two-year-old male junior)

Partiers can be obnoxious, but a lot of people grow out of it when they realize that they actually need to sleep and can't stop vomiting enough to go to class. Then they become a more mellow partier, less obnoxious. These partiers don't bother anyone. (twenty-one-year-old female junior)

Just as students have divergent perceptions of partiers at their school, they are also split in regard to whether they see the "party school" label as positive (23percent) or negative (25 percent), with half not caring either way (52 percent). Not surprisingly, extreme partiers who often choose to attend PU, in part, for its reputation as a party school, are much more likely to see the party school label as positive (86 percent) as compared to less than a third of other types of partiers (29 percent). The following responses illustrate the importance of the party scene, at least initially, for many newer PU students eager to be a part of it. In fact, according to the second response, the more crazy and extreme students behave (at least as it appears to outsiders via ESPN) the more "awesome" the school's reputation becomes as a party school.

I definitely wanted to go to a good party school. You are only young for so long; make the best of it while you can and have fun. (twenty-year-old female sophomore)

Being at a party school is great. How much we party is what makes this school great. I knew I would be getting into some crazy partying, but it's even better than I thought. Every time we are on ESPN or something my friends back home text me saying something like: "Wow, you guys are crazy." It is awesome. (eighteen-year-old male freshman)

In contrast to this positive perspective, there are many students at PU, including many students who party themselves, that express frustration over the school's party image. As conveyed in the following survey responses, some students are embarrassed by PU's reputation and the ways in which students are portrayed by the media. Many students are especially concerned about the negative impact that a party school label could have on their future job prospects.

At first I thought being at a party school was cool, but now I'm worried about it because when I graduate I want employers to take me seriously. (twenty-year-old male sophomore)

I was excited for school. I like to party some, but our reputation sucks and gets worse each year. The bad behavior at games makes us look like uncontrollable animals. The media only shows us when we do something bad and it makes us look terrible. (twenty-two-year-old female senior)

Being the number one party school in America isn't something we should be proud of, and I know that a lot of college students are just going to party anyway, but it would be good if we could eliminate the extreme drunks who get wasted or as high as they possibly can nearly every night. Get rid of those students and the school would be a much better place (twenty-two-year old male senior)

As a freshman, I was super-excited to attend a party school. I thought I would have crazy and wild adventures, and I did. But now that I am older and applying to graduate schools, I'm realizing how negative this label is. I have already had difficulty securing an internship because I attend a school that is known for its partying. I wish this school was known for something else besides the beer. (twenty-year-old female junior)

A final quote from a sophomore represents a more balanced and even practical perspective of PU as a party school. Acknowledging the label as both positive and negative, the student aptly points out that the party school reputation is a large reason why many students choose to come to PU. The label attracts students who want to attend a school that is fun but who, once enrolled, may actually excel academically and become an asset to the school. Without the label, these students might never consider applying.

> I think the party school label is both good and bad. It's negative only because sometimes people will say, "Your degree doesn't count. You went to a party school." But it's positive because it gets us a lot of attention and if people come here because they think it's fun and they end up excelling or realizing how great our school is, then . . . that can't be bad. (twenty-year-old female senior)

This image of the fun-loving party school as a marketing tool that effectively lures students to enroll may help to explain why administrators at PU and other party schools appear rather ambivalent about their reputations (as will be discussed in the book's conclusion). Clearly, a party school label does entice more students to attend PU. But it may also be bringing in too many students whose sole or at least primary purpose is to party and not necessarily to study. These students often become the party subculture's hardcore devotees who party hardest, study least, and cause most of the problems that occur at these schools. Extreme partiers and the problems they cause will be examined more closely in the following chapters.

SUMMING UP

This chapter has begun an investigation of the party school by describing student partiers at PU and their varying commitments to the party subculture. As the chapter describes, not all students at PU party (i.e., drink alcohol or use drugs) or do so to excess. Instead, many students are only minimally committed to the party subculture, and many drift in and out of the party scene while at PU. Nonetheless, the majority of PU's traditional undergraduate students party to some extent. For instance, CCVS data shows that 79 percent of PU students drink alcohol, and approximately 25 percent use marijuana or other drugs. More than half (54 percent) of PU students party in a manner that can be identified as heavy or extreme partying.

For extreme partiers (14 percent of PU students), the party lifestyle can be a substantial part of their student identities. They are PU's most enthusiastic and loyal partiers who typically drink nine or more drinks in a single night, and drink four or more nights in a typical week. Extreme partiers are also more likely to use both marijuana frequently (a few times a month or more) and other drugs at least occasionally to intensify their highs. Extreme partiers are also more likely to have chosen to attend PU due to its reputation as a party school and, fittingly, seek to take full advantage of the opportunities to party while there. But extreme partying can also come at a cost, as will be seen in the next chapter that highlights extreme party rituals and the risks that accompany them.

5

Getting Wasted

EXTREME PARTY RITUALS AND RISKS

As outlined in the previous chapter, students' participation in the party subculture varies, with 21 percent of students using no alcohol or drugs (i.e., non-partiers), 25 percent of students partying moderately (i.e., light partiers), 40 percent of students partying frequently (i.e., heavy partiers), and 14 percent of students partying excessively (i.e., extreme partiers who drink nine or more drinks in a typical night and four or more nights in a typical week, often in combination with drugs). *Extreme partiers* are the most avid champions of a party subculture, most committed to a partier identity, and eager to represent the party school.

This chapter examines more closely some of the extreme party rituals of PU's most hardcore partiers. The term *ritual* is used here to emphasize that the drinking routines and other practices shared by members of a party subculture are often patterned and identifiable events. Rituals express one's involvement and commitment to a group and are learned, like all culture, through a socialization process.[1] Though many of the rituals discussed in the chapter — for example, drinking games, pregaming, tailgating — are common among all partiers at the party school, it is the frequency and extent to which extreme partiers engage in these rituals that make them an exceptional group for closer scrutiny. Even as extreme partiers comprise only 14 percent of PU's traditional undergraduate student population (and 17 percent of PU's partiers), their commitment to the ideals and rituals of the party subculture makes them a formidable presence at the party school. In fact, these are the students who are the public face of the party school, and the MVPs (most valuable players) of the party subculture. They play the hardest and longest, and they take their games most seriously. They are also the most ardent risk takers, willing to gamble it all for their cause.

EXTREME DRINKING ROUTINES

Even as extreme partiers may be admired within the party subculture, they are also the students most maligned by non-partiers as irresponsible and obnoxious drunks who do not know when to stop. And if the typical amount of alcohol that extreme partiers claim to consume is taken at face value, it is not too far-fetched to suggest that many extreme partiers do not know when to stop until, quite literally, they "drop" (i.e., pass out, fall asleep). In fact, the extent to which some students drink while at PU goes so far beyond the typical amounts of alcohol consumed by binge drinkers (as defined by the conventional five-drink minimum) that a simple comparison of binge and non-binge drinkers does not accurately represent the exceptional amounts of liquor consumed by extreme partiers. Examples of their extreme consumption are illustrated in the following responses to an interview question that asked students to describe how much alcohol they typically consumed during a night of drinking.

> Well if it was beer . . . it would probably be north of twelve or thirteen a night. If it were liquor . . . I don't really know, until I black out, maybe five or six shots. (twenty-year-old male junior)

> On a good night I would say I drink about twenty beers. And of course, that doesn't include the drugs, mostly pot . . . mostly. (twenty-year-old male sophomore)

> I never really counted. Ten to fifteen beers will probably keep me from remembering the night . . . and next morning. Let's just say I am always the last one at the keg. (nineteen-year-old male sophomore)

> Probably fifteen beers, something like that, but that's usually on the low side for my friends. I know everyone else is usually way more wasted than I am. (twenty-one-year-old male junior)

> I tend to drink whisky sours, Long Island iced teas, shots of tequila, Jäger bombs, a lot of grain alcohol. How many, who can keep track? (twenty-two-year-old female senior)[2]

> I used to drink grain alcohol . . . purple Jesus. . . . You know, the purple Kool Aid with the grain alcohol . . . but now I just drink beer. How much, God

only knows. If you labeled it in like twelve-ounce drafts I would say at least a case and a half. (twenty-one-year-old male junior)

Note that most students distinguish their alcoholic consumption in terms of beer or hard liquor, with two different standards and rituals for the consumption of each. In fact, excelling in the party subculture seems to require an extensive knowledge and proclivity for the extreme consumption of both beer and liquor. In addition, most PU partiers are well versed in the art of mixology, at least to the extent of knowing what gets them wasted quickly and cheaply. This expertise is demonstrated in the following "drinking recipes" shared by students during their interviews. (Interviewer probes are shown in brackets.)

We like to "bong" jungle juice.[3] [Explain jungle juice for me.] You get the cheapest vodka you can find, gallons of fruit punch, both orange and Hawaiian punch or maybe like a Sprite, throw some gummy bears in there so the vodka soaks in and then once you're done slamming back the jungle juice you can just eat the gummy bears and get wasted off the gummy bears. Or you can use fruit like pineapple. It's usually like 75 percent vodka and 25 percent juice. (twenty-year-old female junior)

Last weekend I had a bottle of Jäger and some kind of vodka. I was taking a bottle of Jäger to the face and then mixing vodka and Mountain Dew . . . and that makes you sick. . . . Don't ever do that.[4] [About how much of these bottles did you drink?] Ummm Jäger, probably the equivalent of four or five shots and then the vodka was probably like half of a bottle. (twenty-one-year-old male junior)

On my twentieth birthday at a friend's house, I wanted to party real hard. I started out by drinking a bottle of Jäger with three people. After that was done I moved onto a bottle of Captain Moran, 100 proof. We finished the bottle and I was pretty much passed out on the couch. Instead of going out, I ended up puking in a thirty-case beer box and then passed back out. I woke up freezing cold with puke all over me. Somehow I walked back home and threw up some more. (twenty-year-old male sophomore)

Based on the previous descriptions of the quantity and variety of liquor that extreme partiers consume, it is not surprising that many of these students lose count of just how much they actually drink during the course of an evening. In fact, many extreme partiers suggest that they drink until there is essentially nothing left to drink, or until they pass out. And apparently, the practice of drinking until they drop is a rather ordinary ending to a night of extreme drunkenness, something they both anticipate and learn to manage. According to Vander Ven (2011), "intoxication management" is an important part of the social learning process of college drinking. It includes learning effective techniques for getting wasted quickly and cheaply, and strategies that help minimize negative consequences such as hangovers or passing out. Properly managing intoxication means that extreme partiers are able to maximize the rewards while minimizing the risks.

DRINKING GAMES AND RITUALS

Some of the most recognizable rituals of party life at any residential college are the drinking games that students play. Though the rules of these games vary, they all share a simple goal: getting wasted. Drinking games, such as beer pong, quarters, and flip cup, are often a significant part of two broader party rituals: pregaming and tailgating. The purpose of both pregaming and tailgating (i.e., a sports-oriented type of pregaming) is to get a "good buzz" or to get completely wasted before moving on to another (often the main) event. In some cases, pregaming is a precursor to the "real" drinking that will take place later that night at house parties or bars, but sometimes students pregame in order to get drunk before heading out to social activities where there will be no alcohol allowed, such as movies or certain athletic events. Pregaming under these latter circumstances is prompted by the assumption that intoxication makes dry events more fun. Pregaming and tailgating are discussed separately in the following sections.

Pregaming

According to the CCVS, 81 percent of students who drink alcohol also pregame before going out at night, and 11 percent of pregamers also use drugs (mostly marijuana) while pregaming. For most of these students, pregaming is a practical or economical ritual that allows them to party hard within a limited budget. The following excerpts from interviews with extreme partiers explain this functional purpose of pregaming, particularly on nights when students go out to bars or clubs, and where the costs of drinks can add up to an expensive tab.[5]

> Pregaming saves money. When you go to the bar and you already have a buzz you save money, and its just a good social event. . . . You get to hang out with friends and chill in someone's house before going out. (twenty-one-year-old male junior)

> Bars become real expensive, so if we do most of our drinking at home, then we only need to buy a couple of drinks when we go out. It works well. We still get wasted, only most of it is done before we get to the bars. (twenty-two-year-old male senior)

> It is far cheaper to pregame before going out, especially when going out to bars and football games. Drinks are real expensive at these places, so by drinking at home, we save a fortune. (twenty-three-year-old male senior)

Most pregaming at PU takes place at someone's house or apartment, and typically involves drinking games. One of the most popular games among college students is beer pong, where cups of beer are placed on a Ping-Pong table (or table equivalent) and players toss balls into the cups. Each time someone gets a ball in a cup an opponent has to chug the contents. According to Seaman (2005) there are at least nineteen versions of beer pong. The following excerpts describe in more detail some of the drinking games and other pregaming rituals at PU.

> When we pregame at a friend's house, we usually play drinking games — I personally like flip cup — where we either drink beer or liquor, and just try to get a nice buzz going before leaving for a party or bar. Most people don't show up to parties or bars stone-cold sober. (twenty-one-year-old male junior)[6]

> Pregaming usually consists of hanging out till around 8 PM, sometimes playing games, sometimes just listening to music and drinking, or smoking pot. Then we usually head over to a friend's house where we will pregame some more until about 10 or 11. Then we go either to a house party 'till around 1 and then around 1-ish we will head to a bar. Saturday nights are usually about the same, except we would head straight to the bar probably

around 11. These nights we pregame from 8 'till 11 and then we head to the bar. (twenty-two-year-old male senior)

Pregaming usually means beer pong, so figure one beer per game plus whatever else you are drinking . . . so figure five to ten beers while pregaming, depending on how good you are at beer pong. (twenty-year-old male sophomore)

Beer, drugs, liquor, beer pong, other games. Pregaming is pretty much a party that doesn't last as long as real parties. Typically, everyone will leave together sometime before midnight and head to another party or to a bar. (twenty-two-year-old female senior)

As described in the above quotes, pregaming is really just the first phase of a much longer night of partying. In fact, pregaming at someone's house is typically followed by a rendezvous to a second destination where students will typically continue to drink if alcohol is available. Aside from local bars and clubs, a popular second destination for partiers is a fraternity party or off-campus "house" party, where there are usually large amounts of beer (and sometimes harder liquor) for a small admission fee.[7] House parties are an ideal setting for extreme partying rituals, since, unlike bars, there are seldom formal agents (e.g., bouncers, bartenders) present to cut patrons off when they have had too much to drink. In addition to the alcohol already consumed while pregaming, it is not unusual for extreme partiers while at parties to drink until the alcohol runs out or they pass out, which ever comes first. It is also not uncommon for students to party for upwards of six hours at "good" parties, at least according to the following student.

A good party will last anywhere from six to eight hours, depending on when you start. If you start at 8, it could last eight hours until 4 in the morning or 3 in the morning, whichever one you want. We usually start at 9, and we could go from 9 until let's say 3 in the morning, and that's six hours of drinking nonstop. Usually you just drink until you kinda, like, pass out (twenty-year-old male junior)

Drinking nonstop until you "kinda, like, pass out" is actually not all that unusual for extreme partiers at the party school. With alcoholic consumption starting as early as 8 PM during the pregaming phase, and then continuing until 3 or 4 in the morning, passing out may simply be a routine ending to an ordinary night of partying.

Tailgating and Game-Day Rituals

Tailgating, a specific type of pregaming that takes place before sporting events (mostly football), is one of the most recognizable drinking rituals at a party school. Tailgating at large sports-oriented universities is a long-honored tradition for sports fans of all ages and usually includes food, music, games (e.g., hacky sack, tossing a football, corn hole), and almost always alcohol, lots of it.[8] According to the CCVS, 95 percent of PU students attend at least an occasional PU football game, and 83 percent of students who attend home games "tailgate" in some manner that includes alcohol. Another 7 percent of students use drugs while tailgating.

Although tailgating is a ritual practiced by many sports fans throughout the country, no one tailgates quite as enthusiastically and excessively as extreme partiers at the party school. For instance, it is not unusual for extreme partiers to begin to drink alcohol at 9 or 10 in the morning on days when football games are scheduled for afternoon or early evening. Many of these students will take a hiatus from partying only to attend the game, and then will promptly continue to party well into the night. In some cases, students may even bypass going into the stadium to watch the football game in favor of an uninterrupted tailgating experience. Under such circumstances, the tailgate and not the actual football game becomes the main event (Vander Ven 2011). The following excerpts from student interviews about tailgating at PU football games illustrate some of the rituals involved in a typical PU tailgate.

> A good tailgate usually consists of drinking about twelve to fourteen beers and also taking about five or six shots while hanging out with a bunch of friends. We walk around to a lot of tailgates, where we are usually offered even more beer. It's a pretty long day. [How long do you typically tailgate for?] We usually start around 11 AM. and sometimes I don't even go to the games . . . so usually from like 11 to 5. [So you actually just tailgate and don't go to the games?] Well, by the time the game starts I'm just too drunk and I don't feel like walking into the stadium and being around a large crowd of people. So, yeah, I just stay put drinking. (twenty-two-year-old male senior)

I usually meet up with my friends at our tailgating spot about five hours prior to kick off. While we are there we drink, cook on a grill, and play games such as corn hole or beer pong. We're all pretty wasted before the game begins. (twenty-year-old female sophomore)

We start tailgating for a Saturday afternoon football game at about 7 in the morning. We mostly stay at my apartment playing beer pong and flip cup and stuff. At some point, we grab some food, but mostly it's about the alcohol, and sometimes pot. (twenty-three-year-old male senior)

Tailgating is fun. Everyone's really excited for the game. And sometimes it will be nuts. Like, people will be crazy, really overdoing it with the drinking. But mostly people will do OK on football days because they want to go to the game. Like, everyone's drunk and trashed, but nobody's, like, doing stupid stuff because they want to end up going to the game eventually, and you got to go through security and stuff. But you can literally do anything on a football day . . . like, I've seen ten-year-olds playing beer pong at tailgates. [laughs] (twenty-one-year-old female junior)

Even though the previous student admits that many students are "drunk and trashed" on football days, she denies that they are doing "stupid stuff" because they "want to end up going to the game eventually." However, she also speculates that "you can literally do anything on a football day," inferring that drunk and trashed students are more apt to get away with reckless behavior on game days. Neal and Fromme (2007) refer to game days at large universities as *dis-inhibited* social environments, where there are different, or at least more relaxed, rules regarding student conduct, which exacerbates bad behavior before, during, and even after games. Some examples of post-game bad behaviors are described in the next section.

POST-GAME AND AFTER-PARTY RITUALS

Once the football game is over, extreme partiers, still hyped up from both the game and their alcohol intake, will often set out for the after-party. Post-game rituals can last for another few hours and will usually include more drinking and, far too often, reckless and even illegal activities (e.g., ripping down street signs, vandalizing private property). Under cover of night and emboldened by alcohol and the disinhibited environment of game days, otherwise well-behaved students behave with little regard to university rules or state and local laws. And it is within this context that one post-game ritual — couch burning — is most likely to take place. In fact, setting couches aflame is not just common at PU but considered somewhat of a tradition.

Couch Burning

One of the more unique post-game rituals at the party school is the act of setting couches, other furniture, or dumpsters on fire, and gathering around to watch such items burn. In the real world, this is considered arson; in the party world, it is often seen as entertainment, and even tradition. As discussed in chapter 3 (see pp. 34–35), couch burning has become so entrenched in PU's public imagery that a portrait of a couch engulfed in flames has been memorialized alongside the school's logo on bumper stickers, T-shirts, and other memorabilia.

According to the CCVS, 16 percent of students at PU admit to having set items on fire or watched other students do so, with 88 percent of these incidents taking place in their own neighborhoods. Despite the stiff penalties if caught, students often fail to see the deviance of burning property. In fact, there is such a celebratory mood among the large groups of students who watch as furniture, dumpsters, and miscellaneous items go up in flames that it is easy to see why students are often ambiguous about its criminality.

Although 68 percent of these intentional fires at PU occur following football and other sports games (no matter whether the team wins or loses), sports are not the only events that inspire PU students to burn things. In the words of one male student: "it wouldn't be a party school if we stopped after football season." Of course, students don't really need a reason to burn stuff at PU (other than being wasted). For instance, one spring day in 2010 someone set fire to a portable toilet that was temporarily stationed in the parking lot near the basketball sports complex. The fire spread to two nearby cars causing $4,500 in damage (Cooper 2010). And at this year's Fall Fest, an event welcoming students back after the summer break, a parking meter wrapped with burlap was set on fire (according to a student who witnessed it). There were no arrests in either incident, and barely any interest among students. After all, these types of fires occur with regularity. In fact, a dumpster is set on fire almost weekly in Ptown, and other "celebratory fires" occur several weekends during the football season. It is apparently just what students do at PU.

Despite PU's attempts to discourage this potentially dangerous practice (as discussed in chapter 3), the practice of setting items on fire is so entrenched within the reputation of the party school, and so seldom seen as real crime by students, that it is difficult to eliminate. For instance, a male student who was asked in an interview whether couch burning is a "problem" in his neighborhood, summed up the general attitude of many PU partiers when he replied: "I wouldn't call it a problem. I would call it entertainment." With the ritual of burning things seen as entertaining, and couch burning in particular seen as tradition, any attempts to curb it, like attempts to prohibit drinking, are not likely to be effective as long as students see such rituals as a integral part of their college experiences.

After-Party Pranks

Another party ritual that, like couch burning, inspires pride and even boasting from students who participate in the party subculture is the "prank," a planned event (or trick, hoax, or practical joke) meant to be funny but is often mean-spirited, and even harmful to the pranked person. Though many pranks take place on game days, they can take place on any day of the week, at any time, but almost always after a long night of partying. Targets of these after-party pranks are sometimes members of one's own peer groups, sometimes members of rival or "enemy" groups, and sometimes "random" targets that can be other students or nonstudents. Pranks that are carried out by peer groups can bond members together in allegiance and forge group solidarity. Pranks are encouraged and rewarded by the party subculture, and it is most likely this reinforcement, or deviance admiration (see Heckert and Heckert 2002), by fellow partiers that motivate pranksters to enact elaborate and sometimes dangerous pranks.

Within the party subculture, pranks can also validate a partier's status. A good party prank can become legendary, and elaborate and "crazy" pranks, along with the retelling of these antics, can bolster and legitimize the university's reputation as a party school. Stories of brash, imaginative, and risky pranks are celebrated and become emblematic of the school's party scene. A cross-section of such pranks, shared by PU partiers during their interviews, are showcased below.

At around noon we started drinking and by 10 PM we were pretty well wasted and we decided it would be a great time to go to the university farm. . . . [How much had you had to drink at that point?] Umm, probably the better part of a twenty-four pack. . . . All of us had our own case so . . . I would say close to a case a piece. . . . It was probably about midnight when we got to the university farm and we go out to one of the barns where the sheep are kept. And we took a big ewe, she was probably about a hundred fifty pounds, threw her in the back of the truck and drove through downtown with one of the guys holding it and then let her loose in the fraternity house and proceeded to pull the fire alarm with her running around inside of it. That was probably one of the better nights. . . . (twenty-three-year-old male senior)

We had an alum of our fraternity that kept coming back. . . . He still comes back every Thursday through Saturday and parties with the freshman kids. . . . One night he was really intoxicated and some of the guys thought it would be funny if they stripped him naked and handcuffed him to the flag poll outside of the house. . . . That was pretty crazy. (twenty-two-year-old male senior)

We had a party at my house a couple years back and my friend got real drunk and went into one of my roommates' rooms and peed all over her purses that were hanging on a rack. I was laughing so hard I almost peed in my pants. Of course, my roommate didn't find it so funny at the time. But we laugh about it now. (twenty-one-year-old female senior)

My first weekend here there was a huge party. Sometime after midnight, someone at the party took an empty keg and threw it right through a car windshield. Everyone at the party started clapping and cheering. I knew right then it was going to be one crazy year. I also learned that I never wanted to park my car anywhere near those crazy-ass party houses! (twenty-three-year-old male senior)

There is a bridge that is about seventy-five feet high right outside of town. One night after playing Edward 40 hands [a drinking game] and shotgunning a few beers, my friends dared me to jump off the bridge. They said it was an initiation of sorts, that everyone did it, and that nobody ever got hurt. It was stupid, but it seemed like a good idea at the time. I stood there for a while debating about it, but finally took the plunge. I bruised my whole butt and back, and had a swollen ankle and chipped two teeth. I don't remember three days of my life because of it. But it's a great story that my friends still talk about. (twenty-two-year-old female senior)

Despite the potential danger and even illegality of some of these prior pranks, students relaying these tales almost always find some humor in them. It is, in part, the shared humor of these situations that make them such a venerable ritual and shared experience among partiers. These larger-than-life tales bond students together and become part of the "good" memories that students take away with them after graduation from the party school. The durability of these shared stories and their potential in helping to establish their school's place in party infamy apparently outweigh the risks of engaging in such pranks.

PARTY RISKS: ILLNESS AND INJURY

Due in part to the endorsement of extreme and risky party rituals by their peers, students at the party school have a rather high incidence (and tolerance) for illness and injury caused by their own partying behaviors. Within the context of the party subculture, students accept a certain amount of risk. For instance, hangovers, or minor injuries and other harms, may simply be seen as collateral damage, an acceptable cost for admission to the party.

Not surprisingly, the more students party, the greater the risks. According to the CCVS, 81 percent of extreme partiers at PU have experienced a blackout while drinking (i.e., being conscious but having no memory of events) as compared to 49 percent of heavy partiers and 11 percent of light partiers (see appendix B, table 9). Moreover, 65 percent of students who have blacked out have done so more than once. The large number of students claiming to have experienced multiple blackouts poses the question as to whether these students really experienced a medically defined blackout or if being "blacked out" has become a convenient excuse that helps students deny responsibility for foolish or regrettable behavior while intoxicated. For example, the following students each describe situations that they say occurred while they were blacked out. But even as their references to blacking out may help to alleviate their embarrassment or regret for bad behavior while intoxicated, blacking out does not appear to concern them, or cause them to slow down.

> My friends tell me one night I was dancing on the table at the bar we were
> at, and flashed the guys at another table. But I have no memory at all. I can't
> imagine ever doing something like that. I was so completely blacked out.
> (twenty-two-year-old female senior)

I don't really know what happened, but I had no recollection of parts of my night. It was the first time I ever blacked out but not the last. It was during the first football game my freshman year, and I ended up waking up in my dorm bed, with bruises on my head, and not knowing who won the football game at all. My roommate told me I had fallen down inside the stadium and hit my head on a railing. (twenty-one-year-old male junior)

In terms of gender, more men than women who party in the extreme category experience blackouts (86 percent versus 66 percent), but more women than men who party in the heavy category experience blackouts (55 percent versus 45 percent). More women than men also experience other types of party-related "illnesses" such as nausea and passing out. For women, 55 percent of extreme partiers and 38 percent of heavy partiers experience illness from alcohol. For men, 42 percent of extreme partiers and 23 percent of heavy partiers experience illness while intoxicated (see appendix B, table 10). These numbers most likely reflect the more severe physical effects of alcohol on women as a group, who tend to be smaller than men on average and metabolize alcohol more slowly than men (Sun and Longazel 2008; Wechsler and Wuethrich 2002).

Considering the super-sized amounts of liquor consumed by heavy and extreme partiers, often combined with drugs, it is not surprising that many students of both genders drink to the point of passing out, blacking out or regurgitating their evening's allotment of liquor. But what is surprising is how entertaining and rather ordinary these incidents appear to be to the students who experience them. Neither women nor men seem overly concerned about the potential or actual dangers that accompany getting sick from excessive partying. Instead, nausea and other physical ailments related to alcohol and drug consumption are often a source of great amusement within the context of the party subculture, as demonstrated in the following survey responses from students.

At a party a couple of weeks ago, I saw some kid funnel a whole bottle of wine in one chug. He was absolutely wasted! It was hilarious. I've never seen someone throw up so much. (nineteen-year-old male sophomore)

Someone right near me threw up in the coliseum [at a basketball game] in the student section. It was disgusting but also pretty funny. Everybody started cheering so I cheered too. Security came and escorted him out. (twenty-one-year-old female junior)

Craziest thing that ever happened to me here was downtown when my friend and I were at a bar and this guy threw up all over her. I wouldn't change it for anything. It is a funny story to tell people about my crazy days in college. (twenty-year-old female sophomore)

In addition to party-related illnesses, extreme partiers also experience the highest rates of injuries while intoxicated. For instance, according to the CCVS, 34 percent of extreme partiers have experienced an injury from an accident while intoxicated, as compared to 20 percent of heavy partiers, and only 3 percent of light partiers. In terms of gender, women are more likely to be injured while intoxicated, with 40 percent of extreme partiers and 24 percent of heavy partiers experiencing injury, as compared to men with 30 percent of extreme partiers and 13 percent of heavy partiers experiencing injury.

Clearly, students who party most excessively put themselves at greater risk of injury. Yet few of these students — women or men — appear overly concerned about such risks. In fact, many of PU's most avid partiers accept the possibility of injury as an acceptable risk for their participation in the party subculture. Furthermore, when injury does happen, most students are readily able to minimize the harms, chalking it up to the old adage "stuff happens." This nonchalant attitude toward injuries brought on by intoxication is illustrated in the following excerpt. In her response to an interview question about drinking, the student refers to her injuries almost as a barometer that allows her to retroactively assess how much she had had to drink. Yet, knowledge of her injuries does not appear to deter her from partying. On the contrary, bumps and bruises seem to be an expected, accepted, and easily rationalized consequence of extreme partying.

I know if I've been drinking too much 'cause I always end up getting hurt. Like I'll wake up with a big scratch or a bruise. . . . The first weekend we came back to school I lost my toenail after one crazy night. I didn't even know how it happened. I wasn't blacked out or anything, I just woke up the next day missing my toenail. But these things don't usually stop me. What's a few bumps and bruises? (nineteen-year-old female sophomore)

In addition to shrugging off their own injuries, most PU partiers also minimize the injuries experienced by other students who get hurt within the context of the party situation. For example, the student in the following excerpt describes an incident where someone at a house party was pushed out of a window. Due to the circumstances of the situation — it was part of a game being played, "no one got seriously hurt," and everyone was "way wasted" — the student is able to minimize the incident's severity. In fact, the incident actually appears to have increased his evaluation of the party that night as "wild," a positive label within the context of the party school.

> About a month ago, I saw a kid get knocked through a window at a party. My friends do this thing when they get drunk called the umpire. You know how sometimes in baseball games when the umpire and coach chest-bump each other? Well a few of them would do that but get a running start and do it to someone who was way wasted and not expecting it. The guy that went crashing through the window was umpired by two people. No one got seriously hurt, but the landlord of the building wasn't happy. That was one wild party! (twenty-two-year-old male senior)

While it may be easy to see a situation as funny or minimize its injuries when no one is seriously hurt, incidents that cause severe injury or send students to the hospital are not as easily rationalized, even within the party situation. According to the CCVS, 12 percent of extreme partiers have been hospitalized due to party-related illnesses or injuries, as compared to 6 percent of heavy partiers, and 2 percent of light partiers. (Women are slightly more likely to be hospitalized than men when they party to the extreme, but men are slightly more likely to be hospitalized than women in the heavy partying category). Perhaps the silver lining of these more serious injuries that require hospitalization, is that they tend to be a wake-up call for students, as expressed in the following excerpts.

> Freshmen year, I drank way too much and had to be taken to the hospital on St. Patrick's Day. It was pretty scary and it definitely got me to change my drinking habits. I no longer party nearly to that extent. (twenty-two-year-old male senior)

> My roommate got kicked out of a club within ten minutes of being there because she was way too drunk for her own good and it wasn't the first time

it had happened. She ended up in the hospital and was very dehydrated. Her knees were banged up along with a few scratches on her face from falling down. Needless to say, she learned her lesson. (twenty-one-year-old female junior)

One time a friend called me from the hospital and asked me to come visit him, and I went over and he told me he had, like, OD'd on "E" [Ecstasy] or speed or something. The cops found him naked [downtown] at 6 PM flipping out. . . . Apparently he had a heart attack or stroke or something, and he had no idea what happened. Wow, that woke him up. I don't think he's used drugs since. (twenty-two-year-old male senior)

One night my freshmen year after a party had been raging for a few hours and I had been drinking Natty and Vlady [Natural Ice and Vladimir] I got completely wasted and I was almost completely blacked out. My buddy filled me in on what happened after. I guess I went downstairs to grab some more beer and after I'd been gone for like thirty minutes, my friends come down to look for me and they found me face down on the concrete floor lying in my own puke [laughs]. Somehow my friends get me up on a chair and at this point, they're extremely wasted too so they're not thinking straight. So they get me to sit up by tying me up to the chair. Idiots [laughs].

[What happened next?]

I don't know how long I was sitting there, but finally this random girl comes down and sees me and my idiot buddies, and gets her friend to take over. He realized my head was bleeding, gets me untied and carries me to his car. At this point I remember a little, because I can remember begging him not to call my parents. So he gets me to the hospital and I am totally embarrassed that I got obliterated at this party and had to be hospitalized. My parents were pissed. It was kind of a wake up call. (twenty-one-year-old male junior)

Clearly, as this prior example illustrates, drunk students can be rather incapable guardians during crises, and may even exacerbate problems and make matters much worse. Yet, within the party situation, the ineptitude of one's intoxicated peers is often viewed as comedic. Even as the student in the previous example is clearly cognizant of how foolish his friends had acted in their misguided attempt to help him, he still finds humor in the situation. Part of his cavalier, and rather forgiving, attitude may be due to his "happy ending" (i.e., he survived). But part of his response may be learned, or even encouraged, by the party subculture. Recall that part of managing intoxication is to minimize harms and reinterpret negative consequences (including crises) in more favorable ways. Like extreme sports, risk and danger is part of the thrill of extreme partying, and surviving extreme wastedness and near calamities can be seen as a triumph, a rite of passage and a positive bonding experience among partying peers.

Aside from drunken ineptitude, another common response to crisis within the party situation is to do nothing. Nonintervention by fellow party-goers can be explained in the following ways. First, in a party setting, there is a "live and let live" attitude that glamorizes risk and makes extreme intoxication appear more adventurous and less dangerous. Witnesses observing potential crises at bars or parties may not interpret what they are seeing as crimes or problems, if they even notice these problems at all. For instance, in a study of bystander responses to sexual assault at parties, Burn (2009) suggests that partygoers often fail to notice sexual assault cues within a party situation because they are too distracted by their own social activities and intoxication. Alcohol and drugs can certainly blur definitions of situations. And students who do not want to appear foolish by misinterpreting or overreacting to a situation that turns out to be nothing, may choose to err on the side of caution by doing nothing (Casey and Ohler 2012).

A second reason for nonintervention is that students, taking their cues from other students who are doing nothing, may not want to stand out as the only one who sees a problem, or what is often referred to as pluralistic ignorance (see Coker et al. 2011, p. 779). This concept is different from the classic "bystander effect" that suggests that persons will be less likely to intervene in large groups, based on the assumption that someone else will help (i.e., diffusion of responsibility) (Michener and DeLamater 1999). Students in a party situation may choose not to intervene specifically when they are fairly certain that no one else will. Nonintervention in this manner is about conforming to group norms. It is also about self-preservation or, rather, concern over possible stigmatization or social disapproval for not doing the "right thing" according to group norms.

One final reason for nonintervention, and also related to self-preservation, pertains to concerns over legal consequences. Students who are engaged in some type of illicit activity (e.g., underage drinking, drug use, property trespass) may be less likely to call 911 or the police to report a crisis in order to avoid getting into trouble for their own illegal behaviors. Such concerns are illustrated in the following excerpt from a student who explains why he did not seek medical help for a friend who he acknowledges should have been taken to the hospital. Although the friend turned out to be fine, fear of self-incrimination and a misguided loyalty to intoxicated friends and peers are often contributing factors in many alcohol-related deaths that have occurred at colleges over the past fifty years (Wechsler and Wuethrich 2002).

One night I went with my friends to watch this band downtown and a couple of friends had taken a few hits from their pipe, which was crack, and took a couple of ecstasy pills. So we were at this bar drinking, dancing, and just having a good time, when I look over, and one of my friends had collapsed. So I rushed over to her and we couldn't get her to open her eyes. We kind of attracted attention, so the bouncer came over and asked us if we needed help. He picked her up and got her outside. My buddy and I were both drunk and had been taking drugs too, so we didn't want to get police involved. Plus we were underage, so that kind of scared us a little. We just wanted to get her home so she could sleep it off. We really should have taken her to the hospital, but we were afraid, I guess. Who wants to get questioned by the police when you're on drugs? We were afraid of getting arrested or kicked out of school. (twenty-two-year-old male senior)

In addition to inhibiting decisions to seek help during medical crises, extreme intoxication can lead students to make other bad and potentially dangerous decisions. For example, the student in the following excerpt describes her decision to get into a car with a stranger who was also drunk and potentially violent. Though this woman did get home safely, extreme intoxication can certainly make partiers much less rational and unable to assess potentially dangerous situations.

I had too much to drink one night and I didn't want to take a bus back home so I got into a car with someone I never met but who agreed to drive me home. While I was in the car I realized he was extremely wasted, too. Then he started telling me that he just got out of jail that morning for beating his wife. Man was I glad to get home alive! (twenty-one-year-old female junior)

Another bad decision that students frequently make while intoxicated is to engage in unprotected sex. The more they party, the more likely they are to engage in this behavior. For instance, according to CCVS data, 33 percent of extreme partiers at PU and 26 percent of heavy partiers have engaged in unprotected sex, as compared to 4 percent of light partiers (see appendix B, table 9). Men are slightly more likely to engage in unprotected sex than women, with 35 percent of extreme partying men engaging in unprotected sex, as compared to 29 percent of women. Extreme intoxication, combined with the pressures for men (and some women) to "hook up" (i.e., find a casual sexual partner) appears to override good judgment when it comes to being safe about sex. These same factors may also help to explain the increased potential of rape for women within the context of the party situation, as will be discussed in the following chapter.

SUMMING UP

This chapter has identified some of the extreme party rituals that take place at the party school, including drinking games, pregaming, and after-party pranks. Although most students at a party school engage in at least some of these rituals, for extreme partiers ritualized drinking (and drug use) is exaggerated to an extreme. With the ultimate goal of getting wasted (and even drinking until they drop), it is no surprise that the most hard-core participants of the party subculture experience the most negative consequences, including illness, injury, and various problems related to bad decisions made while intoxicated.

Yet, within the context of the party subculture, some minor injury and other harms are often brushed aside, laughed away and dismissed as inconsequential. Moreover, it is often the crazy nights, absurd mishaps and even some regrettable decisions while wasted that students remember most vividly when reflecting back upon their college years. The party situation can transform near tragedy into comedy, and convert great pranks and near crises into larger-than-life epic adventures that bond students together and further validate their university's reputation as a party school. With the potential of such rewards, many partiers surmise that the occasional injuries, illnesses, and even crime victimization as described in the next chapter, are simply worth the risks.

6

Flirting with Danger

CRIMINAL CONSEQUENCES
OF THE PARTY SUBCULTURE

In addition to increased risk of illness and injury, as described in the previous chapter, participation in the party subculture increases students' vulnerability to crime victimization. Intoxication dulls a person's awareness of lurking dangers and slows reaction time, making them "attractive targets" for victimization. Participation in the party subculture also increases students' likelihood of perpetrating crime themselves and getting into trouble with the law. Persons who are intoxicated tend to be more careless, reckless, impulsive and aggressive, all of which can contribute to participation in criminal activity. In addition, partiers spend more time at "hot spots" (e.g., bars, clubs, parties), where there is a greater opportunity for crime to occur due to the convergence of motivated offenders, vulnerable victims, and "incapable" guardians, most of whom are intoxicated. In fact, most of the crimes that occur at PU and other party schools — especially vandalism, simple assaults (i.e., fights), and sexual assaults — are "intoxication crimes" that take place when offender, victim, or both are intoxicated. And many of these crimes take place in or near party hot spots.

This chapter examines crime victimization at PU, looking at both the frequencies of crime and the linkages between crime victimization and students' party routines. While chapter 3 of this book described some of the more serious intoxication crimes that have taken place at PU based on official crime statistics and news reports, the findings presented in this chapter draw primarily from the Campus Crime Victimization Survey (CCVS), a self-report survey. In contrast to official crime data such as Clery statistics and Uniform Crime Reports (UCR) that include only incidents known to police (see chapter 1 for discussion), CCVS data include all crimes experienced by students while at PU, irrespective of whether they were reported to police.

Since only a small fraction of intoxication crimes and other party-related disturbances are reported to officials, the CCVS provides a much more comprehensive investigation of criminal victimization at the party school.[1]

CRIME VICTIMIZATION AT PU

CCVS findings show that about half of traditional PU students experience some type of crime during their years at PU. The following sections describe separately three broad categories of crime at PU: property crime (e.g., burglary, vandalism, larceny theft), violent crime (e.g., physical attacks and fights), and sexual crime (e.g., rape and unwanted sexual contact). Rather than providing an exhaustive descriptive account of these crimes, the following sections focus most specifically on intoxication crime, or incidents that occur within the context of the party situation.

Property Crime Victimization

According to CCVS data, just under half of PU students have experienced property crime since their arrival at PU, including burglary, vandalism, and larceny theft.[2] The frequencies and patterns for each of these crimes and their connections to students' party routines are discussed below.[3] (See also appendix B, table 11, for crime descriptives.)

Burglary. Based on CCVS data, almost one in ten students experience a home or car burglary while at PU. A disproportionate number of home burglaries (73 percent) and car break-ins (65 percent) take place off campus in the student-dense neighborhoods adjacent to PU's downtown campus. The majority of burglaries — both home and car — take place at night, with 89 percent of home burglaries occurring at night (55 percent after midnight and 40 percent when students are away on vacations), and 83 percent of car break-ins occurring at night (51 percent after midnight).

Most surprising is the rather large number of students who have experienced multiple burglaries while at PU. For instance, 17 percent of students who have had their homes burglarized have also had their cars broken into (2 percent of the sample experienced both crimes). In addition, 13 percent of home burglary victims have had their homes burglarized twice, while 5 percent have experienced three or more burglaries. Similarly, 15 percent of car burglary victims have had their cars burglarized twice, and 10 percent have had three or more break-ins. The following excerpt from one such serial victim describes two car burglaries while living downtown.

> The car outside my downtown apartment was broken into twice. The first time I had several items such as money, books, and my iPod stolen. I quit leaving stuff in there after this, and the second time only a couple of notebooks were taken but they trashed the inside of the car by throwing things out from the console and glove compartment. (twenty-two-year-old male senior)

Serial burglaries at PU can be explained primarily by where such crimes take place, namely in Ptown's "downtown" neighborhoods. As described in chapter 3, most student-centered neighborhoods near PU are located adjacent to the University's downtown campus. This area is the "hot spot" for PU partiers where most of the student bars, clubs, and parties are located. From a routine activities perspective, a hot spot increases the potential of crime due to the convergence of motivated offenders, attractive targets, and an absence of capable guardians. Aside from students' party routines (which will be discussed shortly), student-dense neighborhoods may be specifically targeted for property crime due to several factors.[4] First, students and young people in general may be less concerned with locking doors and windows. They are also less likely to have alarm systems or use other preventative measures to keep property secure. Student housing in PU's downtown neighborhoods also tend to be older and easier to break into. Students also travel quite frequently on weekends, holidays, and during summer months, which leaves their homes more vulnerable to break-ins during extended absences.

There also tends to be less capable guardians in student-dense neighborhoods, both in terms of formal social control (i.e., police patrols) and informal social control (e.g., neighbors watching out for one another). After all, these neighborhoods comprise the epicenter of the party subculture where students will tend to be especially wary of police and more likely to mind their own business. Additionally, these neighborhoods are exceptionally transient. With residents frequently moving in and out, students who live there are less likely to get to know one another, making it more difficult to distinguish suspicious "strangers" who do not belong from their actual neighbors. Simply stated, these neighborhoods provide motivated offenders with easy access to attractive targets and minimal risk due to an absence of capable guardians.

Vandalism. In addition to burglaries, a large number of students (34 percent) experience vandalism while at PU. More specifically, 16 percent of students experience property damage to their homes, including having windows smashed, eggs, rocks or other items thrown at their houses, and mailboxes or other parts of their homes damaged or removed. Meanwhile, 29 percent of students who keep cars at PU experience damage to their cars, including having side mirrors torn off, car paint scratched or "keyed" and doors, bumpers, or other parts of the car dented or smashed. One in five incidents of car damage is identified by respondents as "hit-and-runs." And, approximately 5 percent of students in the survey attribute damage specifically to eggs, tomatoes, or other food products tossed at their cars; one student claimed she had "caramel poured on the hood." Half of the vandalism incidents at PU cost victims more than $250 in damages.

Like burglaries, a large proportion of vandalism at PU takes place downtown and at night. More specifically, 74 percent of home vandalism and 70 percent of car vandalism take place downtown, and 90 percent of home vandalism and 78 percent of car vandalism occur at night (with 50 percent of each type of crime occurring after midnight). Also like burglaries, it is not unusual for students to experience multiple incidents of vandalism. According to the CCVS, almost half of vandalism victims experience more than one incident while at PU. For instance, 36 percent of students who have had their homes vandalized have also had their cars vandalized (6 percent of student sample have experienced both crimes). In addition, 24 percent of home vandalism victims have experienced two incidents and 14 percent three or more incidents. Similarly, 28 percent of car vandalism victims have experienced two incidents and 17 percent three or more incidents.

Again, like burglary, serial vandalism is largely indicative of where students live and park their cars. Living downtown — a hot spot for PU's party subculture — and parking their cars on the streets near their homes can make students vulnerable to vandalism, as illustrated in the following excerpt. The student, who has had his car vandalized five times while living downtown, refers to a common dilemma for students living in this part of town: whether to pay to park their car, which is very expensive, or risk vandalism by leaving it parked on the streets.

> My car was vandalized five times in two years from drunken idiots coming
> home from the bars and who know they can get away with it. Everyone
> keeps telling me to pay for a parking spot so people would stop messing with

my car. But it is cheaper to pay for the damage than it is to pay for a parking spot. I can't win. (twenty-two-year-old male senior)

Unlike the crime of burglary where an offender's motive is most likely monetary, there appears to be no obvious reason for most vandalism at PU. Instead, most of the vandalism appears to be caused by "drunken idiots," as the prior student suggests, who act out in senseless and destructive ways as they make their way home late at night from bars or parties. And even as vandals may not intend any harm (many of them see their actions as pranks or harmless fun), they clearly cause damage, as demonstrated in the following survey responses that describe some of the costs of these crimes in terms of both time and money.

The front of our house was spray-painted one night probably by a bunch of drunks. Other houses on the street were also vandalized, so the police came door to door asking questions. What really annoyed us was that we had to go out and repaint the front of our house or we would have gotten a ticket from the town. (twenty-one-year-old female junior)

My neighbor was wasted one night and began throwing rocks and other stuff at my car as well as my roommate's car parked in our lot at the time. He shattered a window on my roommate's car and broke the taillights. It was so senseless. (twenty-two-year-old male senior)

I had my windshield wiper ripped off after a football game once, and had to go replace it. And my roommate had eggs thrown at his car on a Saturday night. We were able to scrub it off without too much damage, but what was the point of that? (twenty-one-year-old male junior)

Sometimes when I park just out front of my house I come out in the morning to all sorts of surprises. The idiot drunks walking by from the bars seem to like that spot to pee, so sometimes my tires will smell like urine. There was vomit once on the hood of my car that I had to wash off. But the worst of it was a mess on my passenger windows, something that looked a lot like tomatoes. Just sort of stuck to the window as if my car had been used for target practice. (nineteen-year-old female sophomore)

My landlord needs to replace our mailbox at least once a year. Students tear off parts of it. Sometimes they'll stuff things inside. Like there is sometimes beer cans, cigarette butts stuffed inside. It's only a problem when there is mail still inside. If we forget to pick up the mail, sometimes important stuff gets destroyed. (twenty-one-year-old male junior)

In addition to monetary damages, vandalism that is repetitive and persistent can intimidate entire neighborhoods. In fact, vandalism is Ptown's version of gang warfare, less vicious and lethal than the real thing but nonetheless mean-spirited, disruptive, and intimidating to everyone who lives in the neighborhood. For example, in the following survey response, the student describes a "drive-by" egging on her home turf.

Just last week, we were sitting outside on the porch with some friends drinking when all of a sudden this car drives by and just eggs us. It hit one of my roommates in the arm and just splatters everywhere. But believe it or not, that was not the first time we've been egged. (twenty-year-old sophomore female)

Despite the damages and intimidation caused by vandals at PU, few victims call the police to report these incidents (only one-third of vandalism is reported). In fact, having mailboxes damaged, rocks thrown at their cars, or having to clean vomit, egg, or tomato off their property does not seem all that extraordinary to many students living at the party school. Instead, such incidents are seen as almost ordinary and dismissed as just stuff that happens at a party school.

Larceny theft. One final property crime that occurs with some frequency at PU is larceny theft. According to CCVS data, 17 percent of students have had something stolen from them while at PU, with items ranging from purses and wallets, small electronics (e.g., cell phones, iPods) to books, and ID cards. Although damages from theft is often minimal, 39 percent of stolen items were estimated to be worth $500 or more.

Larceny theft differs from other property crime at PU in a couple of ways. First, more larceny incidents occur during the day (42 percent as compared to 11 percent of burglary and 13 percent of vandalism). Second, unlike other property crime at PU, larceny theft is just as likely to occur on campus as off campus, and incidents are more evenly distributed among off-campus neighborhoods rather than primarily downtown (only 35 percent of larceny thefts occur downtown as compared to approximately 70 percent of burglary and vandalism). However, like other property crimes, it is not unusual for victims of larceny theft to have experienced multiple incidents of theft while at PU. For instance, 21 percent of larceny victims experienced two thefts, and 14 percent experienced three or more incidents. Finally, like other property crimes at PU, many thefts are crimes of opportunity that target victims based on their party routines.

Property crime and party routines. Property crime risk at PU can be explained, in part, by students' routines, including where they live and park their cars, where and with whom they socialize, and especially the extent to which they participate in the party subculture.[5] For almost every type of property crime, risk increases as partying increases (see appendix B, table 12). For instance, 35 percent of heavy and extreme partiers have had their cars vandalized as compared to 20 percent of light partiers and non-partiers. Moreover, 20 percent of extreme partiers and 12 percent of heavy partiers have had items stolen specifically while they were intoxicated, as compared to only 3 percent of light partiers (see appendix B, table 9). Intoxication makes students attractive targets for property crime as they are less aware of their surroundings and less careful in securing their property.

Students' party routines can also explain the higher proportion of car vandalism that occurs downtown, an area with the highest concentration of bars, clubs, and parties. Property damage to both homes and cars in these neighborhoods takes place largely at night, coinciding with the party nightlife. At night in these downtown neighborhoods there is a convergence of attractive targets (e.g., intoxicated students, and cars and homes conveniently located near bars), an absence of capable guardians (e.g., few sober witnesses willing to call police), and motivated offenders who in many cases are intoxicated themselves and, therefore, unconcerned about legal consequences for their actions (Graham, Wells, Bernards, and Dennison 2010).

A routine-activities perspective can also help to explain the sizable percentage of property stolen at bars, clubs, and parties (17 percent of larceny theft takes place at these locales). For instance, within these party hot spots, there are many attractive targets; such as intoxicated students who may be more careless with their property (e.g., purses, car keys, phones). Also, inside these crowded settings, offenders can commit their crimes while maintaining anonymity. A constant jostling of patrons and body contact in crowded bars can increase the ease of picking pockets and other theft without detection

(Thompson and Cracco 2008). In fact, victims may not even realize their property is missing until offenders are long gone. Finally, other bar patrons and party goers are often distracted and not paying much attention to their surroundings, preventing them from serving as capable guardians. Taken together, the crowded and intoxicated climate of bars and parties makes them ideal hot spots for larceny theft.

The amount of time students spend at such hot spots, and their overall commitment to the party subculture, may also explain the slight but statistically significant gender differences in terms of most property crime at PU. (See appendix B, table 11.) At PU, more men than women are victims of home burglary (15 percent as compared to 8 percent), home and car vandalism (21 percent versus 13 percent) and larceny theft (21 percent as compared to 15 percent). Gender differences in property victimization may be explained by gender differences in student routines. For instance, more men than women live downtown while at PU in the most vulnerable neighborhoods for crime (53 percent as compared to 40 percent). More men than women go out regularly to drink at bars (60 percent as compared to 52 percent) or parties (58 percent as compared to 48 percent). Men are also more likely than women to drive their cars when they go out to bars and parties, increasing their risk of car vandalism. And finally, more men than women party in an extreme manner (24 percent versus 8 percent), making them and their property more vulnerable and convenient targets.

Violent Crime Victimization: Physical Attacks and Fights

In addition to property crimes, students at the party school experience a rather large number of physical attacks, with most of these incidents characterized as simple assaults (i.e., attacks without weapons or serious injury) or fights (incidents sometimes referred to as mutual combat with no clear victim or offender). According to CCVS findings, 18 percent of students experience a physical attack or fight while at PU. Of these attacks, 41 percent of victims suffer injuries, with 13 percent of injuries serious enough to require medical attention, and 4 percent of injuries requiring hospitalization. Another 9 percent of attacks involve a weapon.

Like property crime, most violent crime at PU occurs downtown (84 percent) and at night (92 percent), with 65 percent of these incidents taking place after midnight. Moreover, 51 percent of attacks and fights take place specifically at or near party hot spots such as bars, clubs, and fraternity or house parties. And like property crimes, students often experience more than one incident of violence while at PU. According to CCVS, 26 percent of students who experience an attack/fight indicate that they had been involved in two of these incidents while at PU and another 20 percent experienced three or more of these incidents.

Most attacks/fights are perpetrated by "strangers" (68 percent), whereas 8 percent are perpetrated by girlfriends/boyfriends or ex-partners, 3 percent by friends, 7 percent by roommates or neighbors, 7 percent by other students from PU and 7 percent by other acquaintances.[6] Men are more than twice as likely as women to experience an attack or be involved in a fight (28 percent as compared to 11 percent). And the clear majority of offenders (79 percent) are men. Moreover, 41 percent of male-on-male attacks/fights involve multiple offenders. And though the CCVS does not ask if students ever started fights, many male students readily acknowledge during interviews that they are willing to participate in them when necessary (e.g., to "settle the score" to help out in an "unfair" fight).[7] This sense of obligation to "help" fellow fighters by leveling the playing field or restoring some sort of "partier justice" may explain why "simple" fights that start between two persons often escalate into much larger group brawls. For example, the student in the following excerpt describes a fight that began "unfairly" (i.e., three against one) and quickly turned riotous outside a downtown bar.

> My first year here, there was a huge fight downtown. It began with three
> men beating up another guy. But people kept joining in. It got so big that the
> cops kept emptying cans of pepper spray but it wasn't working. By the time it
> was over there were paramedics, and several guys were cut up and bleeding
> pretty bad. (twenty-two-year-old male senior)

Regardless of the size of the fight and the extent of injuries, the common thread for the vast majority of fights at the party school is alcohol, lots of it. Alcohol increases aggression, lowers inhibition and self-control, and can turn even the slightest insult or trivial argument into a provocation to fight (Buddie and Parks 2003; Harford et al. 2003). Within the context of the party situation, simple disagreements or "slights" can quickly escalate into physical altercations. In fact, fights are so common at PU bars, clubs and parties that it is rare to find students who party regularly and who have never witnessed one.

Fighting and party routines.   At the party school, there is an especially strong linkage between violent crime, or more specifically fighting, and students' party routines. According to CCVS data, 55 percent of attacks/fights at PU occur while victims are intoxicated and 79 percent when offenders are drunk or high on drugs.[8] When looking at partier types, 40 percent of extreme partiers and 21 percent of heavy partiers experience an attack or fight while at PU, as compared to 10 percent of light partiers and 7 percent of non-partiers (See appendix B, table 12). And though the potential for experiencing violence while intoxicated increases for both men and women, the increase is especially significant for male students. For men, 48 percent of extreme partiers, 28 percent of heavy partiers, and 15 percent of light or non-partiers experience an attack or fight while at PU. For women, 24 percent of extreme partiers, 16 percent of heavy partiers, and approximately 5 percent of light or non-partiers experience an attack or fight. (See appendix B, table 13).[9]

Even though women are not nearly as violent as men, CCVS data show that women at PU are not merely victims or bystanders (or the impetus for men's fights), but can also be the initiators of aggression, particularly when alcohol is involved.[10] According to the CCVS, 17 percent of offenders of physical attacks are women, with 96 percent of their victims as other women. Like men, women who party hardest may have a greater tendency to be aggressive while intoxicated, which can easily trigger fights and physical attacks. Also like men, women who are involved in fights often experience more than one incident. For example, the student in the following excerpt who describes a physical altercation with a female neighbor, implies that she has been in other fights while at PU, all while intoxicated. Note in this example that alcohol may also be used as an excuse ("it just sorta happens when I get drunk") that allows this student to engage in violence even when such aggression is still typically seen as a masculine trait.

> I got punched in the face by my female neighbor. She was supposed to give me and a friend a ride back from the bar but disappeared. I was so pissed when I got home. I confronted her, was screaming at her and barely pushed her when she punched me square in the face. Then we just sort of started fighting before two of my friends tackled her to the ground. I pretty much think I am invincible when I drink and that is obviously not the case. But it's not like I set out to fight. It just sorta happens when I get drunk. (twenty-three-year-old female senior)

A final pattern regarding fights and party routines at PU pertains to where so many of these incidents occur, namely at party hot spots. Almost half of student-on-student violence at PU takes place at or just outside bars (45 percent), with another 6 percent at parties and 4 percent at sporting events. The combination of alcohol and an atmosphere that encourages aggression, or at least sees aggression as appropriate for resolving conflict, makes the party situation especially prone to violent altercations. The following examples of rather serious violence — all male-on-male incidents — illustrate some of the attacks and fights that take place inside PU's party hot spots.

> I've seen terrible fights at bars and parties. I've seen kids arrested and others taken to the hospital. The scariest had to be at a house party when a fight broke out and a guy was pushed off a platform and fell down onto the grass below. People drink so much at these parties and things get so out of control. (twenty-four-year-old female senior)

> Some dude at a bar broke a bottle over my buddy's head during an argument. He had to go to the hospital and get thirty stitches in his head. (twenty-two-year-old male junior)

> At a bar after the [big] game, a guy hit me in the head with an empty bottle because I wasn't celebrating the football team's victory with them. (twenty-one-year-old male junior)

> At almost every football game there is always some bunch of dudes — usually wasted — and ambling to fight. Guys will fight over anything: the team is winning, team is losing or it is just half-time. They don't seem to need a reason. And it takes security forever to get there once the punches start flying. Seriously, football is a dangerous sport, for the spectators! (nineteen-year-old female sophomore)

While it may be understandable that students fight at unregulated parties (i.e., with lots of alcohol and little supervision), it is more surprising that so many fights occur at bars and sporting events where there are social control agents on hand that should be able to act as deterrents. But the threat of sanctions from these agents seem to do little to prevent or minimize student conflicts. Of course, when fights arise inside bars or clubs, the participants may be merely escorted outside. And since the police are only called to break up large fights, there is seldom any real consequence for bar fighters — legal or otherwise. Similarly, at sports events, as pointed out in the previous excerpt, it can take security "forever to get there." Thus, with no *real* threat of consequences and students' general view of violence as an acceptable means for resolving arguments, fights have become almost normal within the context of the party situation. As one student said in response to why no one called the police to report a four-person bar fight: "It was just a fight, we were drunk; what was there to report?"

Furthermore, a "good fight" is often seen as pure entertainment to enliven an evening. Fights are almost expected at some bars (Lowe, Levine, Best, and Heim 2012), which may help to explain why students often do nothing to stop them or seldom see them as serious violence (Wilkinson 2009). Within these party hot spots, fights are spectacles that can add drama and excitement to the night, as often do other types of intoxication crimes such as arson (i.e., couch burning) and vandalism.

Sexual Crime Victimization

Whereas more men than women are victims of physical attacks and fights at the party school, far more women than men are victims of sexual crimes. This section describes separately two types of sexual crime that occur at PU: rape (defined in the CCVS as forced or coerced sexual intercourse, including attempts) and unwanted sexual contact (defined in the CCVS as unwanted sexual touching, fondling, and grabbing of the body without consent).

Rape. According to the CCVS, 9 percent of female students experience rape while at PU as compared to 3 percent of male students. The data also show that 87 percent of rape offenders are male. All of men's victims are women, and all of women's victims are men. A large proportion of rape (42 percent) takes place during the freshman year. Forty-four percent of rapes occur on campus (in residence halls or fraternity houses), and 87 percent of rapes occur in students' homes regardless of whether their residences are on or off campus. Of the incidents that take place off campus, 57 percent take place downtown. Ninety-three percent of rapes occur at night (82 percent after midnight). Medical attention is required for 11 percent of rape incidents, although none of the incidents reported to CCVS required hospitalization. A weapon is used in 8 percent of rape incidents. (See appendix B, table 11.)

Twenty percent of students who are raped while at PU indicate that they had experienced two incidents of rape, and 10 percent experienced three or more incidents (see appendix B, table 11). Only 13 percent of rape incidents are perpetrated by strangers, whereas 7 percent are perpetrated by boyfriends/girlfriends, 17 percent by ex-partners, 22 percent by friends, with the remaining 41 percent by other acquaintances (including neighbors, coworkers, and other students). In 13 percent of incidents, there were two or more offenders.

Rape and party routines.   Like all crime at PU, rape is highly associated with students' party routines. For instance, most rapes occur when victim, offender, or both participants are intoxicated. According to CCVS findings, 72 percent of rape victims were drunk or using drugs at the time of the incident, and 54 percent of offenders were drunk or high on drugs.[11] Risk of rape triples for heavy and extreme partiers (9 percent), as compared to light partiers and non-partiers (3 percent). For women, risk is even more pronounced, with 15 percent of heavy and extreme partiers experiencing rape as compared to 4 percent of light partiers or non-partiers. (See appendix B, tables 12 and 13.)

Increased risk of rape for students who party the most can be explained primarily by victims' increased vulnerability and inability to resist attacks when intoxicated (Armstrong, Hamilton, and Sweeney 2006; Pezza and Bellotti 1995). As seen in chapter 5, excessive amounts of alcohol (in combination with drugs) increase the potential for students to pass out or black out, making heavy and extreme partiers especially vulnerable to "incapacitated rape." According to Armstrong and colleagues (2006), incapacitated rapes occur most commonly at fraternity or house parties where there is excessive drinking and little supervision. Several studies have specifically identified fraternity parties as "rape-prone environments" due to the large amounts of drinking that take place at such parties, and due to a deeply ingrained sense of sexual entitlement among fraternity members that make it okay to pursue sex any way they can (Boswell and Spade 1996; Menning 2009). For instance, one study found that fraternity men are more likely than other college men to purposefully use drugs or alcohol to get women intoxicated in order to obtain sex (Menning 2009). Other research has found that fraternity men are more likely than non-fraternity men to endorse rape-supportive beliefs (e.g., women say no but mean yes; they really want to be forced or "convinced") that justify the use of aggression in order to obtain sex (Boswell and Spade 1996; Menning 2009).

While surely not all fraternity members — intoxicated or not — pose threats to women at parties or otherwise (see Boswell and Spade 1996 for an excellent comparison of high- and low-risk fraternities), the reputation of fraternity parties as hot spots for rape (and fraternity members as sexual predators) is part of a crime narrative shared by many PU students.[12] In contrast to the rather low number of rapes that actually take place at PU fraternity or house parties (2 percent according to CCVS data), an unflattering depiction of Greek-sponsored parties as hot spots for rape is common among PU students, partiers and non-partiers alike. This negative stereotype is echoed by each of the following students in response to an open-ended survey question asking them to share additional comments about crime and safety at PU.

> I have heard that girls are frequently sexually assaulted and physically detained by frat members during rush week. (twenty-four-year-old female senior)

> I transferred my junior year and the first thing people said was, don't go near fraternity row because you will get roofied, raped, etc. I have heard awful, disgusting things about fraternities at [PU], and I think something needs to be done about it. Sexual assault on campus is a serious problem, and if someone is proven to have raped someone else, they should be kicked out of school permanently. (twenty-one-year-old female junior)

> I was once unfortunate enough to work on a project with a frat guy, and heard open discussions of how to hook up with freshman, how it was a turn-on to see women weep after sex, how best to pass around drunk girls to other frat brothers, how to force anal sex on women who did not want it. I was also shown a video of a "rodeo," which is a fairly common frat practice in which an innocent freshman is lured back to the frat house by a frat brother who treats her lovingly and tenderly. He initiates sex, and at some point he screams "rodeo." (twenty-three-year-old male senior)

Even as many PU students are wary of fraternities and their reputations as hot spots for rape, few students seem concerned about the potential of rape at house parties, the non-Greek equivalent to the fraternity party, and an environment where just as many rapes can occur, and for similar reasons. At house parties, as at fraternity parties, there is a convergence of motivated male offenders (often drunk and looking to have sex), vulnerable female victims (also drunk or even incapacitated), and an absence of capable guardians (i.e., formal social control agents and other persons willing or able to intervene). The following excerpt from a student interview demonstrates just how hands-off fellow partiers can be. As the student describes the crime — an attempted rape of an incapacitated woman at a PU house party — it is clear that no one at the party, including the storyteller himself, tried to do anything to stop the incident.

> One night at a party, I saw a guy trying to shove objects up a girl's ass. It was really weird and freaked me out a little bit. He was trying like hard to shove a beer bottle in her ass and then he started pulling her pants down and trying some more. . . . She was passed out . . . like drunk . . . it was really weird. (twenty-one-year-old male junior)

Note that the student describing this prior event seems more puzzled by the attempted rape than outraged (referring twice to the incident as "weird"). His failure to recognize the incident as a crime (or more specifically as a rape in progress) highlights the ambiguity of defining sexual assaults within the context of the party situation.[13] Generally, recognition of crime requires an assessment of serious injury (or an unambiguous violation of law), a guilty offender (acting with malice), and an innocent victim (see Weiss 2011). Within the sexually charged and overly intoxicated environment of a college party, students may have difficulty recognizing the first two components — serious injury and guilty offender — especially since one of the goals of partygoers, aside from getting wasted, is to "hook up" (i.e., have casual sex) (Armstrong et al. 2006; Peterson and Muehlenhard 2007). In other words, within a party environment, sexual aggression may be less recognizable as criminal behavior, or may even be seen as an acceptable means for obtaining sex.[14] Meanwhile, intoxication provides a ready-made excuse for men accused of crossing the line: "he was wasted and didn't know what he was doing."

Finally, recognizing crime also requires an "innocent" victim. In contrast to men who may be excused for sexual aggression when wasted, there is generally a lack of sympathy for women who drink too much (i.e., they should know their limits). Women are expected to "know better" than to get so wasted that they pass out, and may even be blamed for "getting themselves raped" while intoxicated (Weiss 2010a, 2011). In addition to the expectation that women should know their limits in regard to their alcohol intake, women are also supposed to "know better" than to lead men on and dress seductively or scantily, even though the party subculture tends to encourage them to dress in this manner.

Rape myths and the belief that women sometimes "ask for it" are so ingrained into the social vocabularies associated with these crimes that rape victims may blame themselves for rape, or see themselves for having contributed in some way, especially if they have had too much to drink (see Weiss 2009a; 2010b).[15] Variations of self-blame are illustrated in the following excerpts from two female students who were raped while at PU. In both cases, the women hold themselves responsible while making excuses for their offenders, thereby interpreting their experiences not as rape but as "regrettable sex."

> I was really drunk and I didn't think about what could happen when I started fooling around with some guy at a party. I really have no one to blame but myself. Everybody has people they regret having sex with. (nineteen-year-old female sophomore)

> Coercive sex happens all the time. So I really never thought of it as rape. And I can't say at first I wasn't interested in the guy. He was a football player and I had been flirting with him all night. Besides, it's hard to make a case when alcohol is involved. No one would believe that I didn't want to hook up with him. (twenty-year-old female sophomore)

Ambiguity of definition and self-blame, both alluded to in these previous responses, can certainly explain why only 4 percent of rapes at PU are reported to police. Within a party environment, where "fooling around" and flirtation can easily turn coercive, and where alcohol and drugs can exacerbate opportunity for sexual aggression, as well as excuse and justify it, victims and bystanders may too often be uncertain or reluctant to define situations they experience or witness as rape.

Unwanted sexual contact. In addition to rape, other types of sexual assault involving unwanted sexual touching, fondling, and grabbing of the body occur quite regularly at the party school. Like rape, women are far more likely to be the victims of such incidents. Based on CCVS data, 36 percent of female students experience unwanted sexual contact while at PU as compared to 7 percent of male students. The majority of these incidents are perpetrated by men (93 percent). And while all female victims of unwanted sexual contact are assaulted by men, only 33 percent of male victims of these crimes are assaulted by other men with the remaining 77 percent by women.

Similar to other crimes at PU, 86 percent of unwanted sexual contact occurs downtown and 94 percent at night (56 percent after midnight). (See appendix B, table 11.) Only 21 percent of unwanted sexual contact takes place in homes. Instead, 70 percent of these incidents take place in bars (61 percent) and parties (9 percent). Unwanted sexual contact primarily involves only one offender, but in 15 percent of the cases there is more than one offender. The majority of offenders (61 percent) are strangers, whereas 3 percent are boy-friends/girlfriends and ex-partners, 13 percent are friends, and the remaining 23 percent are other acquaintances. Finally, a rather large percentage of students who experience unwanted sexual contact are victimized more than once, with 20 percent of victims experiencing two incidents, and 51 percent experiencing three or more incidents. These patterns are clearly indicative of students' party routines.

Unwanted sexual contact and party routines. Like rape, most unwanted sexual contact occurs when victim, offender, or both participants are intoxicated. According to CCVS data, 50 percent of victims were drunk or using drugs at the time of an assault, and 74 percent of offenders were drunk or high on drugs. Though there is a statistically significant difference in terms of risk of victimization between non-partiers (13 percent) and partiers (25 percent), the degree to which someone parties contributes much less to risk of unwanted sexual contact than it does for other types of crime. Instead, the more important factor in predicting risk of unwanted sexual contact, at least for female students, is whether or not they spend time in hot spots (e.g., bars, clubs, parties). For instance, 51 percent of women who drink at bars while at PU experience unwanted sexual contact as compared to 20 percent of women who do not drink at bars. In addition, 47 percent of women who drink at parties experience unwanted sexual contact as compared to 28 percent who do not drink at parties. (Only 6 percent of men who drink at bars or parties experience unwanted sexual contact, a similar percentage to men who do not drink at these settings but still experience these incidents.)

In contrast to rape, the bar scene and not the party scene is the ultimate hot spot for unwanted sexual contact, mostly because these crimes are more likely to be perpetrated by strangers and not acquaintances, as with rape. Within the milieu of a highly sexualized and overly intoxicated bar environment, men (and some women) feel entitled to touch strangers in sexual manners without their consent. For instance, in a study that looked at sexual aggression in bars, almost 80 percent of men admitted to grabbing the buttocks of women whom they did not know while in a bar (Thompson and Cracco 2008). Moreover, few of the men who touch women in sexual ways while at a bar see their behaviors as wrong. Perhaps this is due, in part, to the rather ambivalent responses from many of their targets, who, rather than getting angry, tend to dismiss nonconsensual sexual touching inside bars or clubs as harmless play, nothing too serious, and certainly not a crime. In fact, few students at PU who experience unwanted sexual contact complain formally to police or other authorities (less than 2 percent of these incidents are reported to authorities). When asked why they did not report such incidents to someone in authority, respondents suggest that there is an expectation among their peers that they *not* take such incidents very seriously. For instance, one female student said that she did not want to be seen as "the type of girl who can't take a joke." Thus, most bar patrons, as illustrated in the following examples, simply laugh away or shrug aside unwanted sexual contacts that occur inside bars or clubs as minor events. And some students, also illustrated in the following excerpts, excuse their offenders as being too drunk to know any better.

> Just last week some guy pinched me in my butt. I was just waiting at the bar to buy a drink. It wasn't anything truly offensive, just a guy trying to get physical because he was too drunk to know better. (twenty-two-year-old female senior)

> Everyone at the club grabs someone at least once, and it is almost impossible to catch everyone. So you just have to accept it. It can be annoying at times, but it really isn't so bad. Actually it can be pretty funny just how pathetic some of these guys are. (twenty-year-old female sophomore)

> I had a girl grab my ass last year. I guess I should be flattered. But she was wasted, and after I passed by, I could hear her laughing about it with her friends. People grab each other all the time. It is just part of the scene. You get used to it. (twenty-three-year-old male senior)

As these prior quotes demonstrate, unwanted sexual contact within the context of a party hot spot is a rather ordinary occurrence. Even as these same behaviors might be seen as offensive and intrusive in many other situations, at a bar or club they are an ordinary part of the scene. Students get used to it, minimize it, and excuse the behavior. They know the risks going in, and apparently these risks are worth taking.

STUDENT CRIME AND MISCONDUCT AT PU

Participation in the party subculture not only increases risk of victimization at the party school, it also increases the likelihood that students will themselves engage in criminal misconduct. For instance, prior research has found that binge drinkers are more likely to start fights, steal, vandalize property, and get into trouble with the police (Felson and Burchfield 2004; Harford et al. 2003; Sperber 2000; Tewksbury and Pedro 2003; Wechsler and Wuethrich 2002). As discussed in previous chapters, intoxication increases the potential for aggression, inhibits rational decision making, and increases impulsivity to behave recklessly, with little concern for the consequences.

Based on survey responses from the revised CCVS, PU students admit to perpetrating a broad range of criminal offenses while intoxicated, including setting off false fire alarms, defacing school property, and confiscating street signs. The following examples represent a cross-section of criminal misconduct at the party school from students who either participated themselves or witnessed the incidents. (Interviewer probes are in brackets.)

My friends have quite a collection of street signs from all over town taken mostly while they were wasted. They just sort of help themselves as they head home from the bars or parties in the area. You could call them party favors. (twenty-one-year-old male senior)

I have neighbors who like to launch water balloons off the roof of their house at cars passing by. It's juvenile but it seems to entertain them. (twenty-year-old male sophomore)

When we are really drunk we may do something stupid like write on buildings with markers while walking back from the bars. My buddy knocked a mirror off a car one time. That was dumb. If someone did that to my car, I'd be pissed. (twenty-one-year-old male junior)

I got out of control one night at a friend's house and decided to punch through a window. I ended up getting a pretty bad scar from it. (twenty-one-year-old male junior)

Me and my friend stole a table from one of the school buildings on campus. We took it back to my house and now we use it for beer pong. [Why did you take it?] Because we needed a table for beer pong, and it was too easy not to. (twenty-year-old female sophomore)

I threw a brick through the windshield of some girl's car who I hate. I was downtown and wasted, saw her car parked in a lot off the street. I had killed a whole bottle of Smirnoff vodka with some friends before we went out. Then we were drinking more at the club. We were wasted. [Why did you throw the brick?] Because I was drunk and I saw this stupid girl's car. (eighteen-year-old female freshman)

Note that the previous two responses are from women. Even as more men than women commit crimes while intoxicated (or at least admit to or get in to trouble for it), alcohol may be the great gender equalizer in terms of perpetrating bad behavior and excusing it. For instance, neither of the women who acknowledge their involvement in their respective property crimes (e.g., stealing a table, vandalizing a car) exhibit any regret or remorse when asked why they did what they did. Their responses to why they took the table ("we needed a table for beer pong") and why they threw the brick ("I saw this stupid girl's car") are illustrative of a Freudian id impulse, a self-centered, pleasure-seeking response predicated on the simple concept that if you want something, just take it. In Freudian terms, these partiers lack a developed superego to control such impulses and to feel guilt, shame, or to know right from wrong. But, norms are situational, and what is "right" in one context may be wrong in another. In the party world where pleasure seeking is encouraged and rewarded, taking stuff that doesn't belong to you may not seem as bad. In fact, intoxication appears to temporarily relax the rules and codes of conduct that most people live by when sober. For women, who tend to be held to much higher standards than men for their conduct, intoxication can offer a much-appreciated reprieve from their otherwise restrictive gender roles.

Drunk Driving

Irrespective of gender, being wasted appears to absolve students of culpability, empathy for others, and common sense. Students who party feel entitled to do so and invincible while so engaged, and in the process, they sometimes put themselves and others at risk. One potential risk is from drunk driving. Driving while intoxicated, is a rather common event at the party school. For instance, at PU, 28 percent of students who drink alcohol admit to driving drunk. These numbers increase according to party type. Just under half (49 percent) of extreme partiers, 36 percent of heavy partiers and 10 percent of light partiers admit to driving drunk (see appendix B, table 9). Despite public awareness campaigns that emphasize the dangers and criminal penalties of drunk driving, many students at PU continue to put their own and others' lives at risk, in part, because they don't believe they are truly impaired. Recall from chapter 4 that 7 percent of PU students believe they can drink five or more drinks and still drive safety.[16] Based on the following excerpts from students who have driven drunk while at PU, one gets the sense that driving intoxicated is not always considered a very serious offense, even when stopped by the police.

> I've drank and drove many times in the past. I think I've hit a few objects with my car . . . got a few dents. I had a few hit and runs back in high school. So I've done some damage to other cars but I've never gotten caught. I usually just fled the scene. (twenty-two-year-old male senior)

> One Saturday night, well actually Sunday morning, I was with my buddies at a McDonalds and I saw my friend asleep in his car, just sitting in the driver's seat of his car in the McDonalds drive-thru. I pulled up behind him to order food and got out when I noticed he wasn't moving. When I looked in his car window, he was fast asleep. I banged on the window to wake him up and he was slurring his words and you could smell alcohol on him. I asked him if he wanted me to drive him home, but he refused and said he was fine to drive. It was actually pretty funny how functional he was while being so wasted. (twenty-four-year-old male senior)

I drove my car off a rock wall after playing more than five games of twenty-one-cup beer pong and had taken more than five shots and sipped beer in between. I was hammered. I was driving down a road, and it was really dark, and the next thing I know the front of the car was going straight down. I wasn't hurt, but my car had heavy front-end damage. The cops came and gave me a breathalyzer, which I definitely blew over the legal limit. They told me to walk home. (twenty-one-year-old male junior)

Note that the student in the previous excerpt describes a rather lenient encounter with law enforcement. As the student describes it, even as he was not permitted to drive home, he received no legal sanctions at the scene for driving while intoxicated. If his rendition of the incident is accurate, such legal leniency could certainly reinforce students' impression that drinking and driving is not such a serious offense. Coupled with the fact that only 8 percent of extreme partiers, 4 percent of heavy partiers and less than 1 percent of light partiers have been stopped for drunk driving while at PU, students who weigh the risks of getting into trouble with the practicality of needing to get home may conclude that the odds are in their favor. In other words, choosing to drive after drinking may boil down to a simple rational choice. Like partying itself, drunk driving is a risk that many students are willing to take.

Liquor Law and Drug Violations

Aside from the (seemingly rare) occasions when students are stopped for drunk driving, one in five students who party while at PU receive drinking or drug-related citations or disciplinary actions. According to Clery statistics, and as discussed in chapter 3, there were approximately one thousand six hundred liquor law arrests/disciplinary actions in 2009 at PU and just over two hundred arrests/disciplinary actions for drug violations. In terms of percentages, and based on CCVS data, 22 percent of students who drink alcohol receive a citation or disciplinary action for liquor law violations while at PU, mostly for underage drinking.[17] Another 6 percent of students who use drugs are arrested or receive other sanctions from PU, primarily for marijuana possession.[18]

Not surprisingly, students who are most committed to the party subculture experience the most arrests and disciplinary actions while at PU. For instance, 41 percent of extreme partiers, 23 percent of heavy partiers and 9 percent of light partiers receive citations or disciplinary actions for liquor law violations while at PU. In terms of drugs, 6 percent of extreme partiers and 2 percent of heavy partiers receive citations or disciplinary actions for drug law violations while at PU (note: light partiers do not use drugs). (See appendix B, table 9.) Men are much more likely than women to be arrested or to receive citations for underage drinking or drug use combined (27 percent as compared to 12 percent), and a gendered difference is especially pronounced when comparing extreme partiers. Almost 35 percent of men who party in the extreme category have been sanctioned for either alcohol or drug use as compared to 19 percent of women. (See appendix B, table 10.)

Although the CCVS does not ask students how many citations they have received for alcohol or drug violations during their tenure at PU, anecdotally, it is not uncommon for students to receive multiple citations for underage drinking before the age of twenty-one. In fact, receiving such a citation does not appear to be a very effective deterrent for students who participate in the party subculture. Just listen to the following students describe their respective experiences with the police who issued them underage drinking citations, and you get the sense that such encounters and the sanctions they received were rather unremarkable events in their lives.

The first time I got an underage [citation], I was coming out of a bar with a friend. We were drinking inside the club because I had friends in there who were twenty-one. As we were leaving, the cops stopped us. They smelled the alcohol from my breath. They basically asked for our identification and then asked if we drank in the club. At that point, I don't think I denied it. The citation that was issued cost me $235, somewhere around there. And [PU] was notified of the case and I had to take a class and attend six AA meetings (Alcoholics Anonymous) which wasn't too bad.

The second time, I had been drinking vodka at a friend's apartment and we ended up going to a party, and as I was leaving I realized I had a beer in my hand so I drank it. As I was doing that, the cop who was busting the party across the street came up to me and asked for my ID. That's when I got my second underage citation. I was pretty drunk that night. He looked at my ID and realized I was underage and started writing the ticket. He searched me to see if I had any weapons on me but of course I didn't. I had to pay the same cost $235. I had to do more AA classes, six more (twelve total), and I had to go through one more thing with the school where I had to go to meetings and watch a movie, but it wasn't that bad. (twenty-year-old male junior)[19]

My underage citation happened while tailgating before a football game in the fall. We were all hanging out drinking some beers, and randomly three university officers approached us and asked for our IDs. They asked us how old we were even though they had our IDs. They pretty much said "you guys aren't supposed to be drinking," and our response was, "Yeah we know." The officer said, "Well you know I have to give you a ticket." It was pretty basic, we knew we were guilty, and they knew what we were doing, and it was a pretty simple process. (twenty-year-old male sophomore)

Despite the courteous exchanges conveyed by these two students in regards to their confrontations with the police, student-cop interactions at PU are not always so amicable. Considering that the main objective of most partiers is to get wasted, it is certainly not surprising to find that the police, whose jobs include curtailing students' excessive party behaviors, are not always well respected by students who party.[20] In fact, many partiers at PU accuse police of being bullies with nothing better to do than to hassle them, bust up their parties, and impede their good time. Extreme partiers who are most committed to the party subculture and most likely to get into trouble with the law, tend to voice the most resentment toward police. A few of their negative comments are provided below.[21]

The police suck. They just drive around looking for a party to write up. They are quick to write tickets for drinking-related matters, but don't seem to bother to pursue crimes when people's cars are broken into or vandalized. All they care about is seeing how badass they can make themselves seem by messing with drunk college kids. (eighteen-year-old male freshman)

The police here spend too much time arresting underage drinkers, messing with intoxicated students, and busting up parties when they should be attempting to prevent more serious crimes. This is college. Kids are going to party. Hell, that's why some of us are here! (nineteen-year-old female sophomore)

I think the cops here do a pretty good job with crime, but they need to understand that PU is a party school and that is primarily why people come here. They need to back off and let us be young and stupid. (twenty-year-old male junior)

The assumption inherent in the previous comments is that a party school is a unique jurisdiction where kids come to party and, therefore, the police should let students be "young and stupid." Moreover, the supposition that students at a party school have a "right" to party puts PU partiers at odds not only with the police but with other students who do not party. In fact, non-partiers and students who are not at PU primarily to party have a much more positive view of the police, or at least a better understanding of how tough their job is at the party school. The following response from a student who parties only occasionally and has never herself been in trouble with the law represents a more supportive and even sympathetic perspective of the police at PU.

> The cops here have a very tough job. This is a college town and college kids
> don't exactly care what the police say or do. I think they do the best they can.
> It's not easy to control nearly twenty thousand crazy college kids, most of
> whom are partying all the time. (twenty-year-old female sophomore)

Certainly, enforcing the law and keeping peace at a party school cannot be an easy job. The police at PU and in Ptown must walk a fine line between being sensitive to the lifestyle of college students (i.e., letting kids be kids) and not appearing too permissive or soft on crime. No matter what they do, the police are caught in an untenable situation. They are seen as the bad guys by partiers for constricting their fun. At the same time, as discussed in the next chapter, they are seen as too lenient by many non-partiers for not doing enough to keep the peace.

SUMMING UP

Data from the Campus Crime Victimization Survey (CCVS) reveal that about half of PU students experience some type of crime during their college years, including property crime, attacks/fights, and sexual violence. The data also show that the majority of student crimes at the party school are intoxication crimes, incidents where victim, offender, or both parties are drunk or high on drugs at the time of the crime. Such crimes are largely associated with students' party routines, and many of the incidents take place in identifiable party "hot spots," such as bars, clubs, parties, and the neighborhoods that host most drinking establishments and student parties.

Not surprisingly students who party most excessively (i.e., extreme partiers) are at greatest risk of crime victimization, mainly because extreme intoxication makes them more vulnerable and unaware of dangers. Extreme partiers are also most likely to commit offenses themselves, including starting fights, damaging property, and driving drunk. With lowered inhibitions from alcohol and drugs, extreme partiers also have the greatest likelihood of getting into trouble with the law. Yet, at the party school, criminal consequences are often brushed aside by partiers as inconsequential, or considered collateral damage or risks worth taking. Moreover, as we will see in the next chapter, extreme partiers are often so assured in their "right to party" that they are often disrespectful toward police, indignant toward persons who complain, and unconcerned about how their behaviors affect others who live and work in the college community.

1

Party Disturbances

SECONDHAND HARMS TO CAMPUS
AND COMMUNITY

As seen in the previous chapter, students who participate in the party sub-culture are at increased risk for many types of crime. Students who party are also more likely to engage in criminal misconduct themselves, causing a variety of problems for the campus and community. Previous studies, including the PRI documentary *#1 Party School* (see chapter 2, p. 22), have shown that neighborhoods near a party school can be negatively impacted by a variety of party-related disturbances, including noise, litter, and other "nuisance" behaviors such as students vomiting in the street or urinating on private property (Brower and Carroll 2007; Wechsler and Nelson 2008; Wechsler and Wuethrich 2002).

This chapter discusses the various nuisance problems caused by students while intoxicated, or what some researchers have labeled secondhand binge effects (Wechsler et al. 1998, Wechsler and Wuethrich 2002; Tewksbury and Pedro 2003).[1] Like the harms caused by secondhand smoke from cigarettes, the secondhand effects of students' party habits can be far reaching and disruptive to anyone who comes into regular contact with students who party. For instance, according to one study, 61 percent of college students who live on campus and do not drink alcohol themselves say they have had study or sleep interrupted by students who do drink, and 29 percent have been insulted or humiliated by intoxicated peers (Wechsler and Wuethrich 2002). On a broader scale, secondhand harms can negatively impact an entire campus and community, costing millions each year to pay for clean up and police patrols hired to combat the disruption and disorder caused by the party subculture (Brower and Carroll 2007; Pezza and Bellotti 1995; Wechsler and Nelson 2008). This chapter explores the types and patterns of these secondhand party effects.

Most students at PU, irrespective of whether they party or not, consider some aspects of the party subculture to be problems for the campus and community. For instance, approximately half of PU students surveyed in the revised CCVS agreed that noise and loud music, litter, verbal harassment, and vandalism were all problems in the neighborhoods where they lived. One-third of students specifically indicated that missing or damaged signs was a problem. And approximately three-fourths of students agreed that drunk driving and "drunk students" more generally were problems (see appendix B, table 15).

Based on students' responses to survey questions about their experiences with these nuisance problems, it is clear that the majority of secondhand party disturbances at PU occur primarily in two locations: downtown near PU's party hot spots (e.g., bars, clubs, and parties) and at PU's sporting events (primarily football games). The following sections examine separately the problems that occur in each of these two settings.

Downtown Disorder

As seen in the previous chapter, a disproportionate amount of PU's crime occurs downtown in the student-dense neighborhoods closest to campus. This is the area of town that hosts the majority of student bars, clubs, fraternity houses, and "party houses." It is also the area where PU's most enthusiastic partiers choose to live. Not only are these neighborhoods within walking distance to the most popular student bars and clubs, but these neighborhoods consist of mostly large houses with wide front porches that can accommodate beer pong tables and other recognizable props of the party subculture. These houses can also accommodate large numbers of guests, making them ideal for hosting PU's wildest parties. Thus, it should come as no surprise that most of the secondhand effects of the party subculture occur in these downtown neighborhoods, and mostly at night.

Due to the reputation of these neighborhoods as ground zero for PU's party scene, most non-partiers try to avoid living in these neighborhoods. However, this is not always possible considering that the downtown area is also one of the most convenient parts of town for PU students to live without a car. Banks, restaurants, and various stores are located within walking distance from several downtown neighborhoods. As students are not typically provided parking privileges on campus, many students who attend classes downtown, or whose major departments are located there, may also prefer to live in one of the downtown neighborhoods for its proximity to academic buildings, the library, bookstores, and the student activities center.

Regardless of why students live downtown, residents of these neighborhoods have a much greater risk of exposure to secondhand harms, such as property "disruption," noise and verbal harassment. In terms of property disruption, students living downtown can experience many problems ranging from serious vandalism, as discussed in the previous chapter, to litter and other forms of disorder, such as having garbage thrown on their lawns or sidewalks, lawn furniture turned upside down, and trash cans emptied into the streets. These sorts of "littering" incidents can negatively impact neighborhoods in terms of their physical aesthetics and property values.

Although there is no way of verifying how much of PU's litter problem is caused by student partiers, students themselves tend to blame most property disruption in their neighborhoods on their intoxicated peers. In fact, some students complain that excessive partying by other students has caused so much disruption that their neighborhoods have become almost "unbearable after dark." The following survey responses from non-partying students who live downtown describe a cross-section of property incidents in their neighborhoods that they attribute to student partiers. Collectively, these students voice an overwhelming frustration toward their peers who party too hard, study too little, and care even less about their community.

Downtown has become unbearable after dark. The absolute drunkenness of the place is pathetic. And these students don't seem to care at all about the area, or themselves. I have almost run over drunk students on several occasions because they run in front of my vehicle, or because they are sleeping in the road. (twenty-year-old female sophomore)

When I lived downtown, drunks coming home from the bars would throw cigarettes, and even CDs in our yard. There was also a period of time where some bunch of drunks thought it was funny to knock over our lawn chairs at 3 in the morning. But what really got to me was the commotion from the dumpster. Some kids dragged a dumpster from an apartment building down the road and started pushing it down the street. It almost hit my car. I think they eventually set it on fire. Which reminds me, someone once burned my mail. (twenty-two-year-old female senior)

Someone vomited on my car last year. Can you believe that? I just came out one day to head to class and there it was. Disgusting, but I can't say I was all too shocked. Some students are idiots when they drink. (twenty-two-year-old female senior)

People walking home drunk think throwing beer cans at our house is OK. I pay a lot of money to rent my house, and it gets messed up every weekend. (twenty-four-year-old male senior)

What gets me are the kids peeing in public, and the smashing of bottles in the streets. I have to walk in those areas. It is a mess and they don't care at all. (twenty-three-year-old male senior)

Alcohol is a big problem downtown, or the abuse of it. Students act as if they are not accountable for their actions when they drink, as if they are still in high school. The school doesn't need the negativity they bring. And my neighborhood would be a lot cleaner without them. (twenty-year-old female sophomore)

Street signs are ripped down almost every weekend, people's furniture is thrown around, and there is vomit and trash everywhere. I thought I was moving into a great neighborhood, but the place is filthy. No one here seems to care. (twenty-one-year-old female junior)

In addition to litter and other property disruption, students living downtown often complain about the noise caused by excessive partying in their neighborhoods. Repetitive noise can be more than just annoying, it can disrupt sleep and even cause health issues for those subjected to it on a regular basis. Most of the noise disturbances downtown can be attributed to the fraternity and house parties that, according to the following student responses, can last until the early morning hours and can take place any night of the week.

My neighbors go crazy almost every week. They are selfish and don't care about anything or anyone else around them. They start partying at 1 or 2 AM. I hear their parties all night; they are loud and obnoxious. It is impossible to sleep sometimes. (twenty-one-year-old female junior)

I live by a frat house and they never shut up; it's extremely annoying, and the weekend for them evidently starts on a Tuesday night. I've seen a fight literally right outside my house involving two different groups of people. Our trash cans are knocked over repeatedly each night due to fights or just drunk kids "walking" by, oblivious to the time or the concept that others may be trying to sleep. I've also seen kids pee in the middle of the road or on the side walk. But at least they do that quietly! (twenty-two-year-old female senior)

A very different type of "noise" problem that students complain about at PU pertains to verbal harassment, including crude comments and vulgarities that students scream at one another in "fun," and rude and sexually offensive remarks directed at "random" persons walking down the streets.[2] Though the comments vary (including some homophobic and racist themes), the most common scenario involves men yelling crude remarks of a sexual nature at women. And though most of these incidents are more annoying to students than dangerous, comments can sometimes feel threatening, and can interfere with students' sense of safety and well-being. Following are a cross-section of students' experiences with verbal harassment that occur downtown.

I have been frequently harassed and threatened by various drunk assholes and frat boys, including having items thrown at me and being followed. You can't imagine the crude things they will say from inside their cars. (twenty-four-year-old female senior)

I have had drunk students drive by me as I am walking down the street yelling obscenities and sexual comments while swerving around the road like idiots. (twenty-two-year-old female junior)

You can't go out at night around here without having someone yelling something at you. Half the time it doesn't even make sense. Just drunken nonsense. You just learn to ignore it. (twenty-one-year-old female senior)

Several times I have been driving downtown and have had people in another car screaming and shouting obscenities. One night someone attempted to go the wrong way up a one-way street that I was already on, barely missing the side of my car. Then the other driver swerved into the other lane and sped up to pull in front of me. One of the passengers tossed a lit cigarette and matches against my windshield while yelling obscenities and threats. (twenty-two-year-old female senior)

Note that this previous example goes far beyond verbal harassment, as the student describes a reckless driving situation that endangers public safety. Reckless driving is, anecdotally, another problem far too common in Ptown. Of course, considering how many students admit to driving drunk (see chapter 6), this is not too surprising. Still, despite the potential dangers, most students tend to see reckless and harassing behavior from their drunken peers as more childish and annoying than serious, and somewhat expected within the context of the party situation. Recall from the introduction (pp. xxii) that behavior is interpreted based on the situation (and audience). The same behavior can be interpreted as normal in one situation while deviant in another. In a poignant example of "situational normativity," the student in the following excerpt distinguishes the deviance of harassing comments made during the day on her way to class from the more acceptable (or at least expected) comments made at night. While she finds such comments distracting, annoying, and inappropriate during the day, she seems to excuse similar remarks at night when "she is prepared" for them.

> Verbal harassment in the middle of the day is distracting. I understand it when I'm on my way to the club seeing that I am dressed in a certain way that may solicit those kinds of remarks and I am prepared for them. But on my way to class while I am wearing street clothes it is inappropriate and annoying. (twenty-year-old female junior)

Even as many students brush aside rude remarks within the context of the party situation, some students do not feel safe downtown at night due, in part, to such harassment. Borrowing a term from sexual harassment law, downtown PU has become a *hostile environment* at night where many students feel uncomfortable or intimidated by the unwelcome comments and inappropriate behaviors of their peers. As conveyed in the following survey responses, even students who feel very safe during the day at PU tend to perceive some danger at night, largely due to the party subculture.[3]

I don't think [downtown] at night is safe at all. Students are becoming more and more irresponsible and obnoxious. Take a walk downtown after 11 PM and all you hear are threatening and degrading comments coming from one drunk or another. (twenty-four-year-old female senior)

I feel generally very safe here but I keep my eyes open and am aware of my surroundings all the time. The night life is a very different thing. Anything can happen when people are drinking and/or doing drugs. I would suggest people be very cautious about who they drink and party with. (twenty-one-year-old male junior)

I don't think that the campus is a very safe place during the night. Especially downtown. This is a major reason why I don't go out a lot. I don't think the police really take things seriously. Also, the police don't enforce underage drinking laws, which causes more problems. People who are clearly very drunk and who want to pick fights make the area dangerous for all of us. (twenty-one-year-old female sophomore)

As this prior comment suggests, students' perceptions of safety at PU are often related to whether or not they see the police as doing enough to enforce the laws, including underage drinking. In direct contrast to extreme partiers, who see the police as incessantly harassing them for merely trying to have a good time (see chapter 6), non-partiers are more likely to criticize the police as being too hands-off, complaining that they are not doing enough to control the excessive drinking and disruptive parties downtown. Such criticisms are demonstrated in the following responses.

I feel [Ptown] police basically do nothing to make downtown safer. I have personally seen them letting people go when caught drunk driving, underage drinking, public intoxication, even when causing a scene. Their actions (or lack of) only instigates more bad behavior. I honestly believe that if more people were getting in trouble for public intoxication and drunk driving, then many of these crimes would not occur. (twenty-one-year-old female junior)

Anyone who has been downtown during the semester would be astounded by the number of drunk students stumbling toward their cars with no police in sight. I am disgusted by the "boys will be boys" mentality and the lack of law enforcement. Will it take a mass tragedy before someone does something? Why not close a few bars and maintain a drink limit? (twenty-three-year-old female senior)

Frustrations over property and noise disruptions caused by the party subculture, as well as the perspective that police do not do nearly enough to stop it, are sentiments also shared by many nonstudent residents living in Ptown. As discussed in chapter 1 (see pp. 8–9), the recent "invasion" of students moving in to nonstudent and family-occupied neighborhoods has increased conflicts between student and nonstudent residents regarding what it means to be good neighbors and what constitutes acceptable noise. From the perspective of nonstudent residents, their student neighbors are often disrespectful and oblivious to how their party lifestyle can negatively impact their neighbors.

From the students' perspective, their nonstudent neighbors are overreacting. It is a party school, after all, and if they do not like living next door to college students they should move. In fact, many students are genuinely perplexed that nonstudent residents choose to live in *their* neighborhoods. An example of these clashing perspectives is illustrated in the following excerpt from a nonstudent resident who describes an exchange with her student neighbor over noise.

Loud music can be a problem . . . but what gets to us more than anything, worse than the loud music, is when [the students] just stand and yell at random intervals for no reason, like dogs barking at the moon. They were doing a lot of this one Saturday afternoon during a football game. My husband asked them to keep it down, and they just yelled back at us that if we didn't like living next to college students, that we should move. (Nonstudent female resident)[4]

As frustrated as some residents may feel about their recently "mixed" neighborhoods, most residents have become resigned to living with some noise and disturbances. In fact, occasional disorder and disruption have become the "new normal" for many downtown residents of Ptown, at least at night. For instance, during most weekend nights, downtown PU is transformed into party central. In an especially astute articulation of situational normativity, the following dialogue between two nonstudent residents illustrates the metamorphosis of their neighborhood from quiet and peaceful during the day to a nighttime of chaos where otherwise respectful young kids are transformed into "zombies," a reference to students' intoxicated state of unpredictability, stupor, and "obnoxiousness." (Note: A is a male resident, B is a female resident. Interviewer probes are in brackets.)

A: Student obnoxiousness is worst downtown after 7 or 8 when daytime [Ptown] ends and nighttime [Ptown] starts taking over.

B: By 11 PM the zombies come out. [laughs]

A: Yea, you know . . . I don't always feel comfortable when students descend on downtown and when my kids see things. . . .
[What kinds of things are you afraid of them seeing?]

A: Um, well, I mean certainly drunken behavior, kind of aggressive, you know, sort of stand-offs between young men, chest-to-chest kind of stuff. And frankly I don't love the image that my young sons are getting of women when they're dressed, you know, like . . .
[Scantily?]

A: Yea, you know . . . I'm not saying this in a prudish way, just I think it's an unhealthy kind of culture in many ways. [laughs]

B: It's scary. You do not want to be downtown after dark. That's the worst, at 11 PM when they're standing in line for the bars, it's kind of scary.

A: If you go downtown 2 in the morning on a Friday . . . there can be up to ten thousand people in the streets. Because all the bars close at the same time. I rode with a police officer once at 2 in the morning . . . just a ride-along . . . . It was unbelievable. I kept saying, "Oh no, there can't be that many." You cannot walk down the sidewalks, there's so many students in the streets, you know . . .

B: And drunks are unpredictable.

A: Yeah, I think what frustrates me, it's not even so much fear . . . it is partially fear, but it's sort of a frustration that I feel like its my town but I'm sort of an outsider here. When the students take over the downtown or any kind of area, suddenly you're the odd man out. And I live here twelve months a year, I'm raising my kids here. . . . This is the town I live in and I own a home here, and yet I feel like I have to kind of hide in my house at night.

B: . . . and the college students are less respectful of us and feel more entitled . . . or blame us for choosing to live in their neighborhood.

This dialogue not only represents the frustrations shared by many downtown residents in regard to the disrespect and unpredictability of their student neighbors when drunk, but it is also very telling in regard to who controls the downtown turf at night. Similar to neighborhoods overrun by gangs, the party subculture claims domain over PU's downtown neighborhoods, holding its residents hostage at night. Residents living in the shadow of a party school, like residents in high crime neighborhoods, learn to avoid certain parts of town and take other safety precautions, such as staying inside their homes after dark (i.e., a self-imposed curfew) in order to protect themselves and shield their children from exposure to the bad influences of the party subculture that pervades their neighborhoods at night.

Over the years, these once family-centered communities have become less suitable places for raising kids. And, oddly enough, many PU students, even those who party hardest, agree that these downtown neighborhoods are not suitable places for raising families. For instance, in the following responses to an interview question asking whether students plan to stay in Ptown after they graduate, many students indicate that they do not see Ptown, or downtown more specifically, as an appropriate environment for "grown-up" life after college. Even students who have been very happy living downtown while at PU seem to make a clear distinction between its suitability as a place to party and its unsuitability as a place to settle down and raise a family.

I would not want to live here if I wasn't attending school here because it is the stereotypical college town. There's noises every night. There's fights everywhere. After the weekend, there's beer cans and cups everywhere. There are drunk people every night, drunk drivers too. College students here think that nothing bad can happen to them, and I would not want to raise a family in an area that has that view. (twenty-three-year-old female senior)

I wouldn't want to raise my family where there's alcohol everywhere, drugs too . . . you know . . . it's a college town. Everywhere you go, there's a bar and there's, um, college students who love to get wasted, and have competitions to see who can out-drink each other. And I wouldn't want to raise my kids around that. (twenty-two-year-old female student)

No, I can't imagine living here as an adult. I feel like every day I would be looking at students, like "Man, I wish I was still in school." I have had a great time here, but there is a time and place for such stuff in your life, and after I graduate it would be hard to still be around it all. I mean, I definitely love it here. I wouldn't want to have gone to college anywhere else, but it's not where I want to stay. (twenty-year-old male sophomore)

Clearly, even the most extreme partiers at PU acknowledge the temporary status of their participation in the party subculture. There is a time and place for partying and many students understand its limited parameters. Perhaps this is why so many students party to the extent that they do while at PU. They know their time is limited and they want to take full advantage of it while they can. But it may also be this urgency of limited time that cultivates an exaggerated sense of entitlement to party, while exacerbating the conflicts between partiers and those students and residents who have already grown up and moved beyond the desire to party.

Game Day Mayhem

A second environment that can be negatively impacted by extreme partying at PU is the university-sponsored sporting event, most specifically home football games. As described in previous chapters, game days at the party school take on a carnival atmosphere with highly ritualized partying, or tailgating. Considering the large amount of alcohol students consume, the frenetic atmosphere of the game itself, and the more relaxed rules on game days, it is not surprising that secondhand harms are especially evident on game days. Following are examples of students' complaints about party-related problems inside PU's football stadium, particularly in the designated "student section."

At the stadium, people throw whatever they can get their hands on. I've had beer cans and paper cups thrown at me, water bottles, and paper balls. Also I've been pushed and knocked over during a game. (twenty-year-old female sophomore)

During last year's football season, I was in the student section waiting for the game to start. I had a pair of shorts and a jersey on, and the guy behind me reeking of beer kept trying to grab my bottom, and wrap his arms around me. I had no clue who he was, and it made me feel uncomfortable. I asked him to stop several times, then finally I just left the ball game. (twenty-one-year-old female junior)

Students and other fans who get drunk are vulgar and ruin it for the rest of us. Fights run rampant at tailgates; students are belligerent and often pass out during games; there is vomit all over the ground. (twenty-four-year-old female senior)

I hate sitting in the student section at football games where students are so drunk they fight and just act stupid. (twenty-two-year-old female senior)

Students smoke constantly (cigarettes and marijuana) during the football games in the upper student sections. They are not supposed to be doing that, but no one seems to care. (nineteen-year-old female freshman)

In the student section at football games, people are complete drunken idiots. I was constantly yelled at, at one game last year. It didn't stop until I finally got up and left. (twenty-three-year-old male senior)

At a football game last semester, one of my friends got puked on by somebody who was up in the top seating section. They went over the edge and she was just perfectly underneath. So gross things like that happen at games. But stuff happens at any school. It is just part of the game. (twenty-two-year-old male senior)

Note that the behavior described in this last response (i.e., getting puked on) was "gross" but also "just part of the game." In fact, many students who comment on the misconduct of other students at football games do not necessarily see the incidents as anything too disturbing, just "stuff that happens at any school." Still, for some students, the drunk and disorderly behaviors from their peers can ruin their football experience. For instance, several students in the survey suggested that they have stopped sitting in the designated student sections at games in order to avoid some of the problems described above, and a few students stopped attending PU football games all together due to various nuisance behaviors they either experienced themselves or witnessed. Indeed, even when students have not been directly harmed at games themselves, many are indirectly harmed by witnessing other people being victimized or harassed, or even just knowing that such problems exist. For instance, the following survey responses represent a cross-section of some of the crimes and misconduct witnessed by students on game days that may impact their sense of security and safety at PU.

Last semester in a parking garage after a football game I watched as my friends were ambushed with food. Yeah, food. We had come to the game in separate cars, and as I was driving away, I glanced back in time to see them getting sprayed with water from squirt guns and being pummeled with food (looked like assorted fruit) by some dudes in an SUV. (twenty-year-old male sophomore)

As I was walking up to the stadium last year there were a group of people watching someone sledgehammering a car. It was bizarre. I didn't stick around long enough to ask questions. But I decided at that point to never park my car anywhere near those tailgates. (nineteen-year-old female sophomore)

I was with a friend at a game last year when she had a cell phone stolen during the football game. I always hear about stuff being stolen on game days but that was the first time it happened to someone I know. Of course, people are so wasted, I don't know if it was stolen or just somebody who thought it was their own phone. Either way, I make sure to never carry anything important with me to the games (twenty-two-year-old female senior)

My friend's car got broken into one night while we were at a football game. He called the police and they said that they couldn't send a cop since they were all at the game! So to me that means that the game is more important than a citizen's rights being violated. I hope the cops caught a ton of drunk people so they can feel they have achieved their purpose. (twenty-two-year-old male senior)

The criticism voiced in this previous response about the preoccupation of police at sports events with drunks rather than with *real* criminals is a sentiment that is contrary to another common perception that the police do very little to regulate the behavior of drunks at PU on game days. In fact, students who are frustrated with the disruptive behavior of their intoxicated peers tend to take their frustrations out on the police, whom they see as not doing nearly enough to control the (intoxicated) student population at football games. A critical perception of the police and security staff as too soft on students' drunk and disorderly conduct at sporting events is illustrated in the following quotes.

> There needs to be more control of the student population at football games. There are way too many students sneaking in multiple bottles of beer. The event staff clearly sees them drinking in the stands and does nothing while they are endangering all the people around them with their behavior. (twenty-one-year-old female junior)

> Football games are a blast. The atmosphere and energy is amazing, but recently there have been a ton of fights breaking out in the stands. There are simply too many drunks and not enough security. I feel that it might be better to have police not just outside where the vendors are, but also in the stands, to create a sense of safety. Otherwise it's the wild west. (twenty-year-old female sophomore)

> I really think that there needs to be a more strict policy for being intoxicated in the student section of football games. Not everyone that goes to this university enjoys getting so drunk they can't function. I hate sitting in the student section where so many students are so drunk they fight and just act stupid. It is very annoying to go to watch a game and not even be able to enjoy it because of the drunks. It can also be dangerous, especially in the [football stadium], because of the concrete steps, metal bleachers, and very little security. (twenty-four-year-old male senior)

The occurrence of so much disruption and disorder on game days, despite the large number of police and specialized security forces brought in for these events, requires some explanation (or at least speculation). First, it is important to reiterate the magnitude of the task that police are charged with on game days, with so many students and nonstudent sports fans, many of whom are drunk and riled up for the game, converging on Ptown on game days. Even with heightened security (e.g., state police, local police, campus police, and private security), there is bound to be some minor crime and disorder that slips through the cracks. Second, police may adopt a more hands-off approach on game days (i.e., they will only make arrests when someone is in serious danger of hurting themselves or others).[5] Rather than arresting every drunk student who could potentially cause trouble, the police may only arrest students who are causing serious problems, such as fighting, destroying property, and drunk driving. As practical as this policy may be considering the large number of students who are intoxicated during games and at tailgates, it translates into hundreds of drunk students free to mill about and cause minor disruptions to other sports fans. Even as such discretion is probably necessary under the unique circumstances of game days, it inadvertently sends a message to students that they can get wasted on these days with impunity. It also clearly contradicts PU's formal policies on alcohol and other code violations as outlined in chapter 3.

Another factor that may help to explain the frequency of nuisance problems on game days, as well as the perception of insufficient social control inside stadiums and elsewhere, is that the police can not be everywhere at all times. Unless students or other fans are willing to report problems to authorities, there is little that will be done to correct the situation. Yet, despite students' frustrations and informal complaints (as evidenced in CCVS responses), students seldom complain formally to police, choosing instead to deal with matters on their own. Drunken incidents have become so common at these venues that most students do not think it would be worthwhile to involve the police or security. In fact, reporting to police is often a last resort, reserved primarily for serious crime with serious injury. Secondhand problems caused by the party subculture, as annoying as they may be, are seldom considered serious enough to report, or for that matter even seen as *real* crime.

Finally, students sitting among their peers (in presumed solidarity) to cheer on their school's team may not report peer-perpetrated incidents to police or other authorities in order to avoid being seen as a "snitch" or a "troublemaker." Rather than appear disloyal to their peers, or stigmatized as someone who lacks school spirit, most students will suffer in silence. And as mentioned earlier, some students will stop sitting in the student sections at games, or even stop attending football games all together. Since one of the great draws of PU is to experience sports games live and to cheer on their teams, a self-imposed exile from these games can be a substantial sacrifice, and another secondhand harm of the party subculture. In fact, boycotting football games is just one example of the many compromises that non-partying students often make at a party school. Such compromises, including rearranging their lives in some manner to avoid or minimize the negative effects from the party subculture, not only shortchange their college experiences but inadvertently sustain the situational normativity of party-related disturbances at their schools.

SUMMING UP

This chapter has showcased some of the secondhand effects of extreme partying that impact non- and more moderate partiers, as well as everyone else who lives at or near the party school. Party-related problems, including property disruption, noise, verbal harassment, and witnessing intoxication crimes, can negatively impact the quality of life for many students and nonstudent residents who regularly come into contact with the party subculture. Two places of contact highlighted in the chapter are downtown neighborhoods where PU's bars and parties are located, and PU sports events. Conflict between students who feel entitled to party and students who just want a peaceful existence are exaggerated in these two environments. For many partiers at the party school, there is a sense that it is *their* college, their town, their rules. This sense of entitlement perpetuates the party subculture's prominence both on campus and in the community, marginalizes all nonparticipants, and is disruptive to everyone living on or near the party school. Moreover, it is often non-partying students (and more responsible partiers) who must rearrange their lives to accommodate the party subculture, exerting both time and effort in their active avoidance of party hot spots, and even boycotting football games.

Yet, despite their frustrations, non-partying students are seldom willing to complain formally to police, due in part to a concern that they will appear disloyal to their peers or school. Instead, these students may try to convince themselves that the problems caused by their peers who party are not so bad. But by minimizing the harms of the party subculture, or using other rationales that will be discussed in the next chapter, students inadvertently defend the party subculture and sustain its prominence at the party school.

Rationales in Defense of the Party Subculture

As conveyed in previous chapters, more than half of PU students experience some type of crime victimization (e.g., burglary, vandalism, larceny theft, attacks/fights, rape, unwanted sexual contact) while at college, and more than three-fourth of students experience secondhand harms (e.g., property disruption, noise, verbal harassment) caused by the extreme drinking and drug routines of their peers. Most of these student-perpetrated and party-related offenses are "hidden" crimes that are not included in official crime statistics, primarily because they are rarely reported to police. With the exception of burglary (with students reporting 57 percent of incidents to police), most crime at PU goes unreported. For instance, only 33 percent of vandalism at PU (home or car) is reported to police, 20 percent of larceny theft, 11 percent of physical attacks and fights, and only 3 percent of rape/sexual assault (see appendix B, table 14).

Party-related crimes are also underrepresented in the official data because these incidents are not always seen as *real* crimes worth reporting (see Weiss 2011). Recall from chapter 6 (p. 87) that recognition of crime requires three components—an unambiguous violation of law, a guilty offender, and an innocent victim. Within the party situation, minor crime and other bad behaviors while intoxicated are not always recognized as crime. This chapter looks more closely at non-recognition of crime and students' reasons for not reporting party-related crimes and other problems to the police. Three of the most common reasons indicated by students in their survey responses — police as ineffective, incidents as private matters, and intoxication crimes as normal — are discussed below.

POLICE AS INEFFECTIVE

A common reason why victims of crime do not report incidents to police is due to an assumption that police will be ineffective or unwilling to help

(Felson, Messner, Hoskin, and Deanne 2002; Hashima and Finkelhor 1999; Greenberg and Ruback 1992; Sloan et al. 1997). At college, students' impressions of police as ineffective are sometimes based on past negative interactions with law enforcement (as victim, witness or offender), and sometimes based on speculation that police do not care about their problems. Such assumptions are especially prevalent among students who experience secondhand party-related harms. For instance, when asked if they ever call the police to report noise disturbances, less than 10 percent of PU students who experience such problems say yes. Yet, 42 percent say they wanted to. The most common reason for why students do not call police even when they want to is the assumption that doing so would be a waste of time and effort. As expressed in the following response, students assume in advance that the police "wouldn't come or do anything about it, or for that matter even care."

> I lived for almost a year with loud partying and yelling in the apartment next to mine. They would have parties practically every night of the week, and I always had to get up early for class. I never called the police because I know they wouldn't come or do anything about it, or for that matter even care. (twenty-one-year-old female junior)

Another reason why students do not call the police to report crime or nuisance problems is that they may, like many young persons, prefer to have as little interaction with the police as possible. A mistrust and dislike of police and other officials is not uncommon among teens and young adults who often resent the authority that law enforcement represents (Bynum and Thompson 2005; Gumprecht 2008; Hickson and Roebuck 2009; Wilkinson 2007). At the party school, there is an especially antagonistic relationship between student partiers and the police, with police sometimes vilified as the enemy. In light of the main objective of many students at a party school to get wasted, it is not surprising that students who party the most are most critical of the police. From the perspective of extreme partiers, the police are bullies who incessantly harass them for just trying to have a good time. This sentiment is illustrated in the following comments from students who participate regularly in the party subculture.

> The campus cops are worthless. I don't know what they do other than writing up tickets for drunks. And I never see the [Ptown] cops except for

when they are waiting to pounce on students coming out from the bars. Don't they have better things to do? (nineteen-year-old male sophomore)

The police in this town are horrible. I don't think anyone likes them here. They should have better things to do then flirting with our girls and busting up parties. (twenty-two-year-old male senior)

There's little respect for the cops. This past weekend, people were throwing beer bottles off the second-story balcony at a couple of police cars. (nineteen-year-old female junior)

[Ptown] police love to give out underage citations, but it's not the drunk freshman who are dangerous. And no one stops drinking just because they get a citation. All it does is contaminate your record for something that could have been handled with a warning. (nineteen-year-old female sophomore)

In contrast to the opinion (mostly from extreme or heavy partiers) that police spend too much time writing up tickets for underage consumption and public intoxication, many non-partiers criticize the police as not doing nearly enough to curb alcohol-related crime and misconduct at PU. The following excerpts from non-partiers represent the frustration of these students toward what they perceive to be a rather lax attitude on the part of the police (and university administration) toward the party subculture.

Police need to be more aggressive in the downtown area in arresting belligerent drunks. Too many students get wasted and take over. The cops seem oblivious, as does the school. Instead of adding any idiot to our rosters, perhaps the university should concentrate on recruiting students who care about their academics. There are *no* standards in getting in to this school and no enforcement of the rules once they are here. (twenty-four-year-old female junior)

When there are parties going on past 4 AM, the police take forever to show up and break them up. It takes four or five calls for the police to even show up, and then they try to be buddy-buddy and just slap the drunks on the back and leave. (twenty-one-year-old female junior)

Of course, not all students have such disdain for the police. Instead, many students believe that the police do an efficient job under rather difficult circumstances. As illustrated in the following comments, some students acknowledge and appreciate the tough job that police have to do at the party school.

> I feel that [the police] do a good job. They understand that underage drinking will happen and I don't think they let it get out of control. I have never had a problem with the police. (nineteen-year-old male freshman)

> The police are unfriendly, and treat everyone like second-class citizens or guilty of some crime. But they deal with drunk students all week. I'm sure they do the best they can. (twenty-two-year-old male senior)

> Police are too lenient in terms of drinking, but I do feel that they are here to ensure our safety and if I was in danger, I would rely on them and know that they would be available to help me. (twenty-two-year-old female senior)

> The cops are mostly able to calm down loud parties in a proper manner and make sure the party disperses without people getting into trouble. I think it's understanding of them to deal with college kids in a way that warns and helps them without arresting them on the spot for drinking. They control the area without being mean about it. (twenty-year-old female sophomore)

The prior example from "Lilly," a self-identified partier and proud hostess of large and "wild" house parties, echoes this supportive stance for local police, despite her many interactions with them due to noise complaints from neighbors. According to Lilly, her neighbors contact the police "over just about anything." The excerpt that follows from an interview with Lilly reveals both her sense of entitlement to party (i.e., "this town only functions because of the students") and her favorable attitude toward the police. Of course, as the police have never shut down any of her parties, she has no reason to see them as anything but allies.

> [Have your neighbors ever complained about noise or a party at your house?]

> Many times . . . um, a lot of my neighbors actually have said things. On one side of us is all students and one side is all older residents. Our one neighbor . . . he'll call the police over just about anything. He doesn't understand that this town only functions because of the students. He doesn't seem to like students much. Whether it's just him or someone else who calls, the police

have come to my house probably fifteen times. But I've lived here for three years, so that's not that bad. [laughs]

[Have you even been given a citation from the police for your parties?]

Nope, every time they've come in, they've looked at the party and realized that it was just, like, a regular college party and there was nothing crazy going on and they'd just leave. . . . Besides, I know many of them. I, like, wave to them. . . . Sometimes I give them cookies and stuff. I think they do a pretty good job, all things considering.

Assuming Lilly's recollections to be true, it is easy to conclude that calling the police to complain about noise from a "regular college party" would be a waste of time, and could certainly perpetuate the shared assumption among non-partiers of police ineffectiveness. Moreover, as the following student points out, even when police show up and issue citations to students for underage drinking, public intoxication or other noise disturbances, the fines do not necessarily intimidate partiers or deter future parties.

A lot of times loud music from my neighbors or just their constant partying has gotten in the way of a quiet evening of studying. But I don't call the police. These incidents are just too frequent and I doubt whether the police would be able to take the steps necessary to prevent future problems. Besides students at [PU] are not intimidated by fines or citations. They collect them, pay them, or at least their parents do, and life goes on. (twenty-three-year-old female senior)

As the above quote makes clear, underage drinking citations are not typically considered all that serious and are hardly a deterrent for students under twenty-one who want to drink. Whether or not these sanctions are effective may boil down to a simple rational choice: do risks outweigh rewards? For many students at the party school, rewards from partying are apparently too great and risks too small to deter them from engaging in the party lifestyle.

PRIVATE MATTERS

A second reason why students choose not to report crime and student misconduct to police is based on their relationships to offenders. Aside from wanting to protect friends and close acquaintances from getting into trouble, students may also want to protect other students from legal problems, both for their own and for offenders' sake. For instance, making formal complaints against their peers for doing what everyone seemingly does at a party school — getting wasted — can jeopardize students' social standing among their peers. Students who "snitch" on other students may be seen as disloyal, which can place them at risk of stigmatization, ostracism, and other negative consequences (Bynum and Thompson 2005; Finkelhor et al. 2001; Wilkinson 2007; Woldoff and Weiss 2010). In order to avoid negative labels, students who experience or witness crime within the context of the party situation, may choose to keep quiet or to mind their own business.

Students may also remain silent in allegiance to their peer groups or fellow partiers. For instance, students may feel a sense of camaraderie with other students who party and will not want to see them get into trouble. It is this empathy for fellow partiers that apparently prevents the student in the following excerpt from calling the police to complain about her disruptive neighbors.

> There was this blow-out party last year in my apartment building that
> lasted until 5 AM. It was a Thursday night and I had an exam that following
> morning. I was tempted to call the police the later it got, but I never did.
> Though I didn't know them, I did not want to get them in trouble in case
> there were any underage students in the apartment because I know if I
> was there and underage, I'd be pissed if someone called the cops. Besides, I
> remember my crazy party days. I know what its like to lose track of time. I'm
> sure they didn't mean to be so loud or party so late into the night. (twenty-
> one-year-old female junior)

In addition to empathizing with fellow partiers and not wanting to get them in trouble, students may prefer, on principle, to take care of matters themselves rather than involve the police or other authorities. Adolescent and young adult males may be especially resistant to involving police in "private matters," as reaching out to formal authority can be seen as a sign of weakness (Finkelhor et al. 2001). Instead, they may prefer to handle situations privately, engaging in methods of self-help or vigilante justice. At the party school, one common method of vigilantism or "partier justice" involves physical retaliation. For men, fighting demonstrates both self-reliance and physical prowess, two important markers of masculinity (Carlson 2008; Mullaney 2007). But even for women, a physical response to conflict or personal violations is not uncommon. As demonstrated in each of the following survey responses, students who take care of matters themselves by physical means summarily put an end to their respective incidents, and send a strong message that they will not be victims (Weiss 2010b).

> Two guys tried to start a fight with me outside of a bar one night. But, I kicked the shit out of both of them. Police weren't necessary. (twenty-two-year-old male junior)

> One night at a party some guy began groping me. I slapped him and told him (in very strong language) not to let it happen again. (twenty-year-old female junior)

Students at PU also handle conflict or "settle scores" through other means of retaliation (e.g., taking or breaking property, spreading a negative message about someone through social media). Within the party situation, intoxication acts as a social lubricant to lower inhibitions and ethical concerns, and also serves as an excuse afterward for rather unorthodox methods of justice. For instance, the student in the following excerpt who describes a particularly eccentric act of vengeance that he witnessed at a party (i.e., urinating on the target's wardrobe) defends his friend's actions by blaming the victim ("she made him mad") and inferring that intoxication contributed to his actions, insisting that "he's actually a nice guy when he's sober."

> At a party a couple years ago, a guy I know who was really pissed at his girlfriend decided to retaliate by going in to her bedroom and urinating all over the floor, her bed, and clothes. He's actually a nice guy when he's sober, but she made him mad. (twenty-one-year-old male junior)

Another reason why students at a party school may prefer to handle matters privately rather than call police is to avoid getting into legal trouble themselves. For instance, students who are victimized by crimes while drinking underage, using drugs, or engaging in any other illegal activity may not want to involve the police in order to avoid self-incrimination. Clearly, at a party school where two-thirds of students drink while underage, and one-fourth of students use at least occasional drugs, there is a great incentive to avoid involving the police in situations where so many participants have "unclean hands" (i.e., are engaging in illicit activity). But fear of getting into trouble can contribute to more serious injuries for victims who are hurt, and it is often the final straw in many drinking-related fatalities that have occurred at colleges over the past fifty years (Seaman 2005; Wechsler and Wuethrich 2002). Choosing to handle matters privately rather than bring in outside help can end in tragedy for students who party too much, while causing a lifetime of regret for students who choose to stand by and do nothing to help. The following examples, describing two very serious instances of extreme intoxication, illustrate some of the rationales for why students do not to call for help.

> When I was at a party last year, I really overdid it. But when my friends were about to call for help, I begged them not to. I was scared to get in trouble — I'm not twenty-one — and hospitals are expensive. My parents would be pissed and they wouldn't trust me anymore. (nineteen-year-old female freshman)

> A boy in my dorm got wasted at a party and his friends had to carry him out and they dropped him on the sidewalk in the snow and he smacked his head and was bleeding. He had to be taken to the emergency room to have his stomach pumped and his friends found someone over twenty-one to drive him there. When he woke up he didn't know where he was, and his friends had just left him because they didn't want to get in trouble. (eighteen-year-old female freshman)

Due to the potential of tragedy when students are unwilling to intervene over legal concerns, many universities have implemented or are considering implementing "medical amnesty" policies, a pledge of sorts where the university would promise that students who call to seek medical attention for themselves or others would not get into trouble for underage drinking or drug use. The simple logic underscoring this policy is that by eliminating the risk of legal consequences, students will be more willing to call police or 911, thereby saving lives. The vast majority of PU students surveyed in the revised CCVS support such a proposal for reasons that are explicated in the following response.

A medical amnesty policy would ensure that underage drinkers are given the medical help they need. Most students are scared to get involved. Who wouldn't be afraid of getting arrested or kicked out of school? I've been in the situation more than once where I might have called for help when a friend looked like she was in trouble. It would definitely have made a difference if I knew in advance that none of us would get in trouble. (twenty-year-old female sophomore)

Even as most studies suggest that there is an overwhelming amount of support from college students for medical amnesty (Fabian et al. 2008), the policies are not without their critics, who argue that by eliminating the legal consequences for underage drinking and drug use, schools would appear to be endorsing these behaviors. Moreover, critics insist that amnesty policies will increase binge drinking among students by eliminating the legal risks. But this critique has a major flaw in its logic. Many students at college already party irresponsibly despite the legal consequences. Recall that 22 percent of PU students who drink have received citations for liquor law violations, and 6 percent for drug violations (30 percent of extreme partiers have had at least one of these citations). Occasional legal consequences appear to be an acceptable trade-off that most partiers at a party school are willing to make for the rewards of partying. Thus, it is unlikely that introducing amnesty policies that encourage intervention *after* intoxication will impact whether students binge drink or use drugs, only whether they seek help after the fact.

NORMALIZING CRIME

A final reason why students may not report crime or student misconduct to police is that they do not always interpret incidents that occur within the context of the party situation as "real or reportable" crime (see Weiss 2011). While intoxication itself can muddy interpretations of behavior, deviant or otherwise, the party situation can further distort perceptions, making bad behavior seem almost normal, or at least excusable. Recall from the introduction (p. xx) that part of students' socialization into the party subculture is to learn the vocabularies or rationales that enable them to reinterpret extreme behaviors in more favorable ways. These rationales, similar to accounts or techniques of neutralization (see Scott and Lyman, 1968; Sykes and Matza

1957; Weiss 2011) normalize extreme partying and the many problems it causes. Three distinct rationales — minimizing harm, excuses, and condemning complainers — are discussed below.

Minimizing Harm

Within the context of a party school, minor crime and secondhand harms are often trivialized by the participants of the party subculture. Rationales that minimize harm help partiers "manage intoxication" by neutralizing the bad effects that sometimes accompanies it. Rationales may also help students who do not party to make the best of situations that they cannot change. As illustrated in the following quotes from both partiers and non-partiers who live downtown, students who surmise that "stuff happens" everywhere or could be worse elsewhere, are able to conceptualize crime and disorder where they live as manageable or insignificant. (Note: rationales are italicized for emphasis.)

> Stuff happens all the time, people wrecking their cars, getting hit, fighting. I've seen a ton of fights, people getting DUIs *but nothing out of the ordinary.* (eighteen-year-old male sophomore)

> There's a lot of property crime downtown, which I sort of put up with for the first year I lived there. But I moved when I got tired of it all. But it really was OK. I got used to it. It's better to learn that life isn't fair and people are assholes, right? *Learn it while you are young 'cause shit happens.* (twenty-one-year-old male junior)

> In my neighborhood, there are bottles and cans and condoms left in yards after every weekend, trash cans get knocked over. *But nothing really bad happens.* (twenty-one-year-old male junior)

> There've been incidents where every car on the street will get egged, or all of the cars parked there will have the two tires facing the street slashed. *But crime happens everywhere.* (twenty-year-old female sophomore)

> I get woken up almost every weekend by loud parties next door but I don't complain because, hey, *it is what we do here.* Don't live here if that's going to be a problem. (twenty-year-old male sophomore)

While it is easy to understand why students who party would defend the party subculture and the problems it causes as normal, it is more difficult to explain why non-partiers use similar rationales. There are at least two possible explanations. First, non- and more moderate partiers may minimize the harmful effects of the party subculture in allegiance to their peers or schools, as a gesture of solidarity, or as a means to fit in or conform (perhaps begrudgingly) to the norms of the party school. One such norm that both partiers and non-partiers may feel obliged to observe is to *not* "overreact" to certain party-related offenses, such as verbal harassment or unwanted sexual contact. Within the party context, students who want to fit in (or at least not stand out) learn to minimize such incidents by reinterpreting them as funny, flattering or harmless. The influence of peer groups and the social learning process for managing such incidents are demonstrated in the following excerpt.

> A few months ago when I was at a club here in [Ptown], some guy I didn't know grabbed my breast and squeezed pretty hard. Before I could do or say anything, he turned around and started laughing with his buddies. I was actually pretty appalled and a little embarrassed. But when I rejoined my friends, I didn't tell them what happened. I guess I wasn't sure if they'd think I was overreacting. I had just transferred to [PU] and was just getting to know these folks. I didn't want to be seen as someone who can't take a joke. (twenty-one-year-old female junior)

Another reason why non-partiers might use rationales that minimize harms caused by the party subculture is to help them make the best of a bad situation (see Weiss 2011). For instance, non-partiers and nonstudent residents living near "party houses" may minimize the noise and disruptions at night as "normal college stuff" that happens everywhere, or could be worse. By doing so, it makes their lives seem more normal, or at least manageable. The following dialogue between two nonstudent residents living in a downtown neighborhood illustrates how these rationales are integrated into both cognition and conversation. (Note: A is a male resident; B is a female resident. Interviewer probes are in brackets.)

> A: Some nights you have to expect some noise. I mean, you're in a college town, you have a ball game on Saturday, it's going to be noisy Saturday night. I mean, expect that.

B: And I think we're fairly used to it. *And it could be worse.* Based on the physical location of my house, with the creek there and, you know, the bridges, there is a kind of built in insulation from the real craziness. [What do you mean by craziness?]

B: Well, you know, the vulgarity, the peeing in people's yards, the vandalism of property.

A: *But I don't think the problems here are any worse than any other neighborhood, or any other town for that matter.*

Believing that problems could be worse elsewhere and that what happens in their neighborhood is not so bad are coping strategies that allow these residents to acclimate to their "new normal." Similarly, such rationales enable non-partying students to make the best of their lives at a school where they are often marginalized. Minimizing harms caused by the party subculture can help to reduce resentment and conflict, and help non-partiers to fit in at the party school, or at least not stand out.

Excuses

Another means by which crime is normalized at the party school is to excuse students for their bad behaviors while intoxicated. At a party school, being wasted can be a rather effective "get out of jail free" pass that absolves students of culpability for a range of bad behavior. In fact, being wasted has become a catch-all excuse for all types of irresponsible behaviors, from not going to class and missed assignments, to reckless pranks and even minor criminal violations. Of course, the efficacy of excuses will depend upon the audience. Even as there are probably few instructors, law enforcement agents, or parents, who would be willing to excuse students' bad behaviors due to intoxication, such excuses are readily accepted by fellow partiers.

Still, even among the most hardcore partiers, there are limits as to when it is appropriate to use such excuses. For instance, intoxication would probably not be a reasonable excuse for bad behavior at somber events like funerals, or formal events such as graduation. But within the context of the party situation, as illustrated in the following responses, intoxication is a widely accepted excuse among fellow partiers that enables students to be less responsible for their irresponsible behaviors.

Some idiot started grabbing me at a bar one night. *But I should have expected it, he was drunk.* (twenty-one-year-old female junior)

One night there was this altercation outside at a party. Someone threatened to call the cops. But there was really no need to. *It was just a bunch of drunk guys doing what drunk guys do.* (nineteen-year-old male sophomore)

Some really wasted guy followed me home from the bar one night making really crude comments along the way. But it was not a serious issue. *The guy was drunk and did not seem to be dangerous.* (twenty-year-old female sophomore)

It was freshman year and I was in a friend's dorm room who was a close guy friend of mine. We had feelings for each other, but I had a boyfriend back home and did not want anything sexual with this guy. We were sitting on his bed and he just rolled over on top of me and was taking his pants off and humping me. I started yelling at him and he eventually got off of me but not at first. I stormed out of his room and have not heard from him since. I did not say anything to anyone because I did not want to get him in trouble. *Besides he was really wasted, and I don't think he meant anything.* (nineteen-year-old female sophomore)

As suggested by these prior responses, men tend to be excused more often than women for bad behavior while intoxicated. The assumption inherent in men's excuses is that, but for the alcohol, they are really nice guys who would never intentionally hurt anyone. In other words, being wasted makes men's bad behaviors more forgivable, and almost normal under the circumstances (see Weiss 2009a, 2011). By eliminating accountability, excuses enable men at the party school to act recklessly and behave badly with almost no social risk.

Condemning Complainers

A third rationale that normalizes crime and other student misconduct at the party school is diversion of blame, that involves redirecting focus away from the persons causing the trouble and toward the persons who complain. Similar to "condemning the condemner," a technique of neutralization delineated in Sykes and Matza's classic framework (1957), this rationale works by questioning the motives and integrity of the persons who object to some particular offense. Complainers essentially become scapegoats that divert attention away from the actual source of the problems.

At the party school, scapegoated groups include students who complain about the party subculture. These students are often "blamed" for choosing to attend a school known for its parties (e.g., If they don't like to party, then what are they doing at a party school?). Meanwhile, nonstudent residents who complain about students' excessive partying may be labeled as "anti-student," and seen as foolish for choosing to live or buy a home in a college town ("if they don't like students then why are they living in a college town?").

Another scapegoated group consists of students who are victimized while partying and call police to help. When students get hurt from drinking or drug use, they threaten to expose the party subculture as dangerous. Therefore, in order to deflect attention away from the potential dangers of partying, victims who get hurt within the context of the party situation are often blamed for having contributed in some way to their own victimization. Blaming victims for "precipitous behaviors," such as drinking too much, assumes that victims have done something wrong, or failed to do something right, that facilitated their victimization (see Weiss 2009b; 2011). Psychologists who study victim blaming see this rationale as a self-protective function for non-victims that reassures them that the world is predictable and just, and that bad things only happen to persons who deserve them (see Lerner 1980, "just world approach"). Blaming victims who get hurt within the party context can help other partiers feel safe despite the potential dangers. For instance, they may see themselves as different (e.g., smarter, more cautious or responsible) than their peers who get hurt. These rationales are inferred in the following responses from students asked to comment about safety on campus. Within each of the responses, there is an assumption that it is a student's responsibility to avoid putting themselves at risk while at the party school. The implication is that students who do not take the necessary precautions to protect themselves are fools who are "just asking for something to happen."

> Even though it's a college town and there are a lot of things that go down and things tend to happen, I feel safe. Knowing where to go and not to go is a big

part of it. Never walk alone because then *you're just asking for something to happen*, especially if it is late at night. (twenty-two-year-old female junior)

I feel pretty safe on and around campus, and even off campus. There's always going to be crime, so people should obviously take proper precautions. It seems that most of the time people who have these things happen to them could have avoided most situations with a lifestyle change, like not going to places that are shady, or not going to places alone, You know, just being smart. (nineteen-year-old female sophomore)

One night I had a pretty expensive camera with me at a party to take some pictures. And somewhere around midnight, I noticed it was gone. I was wasted and it was my own fault. I wasn't paying attention to where I had put it. (nineteen-year-old male sophomore)

Note that in this last response, the student is the one blaming himself for his victimization. Self-blame is not uncommon among crime victims and it is often triggered by the reactions of others who tend to question the victims' choices prior to a crime. While victims of all types of crime may question and even regret some of the choices they made prior to victimization, no other group of crime victims internalizes more self-blame than female victims of rape and sexual assault (Weiss 2009a; 2010a). Women's sense of responsibility for these crimes is often based on beliefs in rape myths that blame women for "getting themselves raped" for reasons that include leading men on, dressing in provocative ways, not communicating clearly, and drinking too much (Pitts and Schwartz 1997; Weiss 2009a, 2010a). In regard to alcohol, and in direct contrast to men who are often excused for bad behaviors while intoxicated, women are expected to know their limits and to act responsibly even when intoxicated. This double standard is illustrated in the following responses to a survey question that asked students to comment on crime and safety at PU. According to these students (one male and one female), women who get drunk (as well as dress provocatively, or "look slutty") are putting themselves in harm's way and "asking for trouble."

Girls shouldn't go out alone and look slutty. And they shouldn't be stupid, or get drunk. *Dumb girls that walk by themselves and get wasted are asking for trouble* (twenty-year-old female junior)

When it comes to sexual crimes, girls should know better than to put themselves in situations that can be dangerous. For example, avoid drinking like a fish at a Greek party while dressed like a playboy bunny. It's common sense. (twenty-one-year-old male junior)

What these comments suggest is that female students who "get wasted" assume the risks of victimization, including sexual assault. This perspective not only blames victims and discourages sympathy for the women who get hurt, but minimizes outrage for these types of crimes and the persons who commit them. And, of course, condemning victims and other complainers in these manners cultivates a norm of silence that impedes formal complaints to the police. This silence, in turn, perpetuates the normativity of minor crimes and other reckless behaviors within the context of the party situation.

SUMMING UP

This chapter has outlined three of the major reasons why crime at the party school remains "hidden" from official crime statistics, and is rarely brought to the attention of the police. First, police are often seen as incompetent or ineffective within the context of the party school. Many students who party see the police as bullies who interfere with their right (or obligation) to party. As summed up by one sophomore: "It's college, you're supposed to party hard." On the other hand, non-partying students often see the police as too lenient and, therefore, anticipate that reporting minor crime or nuisance problems would be a waste of time. A second reason for students' reluctance to involve police is that they are expected to handle matters privately. In fact, within the context of the party subculture, the norm is to *not* call the police. By handling situations themselves, they are able to remain loyal to their peers. Keeping matters private is also a means of protecting themselves and friends from legal consequences for underage drinking, drug use, or other illicit behavior.

A third reason why crime is not often reported to police at the party school is that students do not always recognize incidents they experience or witness within the party situation as "real crimes" that should be reported. Instead, intoxication crimes and secondhand harms are often rationalized as a normal part of college life. Three rationales — minimizing harms (e.g., "it could be worse," "stuff happens everywhere"), excuses (e.g., "he was wasted," "it's just kids being kids"), and condemning complainers (e.g., "if they don't like to party, what are they doing here?" "she brought it on herself") — perpetuate extreme partying and the problems that accompany it as almost normal, and certainly not reportable. These rationales also defend and, ultimately, sustain the party subculture's prominence at the party school.

Conclusion

SOBERING REFLECTIONS OF
THE PARTY SCHOOL

From drinking games at tailgates to after-party pranks and couch burn-ings, students at Party University (PU) and other party schools across the nation engage in unique and often extreme intoxication rituals that have become as much a part of their college lives as attending classes, taking tests, and graduating. Certainly, life at a party school can be a lot of fun. Students make, and take away with them, many fond memories based on their shared party experiences. In fact, long after course lessons are forgot-ten, students may still recall with vivid detail the nights spent drinking with friends; weekend tailgates; bar crawls in celebration of twenty-first birthdays; and all of the crazy pranks, drinking games, and other rituals of the party subculture.

Of course, excessive drinking, drug use, and other reckless behaviors, so integral to the party subculture and party school, can come at a cost. Students who party the most at these schools experience a variety of negative conse-quences ranging from injury and illness to crime victimization and arrest. Meanwhile, extreme party behaviors are the primary contributor to minor crime and disorder in the surrounding communities. Yet within the context of the party school, many of these intoxication crimes and secondhand harms have become an expected and normalized part of college life.

This book has sought to better understand the party subculture and the problems associated with it. A party subculture comprises a significant part of everyday life at many large residential universities, and is especially prom-inent at sports-oriented schools located in isolated college towns (i.e., the party school). For students who participate in this subculture, it can provide them with an active social life and an identity and sense of purpose that can rival or surpass a more conventional academic role. For students who do not participate, the party subculture can be an impediment to their college experience as they must learn to avoid, accommodate, or even rationalize their peers' extreme party behaviors. Moreover, the perception that students *should* party at a party school can marginalize those who do not, while further perpetuating the normativity of the party lifestyle and the problems it causes for the campus and community.

This final chapter wraps ups an in-depth investigation of the party school by reviewing the key findings from the Campus Crime Victimization Survey (CCVS), including students' drinking and drug routines, extreme rituals, criminal consequences, and secondhand harms caused by the party subculture. The chapter then provides an overview of what colleges and universities are doing today to curtail excessive drinking among their students, to combat party-related crime and disorder, and to improve the overall quality of life for students and residents of their respective campuses and communities. The chapter concludes with some general "solutions" (or rather challenges) for encouraging (sub)cultural changes at the party school.

REVIEW OF THE FINDINGS: PARTY ROUTINES, RITUALS, AND RISKS

At many colleges and universities across the United States, partying or, more accurately, getting wasted, has become *the* extracurricular activity for a sizable proportion of undergraduate students, aged eighteen to twenty-four. Data from the CCVS show that a clear majority of traditional undergraduates at PU drink alcohol (79 percent) and one in four students use drugs (mostly marijuana). Based on their patterns of usage, 25 percent of PU students are identified as light partiers, who drink less than five drinks in a typical night of drinking, drink only one night in a typical week, and use no drugs. Forty percent of students are identified as heavy partiers, who drink five to eight drinks in a typical night of drinking, drink two to three nights in a typical week, and typically use marijuana or other drugs occasionally (less than a few times a month). Finally, 14 percent of PU students are *extreme partiers*, students most committed to the party subculture who drink nine or more drinks in a typical night of drinking, four or more nights in a typical week, and typically use marijuana or other drugs regularly (a few times a month or more).

A closer inspection of the small but consequential subgroup of extreme partiers shows that they are more likely to be men, although women are not far behind when combining extreme and heavy partying. Students over twenty-one party slightly more in this extreme category than students under twenty-one, as do freshmen but only slightly more than upperclassmen. (Sophomores party least, as they often play catch up after partying too much during their freshman year.)

Extreme partiers tend to have lower GPAs, are less likely to work more than twenty hours per week, and are less likely to be involved in academic or religious organizations. However, these partiers are more likely to be involved in two student groups: fraternities/sororities and athletics, two organizations that tend to encourage extreme partying. Finally, students who party the most are more likely to think favorably about their identities as partiers and the label of their university as a party school.

Participation in PU's party subculture includes engaging in many identifiable drinking rituals with the ultimate goal of getting wasted. Drinking games, party pranks and even survival stories of severe "wastedness" bond student partiers together around their shared party experiences. Peer groups play a crucial role in socializing students into the party subculture, teaching them the necessary techniques for successful partying, and providing the rationales that normalize it all.

But even for the most extreme partiers, the partying lifestyle is often temporary and transitory. For most PU students, their partying routines eventually slow down as their priorities shift and graduation approaches. Clearly, the majority of PU seniors transition rather seamlessly from partier to graduate with no permanent damage from their years of excessive drinking, drug use, and other reckless behaviors.

Still, even as permanent damage from excessive partying is rare, partying to such extremes does involve risk that can range from failing classes and minor injuries to crime victimization of all types. For instance, extreme partiers at PU are almost twice as likely as more moderate partiers to experience blackouts or injuries due to intoxication. Partying to an extreme also doubles the risk of injury from fights for men, and significantly increases risks of alcohol-related illnesses and rape for women. Risks of other types of crime victimization, including burglary, vandalism, larceny theft, physical attack, and unwanted sexual contact, increase significantly for extreme and heavy partiers as compared to non-partiers and more moderate partiers.

Crime victimization especially increases for students who spend a lot of their time in party "hot spots," such as bars, clubs, and fraternity or house parties. From a routine activities perspective, the increased risks experienced by students who frequent party hot spots can be explained by the convergence of intoxicated offenders who tend to be more aggressive and reckless, intoxicated victims who are often more careless and vulnerable, and intoxicated bystanders who are often too drunk to be effective or capable guardians.

A routine activities theory can also help to explain why extreme partiers are more likely to commit crimes themselves and experience legal troubles. Intoxication decreases self-control and makes students more belligerent, careless, reckless, and willing to fight and violate laws. CCVS data show that extreme partiers are more than four times as likely as light partiers to receive citations for alcohol or drug violations, and almost five times as likely to drive drunk. Moreover, extreme partiers rarely show remorse, or take responsibility for their bad behaviors while drunk. Within the party situation, being wasted somehow makes it all okay. In fact, students who party most seem least concerned about consequences, including possible legal sanctions.

Apparently, for many PU students the laws and codes prohibiting underage drinking and drug use are merely "suggestions," not taken very seriously by PU's most serious partiers. Most students at PU learn early on how to circumvent the rules (as reflected in a comment from a twenty-year-old male student: "There are always ways to get around the rules"). As cliché as it may be, where there is a will, there is a way. And at the party school, there exists both a strong will and many creative ways to party despite the laws and formal restrictions to the contrary.

With such a strong commitment to partying no matter the costs to themselves, extreme partiers and the party subculture they endorse have contributed to a variety of problems on campus and in the surrounding communities. For instance, about half of PU students (and almost all non-partiers) complain of litter, noise, verbal harassment, and other secondhand problems caused by extreme partying in their downtown neighborhoods and at PU's sports events. These problems can range from minor annoyances to intimidation and crime, creating hostile environments for many students and making it difficult for non-partiers to participate fully in college life.

Yet, despite their collective frustrations, only a small number of students report party-related incidents to the police. Many students at the party school see police as ineffective in dealing with intoxication crimes and party-related disturbances, and many students consider student-perpetrated offenses as private matters that they should take care of themselves. Many of the problems at the party school go unreported because students do not always see them as serious or real problems. Partying is just what students do at college, and "stuff" is bound to happen. These rationales perpetuate the situational normativity of extreme partying routines, rituals, and the risks that accompany them. In fact, many party rituals, such as tailgating and couch burning, are so deeply embedded within the traditions of the party school that engaging in them seems as normal and harmless as studying for exams.

Moreover, party rituals bond students together where they forge a strong loyalty to each other and to their school that lasts well beyond graduation. Many alumni find themselves reflecting back on their years at college with a strong sense of nostalgia for their crazy nights of partying. The "happy ending" for most partying students, and the fond memories toward their alma maters, often translates into a financial generosity in terms of alumni donations. Financial contributions from happy (i.e., nostalgic) alumni may help to explain why administrators at party schools have done very little to curtail the party subculture or to challenge their school's reputation as a party school. The party school is a highly successful entity in today's college marketplace, able to attract thousands of students to attend and, for those students who make it to graduation, provides many lasting and mostly positive memories that encourage generous endowments. In short, the university benefits from the party school imagery and profits from partying students, as does the college town and it's most thriving industry — alcohol. Thus, it is not surprising that no one at the party school or college town wants to rock the boat or bite the hand that feeds them. Simply stated, the party school has become too big to fail.

The following sections investigate the various responses by universities and colleges to the extreme partying on their campuses and the problems it causes, starting with the inaction and ambivalence of administrators at some schools. The section is followed by an overview of some of the proactive efforts undertaken by schools today in an effort to address extreme partying, intoxication crimes and the other party-related problems negatively impacting their college communities.

INACTION AND AMBIVALENCE

Before schools can address the problems related to excessive partying, they must first acknowledge that there are problems and be willing to investigate them. Since knowing that there is a problem makes it harder to ignore, many schools seem content to remain mostly ignorant about the specifics and extent of party-related problems on their campuses. Aside from serious crime that is disclosed to the public as part of Clery or UCR statistics, many incidents that occur at college remain private matters. For instance, fights, bullying and the many alcohol-related medical emergencies that land students in hospitals almost every weekend are handled rather quietly, and treated as unique cases rather than indicative of a much larger problem.

College administrators may also be reluctant to take on excessive drinking on their campuses because, in the long run, the party atmosphere that encourages alcohol consumption has some benefits for them (Seaman 2005). For instance, the party school image — for better or worse — is an effective marketing campaign for schools to stand out among competitors. The party school represents an environment where students can have fun. It is surely not good PR for these schools to reveal just how many injuries or other problems occur while students are engaging in their particular brand of fun. Moreover, excessive drinking goes hand in hand with sports and its most prominent ritual — tailgating. Colleges may be reluctant to implement any restrictions to drinking that may be seen as interfering with the traditions of tailgating and other rituals that encourage school spirit. Doing so could negatively impact both enrollment and alumni donations (Wechsler and Wuethrich 2002).

Meanwhile, party schools and their communities often benefit financially from the business of alcohol. Bars and liquor stores are lucrative industries in a college town, providing a steady stream of revenues. Due to this mutually beneficial business relationship between universities and the alcohol industry, schools rarely challenge the presence of so many bars and clubs near their campuses, or try to regulate the manner in which these establishments conduct business (Sperber 2000). For instance, all-you-can-drink specials at bars (penny pitchers, happy hours, ladies' nights, weeknight specials, etc.) are regularly advertised in college newspapers and campus-endorsed websites, making it seem, even if not true, that colleges themselves sponsor the events (Lanza-Kaduce, Capece, and Alden 2006). Many of these promotional drinking specials endorse irresponsible drinking and entice students to go out on weeknights, contributing to the normativity of five-day weekends that begin Wednesday nights at the local bars.

Rather than confront the dominance of the alcohol industry in their towns, administrators tend to take a hands-off approach, or what Sperber (2000) refers to as "benign neglect," that attempts to keep drinking at a safe distance from campus. This means that many colleges prohibit drinking in the residence halls on campus but ignore what goes on off campus in the town bars and clubs (Sperber 2000, p. 166). Since most of the negative consequences related to students' excessive drinking take place in these off-campus party hot spots (i.e., bars, clubs, parties), the current strategy does little to promote student safety.

Although it may not be possible or even practical to eliminate student drinking off campus, ignoring the problems (or benign neglect) sends a message that encourages extreme partiers to continue doing what they do, as long as it is not on campus. Ignoring the problems associated with extreme partying also contributes to the frustrations felt by many non-partiers, who feel as if the school does not care enough to address the party-related problems that occur regularly in their neighborhoods and at sports events. Simply stated, administrators who remain silent are complicit in perpetuating the situational normativity of extreme partying and the problems it causes to the college community.

ACTIONS AND STRATEGIES

Even as some schools have taken a hands-off approach to extreme partying and party-related problems on their respective campuses, many universities and colleges have implemented a variety of programs and policies in an effort to curtail the excessive drinking and reckless behaviors that characterize the party subculture. The following sections look at some of these strategies, beginning with students' own suggestions for improving their campus and community, followed by some of the policies that schools have already implemented in an attempt to curb heavy alcohol consumption and minimize alcohol-related crime and disorder in their college communities.

What Can We Learn from Our Students?

While acknowledging that problems exist at their schools is a good first step for university administrators, a second step toward positive action and improving safety and student well-being is to listen to what their own students have to say. Students are the ones who live the college experience, and therefore students have both the insight and "expertise" to know what might help to improve their lives at college. Based on survey responses to a question asking PU students what could be done to improve their campus and community, students advocate for three basic changes. First, students suggest that there should be more police patrolling PU's party hot spots, especially the bars and clubs downtown and sporting events, where most crime and student misconduct take place. Students complain that police are mostly reactive (arriving only after something happens) rather than being proactive in preventing crime and disorder in the first place. Many students say they rarely see the police until they are arresting someone. In this regard, students would like to see more community-based policing that would include a greater presence of police downtown at night patrolling on foot rather than driving by in cars waiting for something bad to happen (Barkan 2012, p. 420). Clearly, there needs to be more trust and cooperation between student residents and police officers, as well as between students and nonstudent residents.

A second suggestion from students is to modify the "marketing" of the school from a place known for its parties to a college known for its academic rigor. Many students are embarrassed by the image of PU as a party school. These students are concerned that their degrees will be meaningless when they graduate. They are frustrated by what they see as an inverted priority system where academics are being overshadowed by sports and a party ethic. As one female student stated, "We should not be accepting so many kids with one objective in mind — to party." Statements such as these suggest that students who come to PU primarily to party do not care enough about their education or, for that matter, the school or community.

Certainly, this is a sentiment that could be echoed by many of the faculty who teach at party schools and who struggle to accommodate the ever-increasing enrollments of students with little ambition for studying or academic learning. The large numbers of students who are at college primarily to party rather than to learn create a very frustrating and challenging classroom experience for both instructors and motivated students who want to learn. Students most committed to the party subculture are regularly absent from classes; fail to turn in assignments on time, if at all; and, when they do come to class, are mostly disengaged and apathetic to the course material. In the long run, it is the bright and truly engaged students who are shortchanged by the party school's marketing strategy to promote itself as a fun place to be rather than as a serious place to study.

A final suggestion from students in regard to improving their experiences at college pertains to safety and bystander intervention. Many students, irrespective of whether they party or not, would like to see PU adopt a medical amnesty policy in order to encourage students in need to call for assistance. As discussed in chapter 8, many students involved in the party subculture are reluctant to call police or 911 when they have been drinking or using drugs because they do not want to get into legal trouble. By eliminating the risk of legal consequences, a medical amnesty policy would ensure that more students get help and are treated more swiftly for their alcohol-related injuries and illnesses.

Taken together, students suggestions are insightful and should be taken seriously. After all, students are the ones participating in the party subculture, or coping with the negative effects of other students' irresponsible partying. For this reason, it might also make sense for schools to hold "town hall" meetings that invite students to speak with police and administrators to voice their concerns in person. As the persons most affected by the party subculture, students should be an integral part of the solutions for challenging the party subculture, and addressing problems associated with it.

What Are Schools Doing to Address the Problems?

With or without feedback from their students, many universities have begun to confront some of the party-related problems that occur on their campuses and in the surrounding communities. For instance, many universities and colleges today enforce strict student conduct codes that emphasize zero tolerance toward the use of alcohol and drugs (Vander Ven 2011). Many schools are also getting much tougher on student misconduct while intoxicated and "unruly" parties that disrupt the peace of the college community. This section begins with some of the programs that universities have introduced to reduce excessive drinking on campus, followed by programs that advocate for tougher sanctions for intoxication crime and party-related nuisance problems in the broader community.

Drying out. In an attempt to challenge students' preoccupation with excessive drinking, many universities and colleges sponsor events and activities that serve no alcohol (i.e., dry events). For instance, PU offers a few such dry events as part of an "up all night" program that includes concerts, bowling, and movies. But students seldom attend these events sober. In fact, these programs often backfire because many students who attend alcohol-free events actually increase their pregaming in order to compensate for the absence of alcohol at the sober (main) events (Glass and WBEZ 2009; Seaman 2005). Dry events are destined to fail as long as students are convinced that nighttime events can never be fun without first getting wasted.

Aside from dry events, some schools, such as the University of Oklahoma, have attempted to eliminate alcohol all together from campus facilities and school-sponsored events by creating a "dry campus" (Gumprecht 2008). While most universities and colleges today prohibit alcohol from its residence halls on campus, alcohol is often allowed in certain venues on campus, such as student lounges, alumni centers, and at some sports facilities. When schools mandate a dry campus, they are hoping to make it more difficult for students to obtain alcohol to drink on campus. However, such restrictions seldom eliminate student drinking; they just move it elsewhere. For example, a primary student tailgating hot spot on PU's campus went dry about three years ago, replacing its popular and rather profitable bar service with live bands, but no alcohol. But even music cannot lure students into a dry tailgating spot, and it remains largely empty on game days. The reality is that few students at a party school want to tailgate without alcohol.

For that matter, few students want to attend a college where they cannot drink. Apparently, college students today respond no better to the prohibition of alcohol than Americans did in the 1920s. Students who are determined to drink at college will find a way to drink regardless of the rules. According to some researchers, college crackdowns of alcohol on campus have simply shifted alcohol consumption to off-campus house parties and into the surrounding communities where there are less regulations. In doing so, college drinking has morphed into a much more disruptive presence in the neighboring communities (Hingson et al. 2005).

Researchers also suggest that binge drinking and many drinking-related problems at college began to intensify with the rise of the legal drinking age to twenty-one in 1984 (Gumprecht 2008; Sperber 2008). When students were no longer able to drink legally on campus or in bars, they began to move their drinking "underground" to parties with little supervision. Underage students also stepped up their pregaming activities in order to consume as much alcohol as possible before heading out to events where they could not legally drink. Because alcohol consumption is harder to regulate and control at off-campus parties and pregaming gatherings hosted in private homes, students began to drink more recklessly.

Backed by empirical evidence that suggests that college students are just as likely to drink alcohol before the age of twenty-one as after twenty-one, and that underage students are more likely to drink recklessly, many critics have insisted that the twenty-one minimum drinking age has failed to keep young people safe (see Seaman 2005, pp. 231–44). One notable group of critics in recent years has been university and college presidents. Arguing that the minimum drinking age laws have had counterproductive effects at college, one hundred university and college presidents (as of 2009) have joined a campaign called the Amethyst Initiative to advocate for the lowering of the drinking age back to eighteen (Vander Ven 2011; Wilson 2008).

As stated earlier, prohibition of alcohol did not work very well in this country when attempted in the early 1900s, and prohibiting young people from drinking alcohol before the age of twenty-one is especially bound to fail for the following reasons. First, teens and young adults do not like being told that they cannot do something that adults are able to do. Second, getting wasted is fun. Alcohol and drug awareness programs that focus on a prohibitive message ("just say no") or that highlight the dangers of partying will not be effective as long as young persons see the risks as well worth the rewards. Furthermore, most young people see themselves as invincible, and therefore will fail to see the relevance of the warnings or statistical data about dangers for their own lives. Instead, the information becomes little more than white noise that they block out or dismiss as adults being overly protective. Besides, students at the party school learn to minimize the harms associated with intoxication as part of the social learning process. Finally, students feel entitled to party at college. They see it as a right that they are willing to fight for. As long as students feel entitled to party, and have little regard for the consequences, minimum drinking age laws will have little impact as a deterrent on student drinking at college.

Conceding that prohibition is a losing battle, many universities and colleges have tried to curtail excessive drinking by making it more difficult for students to obtain large amounts of alcohol. One method for making it harder to access liquor is to restrict alcohol-related businesses from operating in neighborhoods closest to campus (Weitzman, Nelson, Lee, and Wechsler 2004). Another strategy, proposed by Hingson and colleagues (2005) is to make alcohol — both beer and harder liquor — more expensive to purchase by raising prices, thereby making binge drinking difficult to accomplish for students on a budget. They also suggest reigning in the proliferation of liquor stores and outlets that provide cheap alcohol in bulk, and make it too easy for students to buy and consume large amounts of liquor. Finally, Hingson and colleagues suggest limiting high-volume drink promotions at student bars and clubs such as happy hours and drink-till-you-drop specials. One example of a school that has implemented this latter suggestion is Frostburg State University in Maryland where administrators have encouraged the Liquor Control Board to pressure local bar owners to stop offering all-you-can-drink specials (Wilson 2008). And at Florida State University (FSU), in an attempt to shed its party-school image, FSU has recently formed a coalition with local bar owners to advocate for responsible drinking that includes outlawing "ladies drink free" nights and other discount specials, as well as stiffening penalties for bars who serve underage drinkers (Gruley 2003).

Getting tough on crime. At the same time that universities and colleges are beginning to address the problems of binge drinking on campus, many schools are also starting to implement tougher penalties for students who commit crimes on or off campus, by forging college-community partnerships between university and local police (Hingson et al. 2005). For instance, PU makes it a mandatory violation of the student conduct code when students violate any local, state, or federal law. Likewise, in 1989, the University of Delaware expanded its judicial system to punish students for criminal offenses that occur off campus, reversing a two-decade-old policy that forbade it from practicing double jeopardy (by penalizing students a second time for the same offenses) (Gumprecht 2008). Penalties for students found responsible for committing crime off-campus can include mandatory counseling, community service, heavy fines, suspension, and, ultimately, expulsion from school (Bromley and Territo 1990; Vander Ven 2011). Some universities and colleges have also started to notify parents when students violate conduct codes while at school.

One particular crime that PU and local police are attempting to combat together is the practice of couch burning. As discussed in chapter 3, Ptown has toughened charges for these crimes from a misdemeanor to a felony. If found guilty, students can also be expelled from PU.[1] At the University of Maryland at College Park, administrators include similar strong sanctions for students found responsible for starting fires and destroying property, as part of its zero-tolerance anti-rioting program (Hoover 2002). Moreover, the city of Boulder, Colorado, has taken a more proactive approach by passing a sofa ordinance that prohibits upholstered furniture from being kept outdoors in neighborhoods near the university, thereby eliminating the convenience and temptation to burn such property (Hoover 2002). However, it is still unclear whether these policies are having any impact on reducing the frequency of this party school "tradition."

Getting tough on parties. Universities and colleges have also begun implementing tougher sanctions against students found responsible for causing noise disturbances most commonly associated with "house parties." For instance, as discussed in chapter 1 (see p. 10), Frostburg State University in Maryland has made it a priority to crack down on rowdy off-campus parties and has reached out to the police to step up patrols in student-dense neighborhoods (Wilson 2008). In other towns, ordinances commonly known as "Animal House Laws" have been implemented that require landlords to begin eviction proceedings against tenants found to have repeatedly violated "quality-of-life" laws (U.S. State News 2007). In Tucson, home to University of Arizona, red tags labeling the house as a site of an "unruly gathering" can be posted on houses that have had too many complaints about loud parties (Wilkins 2012). Unruly gatherings are defined by this ordinance as a disturbance of the quiet enjoyment of private or public property and includes: excessive noise, fighting, obstruction of public streets, and littering. A similar ordinance has been enacted in Narragansett, Rhode Island, aimed at curbing rowdy gatherings from the students of nearby University of Rhode Island (Tucker 2009). The ordinance in Rhode Island allows police to place a ten-by-fourteen-inch orange sticker on homes where parties of five or more people are causing frequent and substantial disturbances (e.g., loud noise, public drunkenness, illegal parking) (Tucker 2009). Stickers that label the house as a nuisance remain up for the duration of the school year.

Although these sanctions and labels are meant to publicly shame and stigmatize the students living in the houses, such methods may be ineffective if students are not ashamed of their parties or deterred by the penalties. In fact, many students at party schools are rather proud of their infamous parties. Therefore, a sticker that identifies the house and its residents as unruly or a nuisance may simply be a validation of their status as serious partiers.[2]

Finally, in a more preemptive stance, the University of Delaware (UD) in collaboration with its host town, Newark, now requires permits for large parties. Newark has also doubled its fines for noise violations and has amended its housing code to require landlords to evict tenants after two disorderly conduct violations (Gumprecht 2008, p. 306). However, according to a case study of UD by Gumprecht (2008), these policies have done little to quell the enthusiasm of student partiers or to change the school's reputation as a party school. Trying to ameliorate alcohol-related problems by getting tougher on violators is unlikely to work within the current cultural climate of the party school that endorses partying as a basic right and rewards bad behaviors associated with it. Change can only be accomplished by confronting the party subculture head on.

The (Sub)cultural Challenge

Strategies for minimizing extreme partying and the problems it causes must begin with an understanding of students' commitment to a party subculture, and the situational normativity of extreme drinking, drug use, and other reckless behavior within the context of the party school. In other words, strategies for (sub)cultural change must challenge the accepted values, norms, rituals and rewards of the party subculture. Strategies for change must especially begin to disentangle drinking as a leisure activity from the goal of getting wasted. Advocating for "responsible drinking" is already part of many alcohol-awareness programs that draw upon a harms-reduction approach that teaches safe and moderate drinking rather than abstinence. One popular program undertaken by many colleges today is the *social norms approach* based on the view that people act according to their perceptions of how "normal" people behave. These programs suggest that if students think their peers are drinking a lot, they are more likely to drink just as much in order to fit in and appear normal. Marketing for these programs generally involves ads that provide numbers and quotes emphasizing students' moderate drinking and drug use that are meant to dispel the image that irresponsible partying is the norm. The premise is that if students see that the actual rates of alcohol use are much lower than their perceptions of it, then they will decrease their own usage (NIAAA 2007, p. 7).[3] However, this approach has had mixed results, and some researchers have discounted the effectiveness of such programs all together (Durkin et al. 2005; Murray and Gruley 2000; Vander Ven 2011). Part of the reason why a social norms approach may not be effective at the party school is that empirical evidence suggests that college students at such schools do drink a lot (Wechsler and Wuethrich 2002). It is not some fabricated story or misconception. For instance, at PU more than half of college students drink heavy or extreme amounts of liquor three or more days a week. Not only is excessive partying real, it is quite normal, both statistically and situationally (i.e., within the context of the party situation).

Thus, rather than trying to convince students that their peers are not drinking as much as they really are, a better approach would be to try to change students' actual routines and rituals by challenging their value system that encourages excessive drinking in the first place. This, of course, is not an easy task, as it would require replacing the values so intrinsic to the party subculture with an alternative set of norms that stresses moderation. It would also require that students be resocialized so as to unlearn behaviors favorable to extreme partying and risk taking. Instead, students would learn that reckless partying is disrespectful and embarrassing to themselves, their peers, their sports teams, their university, and the community. They would also learn that drinking irresponsibly is not funny, fun, or memorable. In other words, the risk-reward structure currently in place would need to be toppled and inverted. Rather than be rewarded or admired for risky behavior, extreme participants of the subculture would be shamed and seen as disloyal to their peers and to the school. Finally, students' bad behaviors while intoxicated would no longer be excused or normalized. Partiers would be held accountable.

Such a massive (sub)cultural transformation would have to come from students' own peer groups, and not from college administrators, police, policy makers, or health advocates. Part of the prominence of the current party subculture is that it is student operated and controlled. Students are the rule makers, socializing agents, enforcers, and gatekeepers. Therefore, students themselves would need to be the ones to spearhead any meaningful changes to their party routines and rituals.

SUMMING UP

There can be little doubt that the years spent at college are a substantial and memorable time for millions of Americans. For students who attend one of the many large public residential and sports-oriented universities located in isolated college towns, it can also be a time of excessive partying. And though students party at almost all residential universities and colleges, nowhere do they do so with such gusto and to such extremes as they do at the so-called party school. Extreme drinking, drug use and bad behavior while intoxicated have become all too common at the party school, endorsed by a prominent party subculture that encourages and rewards extreme routines, rituals and risk-taking, while providing the rationales that defend it all.

Party School: Crime, Campus, and Community has attempted to shed some light on the unique party subculture, the problems it can cause, and the normativity of it all at the party school. Students' sense of entitlement to party no matter what the cost to themselves and others has had a substantial impact on the social landscape of many residential universities and colleges, but most especially at the party school. At these schools, a party subculture holds the campus and community hostage. Students who do not party are often marginalized and must actively avoid and accommodate the party subculture. Meanwhile, nonstudent residents are often treated as intruders by their partying neighbors. And anyone who complains formally about the party subculture may be stigmatized, labeled as unreasonable, or even seen as anti-student or disloyal to their school.

Despite the havoc that a party subculture can cause to the college community, many university administrators have done little to address the problems caused by extreme drinking and drug use at their schools. On the other hand, some schools have toughened their policies in an attempt to deter students' drinking and their bad behaviors while intoxicated. Still, few schools have been successful in dampening an enthusiastic party climate. Programs that try to convince students of the dangers of partying fail because, from the students' perspective, their behaviors are harmless and rather ordinary. Meanwhile, negative consequences from partying are often rationalized by student partiers as well worth the risks. Thus, the challenge for administrators at the party school is to discourage students from engaging in behaviors that they currently see as harmless fun. It is a challenge that requires a destabilization of a formidable party subculture that has become a prominent and normalized part of student life at the party school.

Appendix A

RESEARCH METHODS

The findings in this book draw from three data sources: the Campus Crime Victimization Survey (CCVS) based on a probability sample of undergraduate students at Party University (PU), a revised CCVS distributed to a convenience sample of PU students, and interviews using a snowball sample of students and nonstudent residents in Ptown, the college town where PU is located. Separate Internal Review Board approvals were obtained for each project. The methodical procedures for each research project are described below, starting with the original CCVS.

CAMPUS CRIME VICTIMIZATION SURVEY (CCVS)

The Campus Crime Victimization Survey (CCVS) is a self-administered survey that was implemented in spring 2009 at PU, a large public university with an undergraduate population of approximately 22,000. The preliminary objective of the survey was to investigate "hidden" crime victimization on campus (e.g., incidents unknown to police and, therefore, not part of official statistics), and most especially "intoxicated crimes," offenses perpetrated when victim, offender, or both parties are intoxicated. Thus, findings from the CCVS focus primarily on students' drinking and drug use, and the criminal consequences and other harms related to these "party" routines.

Data Collection Procedures

The sampling frame for the CCVS consisted of undergraduate students enrolled at PU in 2009. After receiving Internal Review Board approval for the project, e-mail addresses for 5,000 randomly selected undergraduates were provided by the university's Records and Admissions office in mid-spring 2009. Graduate students and students under eighteen years of age were excluded from the sampling frame.

A preliminary e-mail introducing the upcoming survey was sent out to the selected students in early April 2009. The e-mail correspondence introduced the research project as a survey interested in gathering information about campus crime and student safety on campus. It also informed students that they would be receiving another e-mail within a week that would formally invite them to participate in the survey. During the second week in April, invitation e-mails were disseminated to the randomly selected students and provided them with a link to the web-based survey. The e-mail informed students that the survey would take them approximately fifteen minutes to complete, and assured students that their participation was voluntary and anonymous (i.e., the survey was encrypted to ensure that students' identities were not traceable and that their responses could not be linked back to their e-mail addresses). The instructions also reminded students that they could skip questions that made them uncomfortable or quit the survey at any time. Included in the e-mail were some important phone numbers and website addresses for victim-assistance resources (e.g., student health services, rape crisis counselors, campus police).

Two follow-up reminder e-mails were disseminated to the randomly selected students. The first reminder e-mail was sent out one week after the initial invitation and the final reminder was sent out one month later (after the semester had ended). The follow-up e-mails replicated much of the information from the original invitation e-mail and contained the same link to the Web-based survey questionnaire. In order to make sure that students' anonymity was maintained, follow-up e-mails were sent out to all of the selected participants, thanking those who had already responded for their participation.

Survey design. Students who participated in the CCVS completed the survey via a link in an invitation e-mail that connected them to the survey questionnaire in SurveyMonkey, a user-friendly Web-based survey program that allows respondents to navigate easily through a series of questions. An advanced version of SurveyMonkey with encryption was used to ensure respondents' privacy. The decision to implement the survey questionnaire online was based on a number of factors. First, online surveys are cost efficient and easier to distribute to a broad range of respondents. For instance, disseminating the survey online allowed for a much more representative sample of PU students from diverse academic majors. Second, online surveys are better for sensitive information such as crime victimization. Respondents have more privacy while taking the survey and more time to think about their responses. Third, online surveys allow researchers immediate access to data responses and make it easier to sort and transfer responses to statistical programs for analysis. Finally, online surveys (versus a self-administered "pen and pencil" format) also correct for problems that may arise from complicated skip patterns, as the programs automatically "skip" respondents over sections of questions that are not relevant to them.

Response rate. Despite the advantages of online surveys, these methods often produce low response rates (i.e., the percentage of completed surveys with usable data). Indeed, the response rate for the CCVS was rather disappointing. Of the 5,000 students who were sent e-mail invitations to participate in the survey, only 903 students responded, for a response rate of 18 percent. Still, this response rate is comparable to many online surveys today with response rates ranging from 11 to 35 percent (see Cook, Heath, and Thompson 2000).

Aside from a general apathy among students toward participating in surveys, there are two other possible explanations for the low response rate for the CCVS. First, the list of e-mail addresses provided by the office of Records and Admissions in late spring may not have been current. In fact, approximately fifty e-mails were returned as undeliverable. Invalid e-mail addresses may represent students who had already left the institution after the fall semester by transferring, withdrawing, or flunking out. A second reason that may help explain the low response rate was the unfavorable timing of the survey. The survey was launched very late in the spring semester right before the final week of classes. By this time of year students are tired and are extremely busy preparing for final exams, graduation and summer break. Additionally, some students may have already left campus early for summer break or may have stopped checking their student e-mail accounts. Also, with the survey's dependence on e-mail dissemination, students who were not regularly checking their student e-mail accounts may not have received the CCVS invitation or follow up correspondence in a timely manner to enable them to participate.

Survey questions. The final CCVS instrument borrowed some of its crime questions from the National Crime Victimization Survey (see U.S. Department of Justice 2010), and some of its drinking and drug questions from the Monitoring the Future survey (see Johnson, O'Malley, Bachman, and Schulenberg 2007). Questions were revised based on their relevance to a sample of college students. Additional questions for the CCVS were added based on insights and anecdotal experiences shared by criminology students in an advanced survey-writing course during spring 2008. A preliminary draft of the CCVS questionnaire was pretested in two research methods courses during the fall 2008 semester. The primary purpose of the pretest was to correct for any problems related to question ordering and skip patterns, and overall comprehension of questions and responses. Revisions were made to the survey instrument in early February 2009. The final CCVS questionnaire was transcribed into the SurveyMonkey program in March 2009. A pretest in SurveyMonkey was conducted using a convenience sample of students from criminology, sociology, and anthropology courses ($n = 88$). The pretest verified that there were no technical or formatting problems with CCVS questions or response categories.

The final survey instrument consisted of approximately three hundred closed-ended questions (i.e., respondents were asked to select answers from predetermined response categories). Some questions allowed respondents to choose only one answer, while others allowed them to "click all that apply." There were also two open-ended questions at the end of the survey. One question asked respondents to add any additional comments regarding the crimes they had experienced while at PU that had not already been addressed in the survey. A second question asked them to comment on their perceptions of police and campus safety. In addition to these two questions, respondents were asked on several occasions throughout the survey to expand upon or explain in comment boxes their closed-ended responses.

The final CCVS survey contained questions in three general areas: student demographics, drinking and drug usage, and types of crime victimization. Demographic questions asked respondents about their gender, age, and other personal characteristics (e.g., race, marital status), as well as several student-related characteristics (e.g., class rank, grade point average, involvement in campus and student organizations). A second series of questions asked respondents about their "party" routines, such as drinking and drug use, and certain consequences associated with these routines (e.g., failing classes, injuries, illnesses, arrests). The final section of questions in the survey asked about several types of crime victimization "while at [PU]," including incidents both on and near campus.[1] Incidents included: car break-ins and home burglary, car and home vandalism, larceny theft, physical attacks and fights, rape, unwanted sexual contact and arson.[2] Respondents who were victimized by any type of crime were asked a series of follow-up questions regarding the context and consequences of their victimization experiences, and whether or not they reported their incidents to the police. Students who experienced more than one incident of any crime were asked to answer questions about their most recent incident. Respondents who were not victims of any specific type of crime were automatically skipped to the next crime section.

Data clean up and analysis. Survey responses from SurveyMonkey were downloaded into Excel spreadsheets and then transferred into a statistical software program (SPSS) and cleaned up for analysis. Data cleanup included the elimination of 24 cases due to incomplete responses, leaving a final usable data set of 879 cases (although this sample was further filtered for analysis of only traditional students, $n = 787$). Aside from deleting cases with incomplete information, data was also cleaned up in the following ways. First, there were some inconsistent responses (e.g., "yes" responses to follow-up questions that should have been blank) that were corrected. Also, dummy variables were created for the many multiple-response questions that asked respondents to "check all that apply." Finally, many variables required recodes for appropriate analysis.

Analysis in SPSS included descriptive statistics of students' demographics, participation in organizations and work, drinking patterns, drug use, party-related consequences, and crime victimization. Bivariate tests using cross-tabulation and chi-square statistics to determine statistical significance were conducted to examine the patterns of drinking, drug use, and crime victimization by student characteristics and partier type. In addition, gender was added to the analyses in order to examine patterns between women and men in regards to party routines and consequences.

Qualitative responses from the two final open-ended survey questions were read and coded according to themes found within the text (e.g., additional types of crime, perceptions of police and safety, excuses and other rationales) to enable them to be more easily sorted and analyzed. Many of these responses were used as excerpts in the book to illustrate theoretical concepts and to provide more descriptive detail to help enhance the quantitative patterns regarding students' routines and crime victimization.

CCVS Sample biases. Although the final sample (n = 879), with a filter for traditional students aged eighteen to twenty-four (n = 787), is much smaller than anticipated, it adequately represents the undergraduate student population in regard to all demographic variables except for two: sex and class rank. In terms of sex, there is a disproportionate percentage of females (63 percent) as compared to males (37 percent) in the sample, possibly reflecting women's greater willingness to respond to surveys in general, and a crime victimization survey in particular (i.e., men may not be as willing as women to admit being victimized). Since PU reports that 51 percent of enrolled students are male, and 49 percent are female, the CCVS sample does not adequately representative the gender composition of undergraduate students at the university. Another potential bias of the sample is the disproportionately low number of students in the early class ranks (i.e., freshman and sophomore). For instance, only 9 percent of the CCVS sample are freshmen, as compared to 20 percent sophomores, 34 percent juniors, and 37 percent seniors. High rates of freshmen who drop out or transfer, in addition to the exclusion of seventeen-year-olds from the sampling frame, may help to explain why freshmen (and sophomores to a lesser degree) represent smaller proportions of the sample.

Aside from sex and class rank, other student characteristics (e.g., race, ethnicity, GPA), and involvement in student organizations, Greek life, and sports are mostly representative of the undergraduate population at PU, as well as representative of many other large public residential, sports-oriented universities and colleges. (See appendix B, table 1 for sample descriptives.)

REVISED CAMPUS CRIME VICTIMIZATION SURVEY (CCVSr)

The original CCVS was amended in spring 2011 to incorporate additional questions that would elicit more detail from student respondents regarding their drinking and drug routines and party-related victimization experiences. Many open-ended questions were also added to elicit more detail from respondents about their experiences with secondhand harms on campus, such as property disruption, litter, noise, and verbal harassment. Questions were also added that asked about students' perceptions of the "partier" and "party school" labels. And an entire section of questions was added in order to gather descriptive detail about pregaming and tailgating. Findings from this revised survey are used throughout the book to supplement the quantitative findings from the original CCVS.

Data Collection Procedures

Like the original CCVS, The CCVSr was pretested in order to correct for any potential technical and grammatical problems with questions and response categories. Once the pretest was completed in early spring 2011, the survey was administered to a convenience sample of approximately one hundred fifty undergraduate students in sociology and anthropology courses. Students under eighteen years of age were excluded. And like the original CCVS, students participated in the survey through a link in an invitation e-mail. The e-mail provided information about the survey and contained instructions on how to access the survey questionnaire via a link to SurveyMonkey.

The final sample for the CCVSr consisted of ninety-seven undergraduate students, a 65 percent response rate (much higher than the original CCVS, probably due to an endorsement by course instructors in several classes). The sample consisted almost exclusively of upperclassmen, with a mean age of 22. Only one of the respondents lived on campus, and all but one of the students were sociology or criminology majors. In regard to sex, race, and other basic demographics, the sample was mostly representative of the larger population of PU undergraduate students.

Cleanup and procedures for analyzing the quantitative data from CCVSr were similar to the procedures used for the original CCVS, as discussed above. Open-ended responses from the CCVSr were downloaded into an Excel spreadsheet to facilitate an easier reading of the responses and to identify predetermined themes (e.g., tailgating, party pranks, police perception). Excerpts from these responses are integrated throughout the book's chapters to provide more descriptive detail regarding students' party routines, rituals, risks, and secondhand harms.

INTERVIEWS

A final source of data used in this book comes from interviews with approximately twenty students (and five nonstudent residents). The overall objective

of these interviews was to increase an understanding of students' perceptions of the party subculture and its impact on campus and community. It
specifically sought to investigate students' interpretations of the risks and
consequences from their own participation in the party subculture, as well
as to understand the perspectives of non-partiers toward their peers who
party and, more generally, their lives at a party school.

Data Collection Procedures

Students who participated in interviews did so primarily by word of mouth
(i.e., snowball sample) beginning with friends of students in a criminology
course who agreed to be interviewed. Although interviewees are part of a
convenience sample rather than a random sample, the selected students
adequately represent the variability within the student undergraduate population in terms of sex, age, class rank, and other student routines. Students
under eighteen years of age were not permitted in the sample. Students who
agreed to be interviewed were informed about the study in a letter and told
orally at the start of the interview that the process would take approximately
thirty minutes and that the interview would be tape recorded. They were also
told that their names and information would be protected and kept strictly
confidential.

Interview questions were written and pretested by students in an advanced
research course in spring 2010. A final interview protocol of approximately
twenty semistructured questions and various probes asked students about
their drinking activities on campus (including pregaming) and about their
perceptions of the party subculture and party school, attitudes toward police,
and overall safety on campus. Interview data were transcribed from tape
recorded interviews into a Word document, and passages were highlighted
according to both predetermined and unexpected themes. Excerpts from
these interviews are used in this book to provide detailed descriptions of
students' experiences at the party school, especially as they underscore the
theoretical concepts of routine activities, social learning, and subcultural
theory. They are also used to illustrate students' rationales in defense of the
party subculture. The language was cleaned up and edited for readability
and, where needed, interviewer probes are included in brackets in order to
maintain continuity of the dialogue.

In addition to interviews with students, a second and related interview
project (primarily for a future project on neighborhood conflict and disorder)
was conducted with nonstudent residents. A focus group, consisting of five

participants from a snowball sample, was conducted that took about an hour and a half. The main objectives of these interviews were to learn more about residents' perspectives of neighborhood disorder caused by the party subculture, and to learn more about the social interaction and conflict between students and nonstudent residents living in communities together. A small portion of the dialogue from nonstudent residents is included in this book.

LIMITATIONS OF THE RESEARCH

In addition to the low response rate for the CCVS (as discussed earlier), there are a few other limitations of this research project that warrant mentioning. First, even though self-administered questionnaires offer many benefits in terms of privacy and allowing respondents to work at their own pace to answer questions, one of the disadvantages is that respondents are unable to get clarification of questions, terms used, or instructions during the survey process. Although the CCVS defines all of its terms and does not use crime-specific jargon, some of the questions may not have adequately reflected the important distinctions among these crimes, or may have appeared redundant to respondents. For instance, the questionnaire contained separate sections on burglary and larceny, crimes that are distinct from a legal perspective but may have appeared redundant to persons taking the survey. Similarly, we asked separate questions for rape and unwanted sexual contact, which may also have seemed repetitive to respondents.

Additionally, when respondents had experienced multiple incidents for a specific type of crime, they were not asked to complete follow-up questions for each incident separately (the procedure used by the National Crime Victimization Survey). Instead, due to time constraints, students who had been victimized more than once while at PU were asked to answer the follow-up questions based on only the most recent incident. In doing so, some important information regarding repeat victimization and multiple incidents was lost.

Moreover, in an attempt to be comprehensive and include all relevant types of crime, the survey was very lengthy for respondents who had experienced multiple types of crimes. This may explain why the number of respondents answering questions about types of crimes that appear later in the survey (e.g., rape and unwanted sexual contact) were much smaller than the number of respondents who answered questions about types of crime asked earlier (e.g., property crime). Certainly, with a lengthy survey questionnaire, there is a potential that respondents will quit the survey before completing all of the questions.

Another limitation that should be noted has to do with the types of persons willing to take surveys in general, and crime surveys in particular. Simply stated, persons who have been victimized by crime may be more interested and more motivated to respond to a crime survey. Thus, even though respondents for the CCVS were solicited from a random sample, frequencies of crime victimization may be distorted somewhat based on the possibility that persons who had experienced crime during their college years may have been more willing to participate in the survey. This may distort actual crime frequencies and may also explain the disproportionate amount of criticism toward police and perceptions of PU as unsafe.

Finally, the "accuracy" of survey and interview data is dependent upon respondents' honesty in answering questions. Even though anonymity or confidentiality was assured, students may not have been comfortable admitting to underage drinking, drug use, or certain types of victimization (i.e., rape). On the contrary, there is also the potential that some respondents exaggerated their responses, particularly around their drinking routines and rituals. After all, many students at a party school take pride in their alcohol consumption and therefore may over-report their party prowess (e.g., drinking routines, party pranks). For this same reason, it is possible that the incidents that students describe in vivid detail in their open-ended survey and interview responses are largely exaggerations or even fabrications of how partiers are supposed to behave at a party school. Still, since it is students' hyperbole that keeps PU on a party school list, it seemed appropriate to let their sometimes larger-than-life responses allegorize life at a party school, regardless of whether these anecdotes accurately reflect "reality."

Appendix B

DATA TABLES

From Campus Crime Victimization Survey (CCVS)

Table 1. Sample descriptives (*n* = 787)[a]

	Base *n*	Sample %		Base *n*	Sample %
Victim characteristics			*Major*[b]		
			Social science	244	31.0
Sex			Health science	70	8.9
Male	291	37.0	Engineering,		
Female	496	63.0	physical science	122	15.5
			Other	351	44.6
Age					
Under 21	392	49.8	*Residence*		
21 and older	395	50.2	On-campus	161	20.5
			Greek housing	16	9.9
Race			Non-Greek housing	145	90.1
White	732	92.9	Off-campus	626	79.6
Black	20	2.6	Downtown	307	48.8
Other	35	4.6	Elsewhere	319	51.2
Latino					
Yes	28	3.6	**Involvement in school groups and work**		
No	759	96.4			
			Fraternity/sorority		
U.S. Citizen			Yes	119	15.1
Yes	781	99.2	No	668	84.9
No	6	0.8			
			Varsity/club or intramural sports		
Married[b]			Yes	237	30.1
Yes	14	1.8	No	550	69.9
No	773	98.2			
			Academic club/honor society		
Children			Yes	284	36.1
Yes	12	1.5	No	503	63.9
No	775	98.5			
			Work		
Class rank			Over 20 hours	144	18.3
Freshman	71	9.0	20 hours or under	243	30.1
Sophomore	158	20.1	Does not work	400	50.8
Junior	266	33.8			
Senior	292	37.1	**Financial obligations**		
Full time student[b]			*Tuition*		
Yes	767	97.4	Yes	157	19.9
No	20	2.6	No	630	80.1
Grade Point Average[b]			*Rent*		
3.5–4.0	302	38.5	Yes	360	45.7
3.0–3.49	281	35.7	No	427	54.3
2.5–2.99	147	18.8	*Other bills (groceries, utilities, gas)*		
2.0–2.49	47	6.0	Yes	653	83.0
under 2.0	10	1.3	No	134	17.0

[a] Sample contains only undergraduate "traditional" students 18–24 years of age.

[b] Missing cases allocated: race and Latino (3), married (8), full-time (3), GPA (3), Major (36).

Table 2. **Drinking routines (n = 617)**[a]

	Base n	Sample %	Men	Women
Number of drinks on average per night				
1–2	77	12.5	11.4	13.2
3–4	173	28.0	19.6	33.6
5–6	172	27.9	17.1	34.9
7–8	93	15.1	20.4	11.6
9 or more	102	16.5	31.4	6.7
Number of nights drink per week				
1	252	40.8	32.2	46.5
2–3	307	49.8	54.7	46.5
4–5	43	7.0	9.0	5.6
6 or more	15	2.4	4.1	1.3
Nights intoxicated in past 2 weeks				
None	162	26.3	19.2	31.1
1	156	25.2	24.1	26.0
2–3	195	31.6	36.3	28.4
4 or more	104	16.8	20.4	14.5

[a] 79.4% of sample drink (n = 625); 20.6% do not drink (n = 162). Eight drinkers did not answer the drinking questions.

Table 3. **Drug usage** (*n* = 787)[a]

	Base *n*	Sample %	Men	Women
Marijuana	172	21.7	30.4	21.2
Other illicit drugs[b]	66	8.4	11.7	6.5
Cocaine	38	4.8	6.9	3.6
Heroin	6	.08	1.0	0.6
Ecstasy	27	3.4	3.8	3.2
Hallucinogens/psychedelics	44	5.6	7.9	4.2
Methamphetamines	4	0.5	1.0	0.2
Pharmaceutical *(without a legal prescription)*	98	12.5	15.5	10.7
Xanax	39	5.0	6.2	4.2
Vicodin	34	4.3	7.2	2.6
Oxycotin	26	3.3	5.2	2.2
Adderall	87	11.1	13.4	9.7
Ritalin	14	9.8	2.7	1.2

[a] 24.6% of sample uses drugs (*n* = 191).

[b] Steroid use (*n* = 1) and GHB use (*n* = 2) excluded.

Table 4. **Frequency of marijuana, illicit and pharmaceutical drug use**

	Base *n*	Sample %	Men	Women
Frequency of marijuana use (*n* = 172)				
Few times a year	59	34.3	31.6	36.6
Once a month	19	11.0	8.9	13.9
Few times a month	17	9.9	10.1	9.7
Once a week	9	5.2	5.1	5.4
Few times a week	26	15.1	15.2	15.1
Daily	42	24.4	29.1	20.4
Frequency of other illicit drug use (*n* = 66)				
Few times a year	48	72.7	67.5	83.3
Once a month	6	9.2	15.0	0.0
Few times a month	7	10.8	7.5	11.9
Once a week	1	1.5	2.5	0.0
Few times a week	2	3.0	2.5	4.8
Daily	2	3.0	5.0	0.0
Frequency of pharmaceutical drug use (*n* = 98)				
Few times a year	44	44.9	54.9	44.8
Once a month	10	10.2	2.0	15.5
Few times a month	30	30.6	25.5	29.3
Once a week	3	3.1	3.9	3.4
Few times a week	10	10.2	11.8	6.9
Daily	1	1.0	2.0	0.0

Table 5. **Type of drinker (*n* = 787)**

	Base *n*	Sample %	Men %	Women %
Non-drinker	169	21.5	15.8	24.8
Light drinker	209	26.6	18.9	31.0
Heavy drinker	302	38.4	41.2	36.7
Extreme drinker	107	13.6	24.1	7.5

Non-drinker: Does not drink.

Light drinker: Drinks less than 5 drinks in a typical night of drinking, drinks only one night in a typical week, was intoxicated no more than once in past 2 weeks.

Heavy drinker: Drinks 5–8 drinks in a typical night of drinking, drinks 2–3 or more nights in a typical week, was intoxicated more than once in the last 2 weeks.

Extreme drinker: Drinks 9 or more drinks in a typical night of drinking, drinks 4 or more nights in a typical week, was intoxicated more than twice in the last 2 weeks.

Table 6. Type of drug user ($n = 787$)[a]

	Base n	Sample %	Men	Women
Non-drug user	605	76.9	71.5	80.0
Light drug user	74	9.4	10.3	8.9
Heavy drug user	108	13.7	18.2	11.1

Non-drug user: Does not use drugs.

Light drug user: Uses marijuana or other drugs less than a few times a month.

Heavy drug user: Uses marijuana or other drugs a few times a month.

[a] With so few illicit and pharmaceutical drug users, all drugs were combined to examine frequency rather than looking at types of drugs separately.

Table 7. Type of partier ($n = 787$)

	Base n	Sample %	Men	Women
Non-partiers	168	21.3	15.8	24.6
Light partier	194	24.7	16.8	29.2
Heavy partier	318	40.4	43.3	38.7
Extreme partier	107	13.6	24.1	7.5

Non-partier: Does not drink alcohol or use drugs.

Light partier: Light drinker, non-drug user.

Heavy partier: Heavy drinker, non- or light drug user.

Extreme partier: Extreme drinker, light or heavy drug user.

Table 8. Partier type descriptives (n = 787)[a]

	Base n	Non-partier	Light partier	Heavy partier	Extreme partier
Victim characteristics[b]					
Sex					
Male	291	15.8	16.8	43.3	24.1
Female	496	24.6	29.2	38.7	7.5
Age					
Under 21	392	31.4	22.7	34.9	11.0
21 and older	395	11.4	26.6	45.8	16.2
Race					
White	732	21.4	24.2	40.8	13.6
Black	20	15.0	35.0	30.0	20.0
Other	35	25.7	31.4	34.3	8.5
Latino					
Yes	28	14.3	28.6	39.3	17.9
No	759	21.6	24.4	40.4	13.5
Class rank					
Freshman	71	33.8	12.7	35.2	18.3
Sophomore	158	33.5	28.5	30.4	7.6
Junior	266	22.9	20.7	40.6	15.8
Senior	292	10.3	29.1	46.9	13.7
Major					
Social science	244	16.8	19.7	47.5	16.0
Health science	70	31.4	37.4	29.6	2.9
Engineering, physical science	122	26.7	32.9	35.6	4.8
Other	351	20.3	23.0	40.2	16.5
Grade Point Average					
3.5–4.0	302	28.8	26.2	36.4	8.6
3.0–3.49	281	20.1	26.6	37.4	15.8
2.5–2.99	147	10.2	21.8	53.1	15.0
2.49 and under	57	14.0	15.8	45.6	24.6
Residence					
On-campus	161	32.9	23.0	30.4	13.7
Greek housing	16	0.0	6.3	62.5	31.3
Non-Greek housing	145	35.9	23.4	30.0	17.2
Off-campus	626	18.5	25.0	43.2	13.3
Downtown	307	11.7	17.6	49.8	20.8
Elsewhere	319	24.2	31.7	37.9	6.2

Table 8. (continued)

	Base *n*	Non-partier	Light partier	Heavy partier	Extreme partier
Involvement in school organizations and work					
Fraternity/sorority					
Yes	119	10.9	20.2	48.7	20.2
No	668	23.2	25.4	38.9	12.4
Varsity/club or intramural sports					
Yes	225	17.8	19.6	47.1	15.6
No	562	22.8	26.7	37.7	12.8
Academic club/honor society					
Yes	284	25.4	26.1	40.1	8.5
No	503	19.1	26.9	40.6	16.5
Work					
Over 20 hours	144	17.4	22.9	52.1	7.6
20 hours or under	243	18.5	29.2	37.9	14.4
Does not work	400	24.8	22.3	37.8	15.0
Financial obligations					
Tuition					
Yes	157	24.2	29.9	36.3	9.6
No	630	20.6	23.3	41.4	14.6
Rent					
Yes	360	18.1	28.9	42.8	10.3
No	427	24.1	21.1	38.4	16.4
Other bills (groceries, utilities, gas)					
Yes	653	20.5	26.3	40.3	12.9
No	134	25.4	16.4	41.0	17.2

[a] Sample contains only undergraduate "traditional" students 18–24 years of age.

[b] Due to small *n*s, the following variables were eliminated from analysis: U.S. citizen, married, children, full-time.

Table 9. Consequences while intoxicated by partier type[a]

Consequences	Light partier	Heavy partier	Extreme partier
Academic Consequences			
Missed class	19.6	62.9	80.4***
Failed a class, dropped a grade	0.5	11.6	20.6***
Criminal consequences (while intoxicated)			
Had property stolen	2.6	12.3	19.6***
Injured while fighting	1.5	7.2	22.4***
Sexually assaulted	4.1	5.3	6.5
Health-related consequences			
Blackouts	11.3	49.1	81.3***
Injury due to accidents	3.1	19.8	33.6***
Illness from alcohol/drugs	17.0	31.8	46.7***
Hospitalized	1.5	5.7	12.1***
Engaged in unprotected sex	4.1	25.8	32.7***
Legal consequences			
Arrests for alcohol violations	4.6	15.1	30.8***
University disciplinary action for alcohol violations	5.7	15.7	28.0***
Arrests for drug violations	0.0	1.3	5.6**
University disciplinary action for drug violations	0.0	1.3	2.8*
Driving while intoxicated			
Drove intoxicated	9.8	35.5	48.6***
Stopped for driving while intoxicated	0.5	3.5	8.4***

[a] Non-partiers ($n = 168$) are excluded. Numbers are based on combined results from questions:

Which of the following consequences, if any, have you experienced as a result of your alcohol consumption? (check all that apply)

Which of the following consequences, if any, have you experienced as a result of your drug use? (check all that apply)

*$p < .05$

**$p < .01$

***$p < .001$

Table 10. Consequences while intoxicated by partier type and sex[a]

Consequences	Male			Female		
	Light partier	Heavy partier	Extreme partier	Light partier	Heavy partier	Extreme partier
Academic Consequences						
Missed class	16.3	52.4	80.0***	20.7	69.8	81.1***
Failed a class, dropped a grade	1.7	10.6	20.3**	0.6	13.6	21.1***
Criminal consequences (while intoxicated)						
Had property stolen	3.4	9.2	20.3**	2.4	15.1	15.8***
Injured while fighting	5.1	10.6	27.0***	0.6	5.0	10.5**
Sexually assaulted	0.0	0.7	5.4*	5.4	8.0	7.9
Health-related consequences						
Blackouts	8.5	39.7	86.5***	11.4	54.8	65.8***
Injury due to accidents	5.1	12.8	29.7***	2.4	23.6	39.5***
Illness from alcohol/drugs	13.6	22.7	41.9***	18.0	38.2	55.3***
Hospitalized	1.7	6.4	10.8	1.2	5.0	13.2**
Engaged in unprotected sex	3.4	26.2	35.1***	5.4	25.1	28.9***

Table 10. (Continued)

Consequences	Male				Female		
	Light partier	Heavy partier	Extreme partier		Light partier	Heavy partier	Extreme partier
Legal consequences							
Arrests for drinking violations	3.4	18.4	33.8***		4.2	11.6	21.1**
University disciplinary action for alcohol violations	3.4	18.4	36.5***		5.4	12.6	10.5
Arrests for drug violations	0.0	1.4	8.1**		0.0	1.0	0.0
University disciplinary action for drug violations	0.0	2.1	4.1		0.0	0.5	0.0
Driving while intoxicated							
Drove intoxicated	10.2	33.3	54.1**		10.2	36.2	34.2***
Stopped for driving while intoxicated	0.0	3.5	8.1		1.2	4.0	7.9

[a] Non-partiers ($n = 168$) are excluded. Numbers are based on combined results from questions:

Which of the following consequences, if any, have you experienced as a result of your alcohol consumption? (check all that apply)

Which of the following consequences, if any, have you experienced as a result of your drug use? (check all that apply)

*$p < .05$

**$p < .01$

***$p < .001$

Table 11. Crime descriptives (n = 787)

	Home burglary[a] n = 80	Car burglary[a] n = 53	Home vandalism n = 123	Car vandalism[a] n = 170	Larceny theft n = 132	Physical attack/fight n = 133	Rape n = 51	Unwanted sexual contact n = 194
Victim sex[b]								
Male (n = 291)	14.7	9.3	21.1	34.4	21.7	28.5	2.9	6.3
Female (n = 496)	8.1	8.7	13.3	25.1	15.0	11.3	9.0	37.4
Number of incidents[c]								
One	82.1	75.0	61.8	55.3	64.3	54.1	69.4	29.1
Two	12.8	15.4	24.4	27.6	21.4	26.3	20.4	19.9
Three or more	5.1	9.6	13.8	17.1	14.3	19.5	10.2	51.0
Where crime took place (campus/off-campus)								
On campus (dorms, fraternity houses)	24.3	24.5	17.1	36.6	52.8	35.9	43.5	41.3
Off campus	75.7	75.5	82.9	63.3	47.2	64.1	56.5	58.7
Off campus downtown	72.6	65.3	73.9	69.5	64.5	83.5	56.5	86.2
Off campus elsewhere	27.4	35.7	27.1	31.5	35.5	16.5	43.5	13.8

Table 11. (Continued)

	Home burglary $n = 80$	Car burglary[a] $n = 53$	Home vandalism $n = 123$	Car vandalism[a] $n = 170$	Larceny theft $n = 132$	Physical attack/fight $n = 133$	Rape $n = 51$	Unwanted sexual contact $n = 194$
Where crime took place (specific location)[d]								
Home (respondent's or friends)	—	67.3	—	54.9	40.3	13.5	87.0	21.0
"Party" hot spots								
Bars	—	—	—	—	9.7	45.2	2.2	61.0
Fraternity or house parties	—	—	—	—	6.5	5.6	2.2	8.6
Sports events	—	—	—	—	0.8	4.0	0.	2.7
When crime took place								
Day	10.8	12.2	7.6	16.4	32.5	7.9	6.7	5.9
Night	20.3	22.4	19.5	20.6	29.3	27.0	11.1	37.4
Late night/after midnight	37.8	36.7	52.5	36.4	16.3	64.3	82.2	56.1
Don't know	31.1	28.6	20.3	26.7	22.0	—	—	—
Cost of damage[e]								
Under $250	36.6	60.4	73.4	48.5	29.0	—	—	—
$250–500	14.1	22.9	7.0	23.9	22.6	—	—	—
$501–1,000	9.9	4.2	10.5	14.7	38.7			
More than $1,000	39.4	12.5	9.3	12.9	9.7			

Injury requiring medical attention[f]

Yes	12.7	11.1	—
No	87.3	88.9	—

Victim was drunk or using drugs at time of incident[f]

Yes	55.2	71.7	49.7
No	44.8	28.3	50.3

Victim-offender relationship[f]

Acquaintance	32.0	87	39.8
stranger	68.0	13.0	61.2

Offender(s) Sex[f]

Male	79.3	84.8	92.8
Female	17.2	13.0	5.4
Both	3.4	2.2	1.8

Offender was drunk or high on drugs at time of incident[f]

Yes	79.3	54.3	73.8
No (or don't know)	20.6	46.7	26.2

[a] Car burglary and car vandalism questions were asked only of students who have a car on campus ($n = 597$). 76% of students have cars at PU.

[b] Percentages based on sex denominators rather than type of crime.

[c] If victims experienced multiple incidents, crime descriptors are based on most recent incident.

[d] Not asked for burglary or home vandalism.

[e] Don't knows excluded. Also, these questions were not asked for violent and sexual crimes.

[e] Because victims of property crime do not often see their offenders, respondents were not asked questions pertaining to offender characteristics.

Table 12. **Crime victimization risk by partier type**

Crime offense	Non-partier	Light partier	Heavy partier	Extreme partier
Home burglary	5.0	5.8	13.2	20.4***
Car burglary	2.8	9.6	9.2	15.2*
Home vandalism	8.2	9.5	19.8	30.3***
Car vandalism	19.4	22.2	33.7	36.7**
Larceny theft	10.7	14.1	22.3	19.4**
Physical attack/fight	7.0	9.9	20.8	40.2***
Rape	3.2	3.6	10.1	8.4**
Unwanted sexual contact	12.3	28.4	31.6	25.5***

*p < .05

**p < .01

***p < .001

Table 13. Crime victimization risk by partier type and sex

Crime offense	Male				Female			
	Non-partier	Light partier	Heavy partier	Extreme partier	Non-partier	Light partier	Heavy partier	Extreme partier
Home burglary	7.0	6.3	13.8	27.7**	4.3	5.6	12.8	6.2*
Car burglary	3.1	5.4	8.8	16.7	2.6	10.8	9.5	12.0
Home vandalism	14.0	6.3	21.8	35.4***	6.0	10.6	18.5	20.6**
Car vandalism	18.8	15.8	42.4	43.4**	19.7	24.2	28.7	23.1
Larceny theft	18.6	23.4	23.0	20.0	7.8	11.1	21.8	18.2*
Physical attack/fight	16.3	14.6	27.9	48.4***	3.5	8.3	16.1	24.2***
Rape	2.3	.0	3.3	4.9	3.5	4.8	14.6	14.7***
Unwanted sexual contact	4.9	4.2	5.8	9.7	15.0	36.6	48.4	56.3***

*p < .05
**p < .01
***p < .001

Table 14. Crime victimization reported to police

	Base *ns*	Percentage reported to police
Home Burglary	80	66.2
Car burglary	53	42.9
Home vandalism	123	35.9
Car vandalism	170	31.5
Larceny theft	132	19.5
Physical attack/fight	133	11.3
Rape	51	4.3
Unwanted sexual contact	194	1.6

From Revised Campus Crime Victimization Survey (CCVSr)

Table 15. Perceptions of party-related problems at PU (*n* = 97)

	Frequency	Percentage consider a problem
Noise	45	46.4
Litter	62	63.9
Graffiti	21	21.6
Verbal harassment	44	45.4
Missing or damaged signs	35	36.1
Vandalism	54	55.7
Drunk students	69	71.1
Drunk driving	74	76.3

Table 16. Perception of party identity and party school label (*n* = 97)

	Frequency	Percentage
Identify as partiers		
Yes	34	35.1
No	63	64.9
Is label positive or negative?		
Positive	22	22.9
Negative	24	25.0
Doesn't matter	51	52.1

Table 17. Perception of "responsible" drinking (*n* = 83, drinkers only)

	Frequency	Percentage
Maximum amount of alcohol can drink without getting drunk		
1–2 drinks	13	15.7
3–4 drinks	38	45.8
5–6 drinks	22	26.5
7–8 drinks	10	12.0
Maximum amount of alcohol it is safe to drink and drive		
0 drinks	39	47.0
1–2 drinks	36	43.4
3–4 drinks	2	2.4
5–6 drinks	4	4.8
7–8 drinks	2	2.4

Appendix C

STUDENT CONDUCT CODE

AND REGULATIONS

*Party University Student Conduct Code (2010) [Distributed to PU
students from the Office of Student Conduct and available on PU website.]*

A. Jurisdiction of the Student Code

The University Student Code shall apply to conduct that occurs on University
premises, at University sponsored activities, and to off-campus conduct that
adversely affects the University Community and/or the pursuit of its objectives.
Each student shall be responsible for his/her conduct from the time of application
for admission through the actual awarding of a degree, even though conduct may
occur before classes begin or after classes end, as well as during the academic year
and during periods between terms of actual enrollment (and even if their conduct
is not discovered until after a degree is awarded).

B. Conduct: Rules and Regulations

Any student found to have committed or have attempted to commit the following
misconduct is subject to the disciplinary sanctions:

1. Acts of dishonesty, including but not limited to the following:
   a. Plagiarism: Plagiarism is defined in terms of proscribed acts. Students are
   expected to understand that such practices constitute academic dishonesty
   regardless of motive. Those who deny deceitful intent, claim not to have
   known that the act constituted plagiarism, or maintain that what they did
   was inadvertent are nevertheless subject to penalties when plagiarism has
   been confirmed. Plagiarism includes, but is not limited to, the following:
   i. Submitting as one's own work the product of someone else's research,
   writing, artistic conception, invention, or design; that is, submitting as
   one's own work any report, notebook, speech, outline, theme, thesis,
   dissertation, commercially prepared paper, musical piece or other written,
   visual, oral or electronic/computerized material that has been copied in
   whole or in part from the work of others, whether such source is published or unpublished;

    ii. Incorporating in one's submission, without appropriate acknowledgment and attribution, portions of the works of others; that is, failing to use the conventional marks and symbols to acknowledge the use of verbatim and near-verbatim passages of someone else's work or failing to name the source of words, pictures, graphs, etc., other than one's own, that are incorporated into any work submitted as one's own.

  b. Cheating and dishonest practices in connection with examinations, papers, and projects including, but not limited to:

    i. Obtaining help from another student during examinations;

    ii. Knowingly giving help to another student during examinations, taking an examination or doing academic work for another student, or providing one's own work for another student to copy and submit as his/her own;

    iii. The unauthorized use of notes, books, or other sources of information during examinations;

    iv. Obtaining without authorization an examination or any part thereof.

  c. Forgery, misrepresentation, or fraud:

    i. Forging or altering, or causing to be altered, the record of any grade in a grade book or other educational record;

    ii. Use of university documents or instruments of identification with intent to defraud;

    iii. Presenting false data or intentionally misrepresenting one's records for admission, registration, or withdrawal from the university or from a university course;

    iv. Knowingly presenting false data or intentionally misrepresenting one's records for personal gain;

    v. Knowingly furnishing the results of research projects or experiments for the inclusion in another's work without proper citation;

    vi. Knowingly furnishing false statements in any university academic proceeding.

2. Disruption or obstruction of, or leading or inciting others to disrupt or obstruct, teaching, research, administration, disciplinary proceedings, other University activities, including its public-service functions on or off campus, or other authorized non-University activities when the act occurs on University premises.

3. Physical abuse, verbal abuse, threats, intimidation, coercion and/or other conduct which threatens or endangers the health or safety of any person. Engaging in harassment or repeated unwanted contact, rising to the level of illegal harassment, including, but not limited to, stalking.

4. Attempted or actual theft of and/or damage to property of the University or property of a member of the University community or other personal or public property.

5. Hazing, which means to recklessly or intentionally cause any action or situation which endangers the mental or physical health or safety of another person

or causes another person to destroy or remove public or private property for the purpose of initiation, admission into, affiliation with, or as a condition for continued membership in a team, a group or student organization. The express or implied consent of the victim will not be a defense. Knowingly witnessing or acquiescing in the presence of hazing are not neutral acts; they are violations of this rule.

6. Sexual Offenses, including, but not limited to:
   a. Sexual intercourse with, and/or sexual intrusion against, a person capable of giving consent, without such person's consent, or a person incapable of giving consent;
   b. Sexual assault or abuse, statutory or acquaintance rape, sexual harassment.

7. Failure to comply with directions of University officials or law enforcement officers acting in performance of their duties and/or failure to identify oneself to these persons when requested to do so.

8. Unauthorized possession, duplication or use of keys to any University premises or unauthorized entry to or use of University premises.

9. Violation of any published University policies, rules or regulations in hard copy or available electronically on the University website.

10. Violation of any federal, state, or local law.

11. Use, possession, or distribution of narcotic or other controlled substances except as expressly permitted by law.

12. Use, possession, manufacturing, or distribution of alcoholic beverages (except as expressly permitted by University regulations), or public intoxication. Alcoholic beverages may not, in any circumstance, be used by, possessed by or distributed to any person under twenty-one (21) years of age.

13. Illegal or unauthorized possession of firearms, explosives, other weapons, or dangerous chemicals on University premises or use of any such item, even if legally possessed, in a manner that harms, threatens or causes fear to others.

14. Improper obstruction of the free flow of pedestrian or vehicular traffic on University premises or at University-sponsored or supervised functions.

15. Conduct which is disorderly, lewd, or indecent; breach of peace; or aiding, abetting, or procuring another person to breach the peace on University premises or at functions sponsored by, or participated in by, the University.

16. Theft or other abuse of computer time, including but not limited to:
    a. Unauthorized entry into a file, to use, read, or change the contents, or for any other purpose.
    b. Unauthorized transfer of a file.
    c. Unauthorized use of another individual's identification and password.
    d. Use of computing facilities to improperly interfere with the work of another student, faculty member, or University official.
    e. Use of computing facilities to send obscene or abusive messages.
    f. Use of computing facilities to improperly interfere with normal operation of the University computing system.

    g. Use of computing facilities and resources in violation of copyright laws.

    h. Any violation of the University Computer Use Policy.

17. Abuse of the University Student Code of Conduct and hearing procedures, including but not limited to:

    a. Failure to obey the notice from a Student Conduct Board or University official to appear for a meeting or hearing for violations of the University Code of Student Conduct.

    b. Falsification, distortion, or misrepresentation of information before a Student Conduct Board.

    c. Disruption or interference with the orderly conduct of a judicial proceeding.

    d. Institution of a student conduct code proceeding in bad faith.

    e. Attempting to discourage an individual's proper participation in, or use of, the judicial and other proceedings associated with the University Student Code of Conduct.

    f. Attempting to influence the impartiality of a member of a Student Conduct Board prior to, and/or during the course of, the judicial proceeding.

    g. Harassment (verbal or physical) and/or intimidation of a member of a Student Conduct Board prior to, during, and/or after a judicial proceeding.

    h. Failure to comply with the sanction(s) imposed under the student code.

    i. Influencing or attempting to influence another person to commit an abuse of the judicial system.

18. Actions which cause or attempts to cause a fire or explosion, falsely reporting a fire, explosion or an explosive device, tampering with fire safety equipment or intentionally failing to evacuate university buildings during a fire alarm.

C. Violation of Law

1. When a student is charged by federal, state, or local authorities with a violation of law, the University will not request or agree to special consideration for that individual because of his or her status as a student. Proceedings under this Student Code may be carried out prior to, simultaneously with, or following civil or criminal proceedings off campus at the discretion of the Vice President of Student Affairs or his/her designee.

2. If the alleged offense is also the subject of a proceeding before a Student Conduct Board under the Student Code, however, the University may advise off-campus authorities of the existence of the Student Code and of how such matters will be handled internally within the University community.

3. The University will cooperate fully with law enforcement and other agencies in the enforcement of criminal law on campus and with the conditions imposed by the criminal courts for the rehabilitation of student violators.

4. Individual students and faculty members, acting in their personal capacities, remain free to interact with governmental representatives as they deem appropriate.

Student Conduct Code Procedure

A. Charges and Hearings

1. Any member of the University community may file charges against any student for misconduct. Charges shall be prepared in writing and directed to the Student Code Administrator. Any charge should be submitted as soon as possible after the event takes place or the discovery of the same, but in no event later than ninety (90) days after the event takes place or the discovery of the same.

2. In cases where suspension or expulsion is a possible outcome, the Student Code Administrator shall refer the case to the Student Conduct Board. In all other cases, the Student Code Administrator shall seek to determine whether the charges can be disposed of administratively by mutual consent or refer the matter to the Student Conduct Board. In the event that the charges are disposed of by mutual consent, that decision shall be final and there shall be no subsequent proceedings.

3. Hearings shall be conducted by the Student Conduct Board:
   a. such determination shall be made on the basis of whether it is more likely than not that the Accused Student violated the Student Code.

B. Sanctions

1. The following sanctions may be imposed upon any student found to have violated the Student Code:
   a. Warning: A notice in writing to the student that the student is violating or has violated institutional regulations.
   b. Probation: A written reprimand for violation of specified regulations. Probation is for a designated period of time and includes the probability of more severe disciplinary sanctions if the student is found to be violating any institutional regulation(s) during the probationary period.
   c. Loss of Privileges: Denial of specified privileges for a designated period of time.
   d. Fines: Previously established and published fines may be imposed.
   e. Restitution: Compensation for loss, damage, or injury. This may take the form of appropriate service and/or monetary or material replacement.
   f. Discretionary Sanctions: Work assignments, service to the University or other related discretionary assignments (such assignments must have the prior approval of the Student Code Administrator).
   g. Residence Hall Suspension: Separation of the student from the residence halls for a definite period of time, after which the student is eligible to return. Conditions for readmission may be specified.
   h. Residence Hall Expulsion: Permanent separation of the student from the residence halls.
   i. University Suspension: Separation of the student from the University for

a definite period of time not to exceed one year, after which the student is eligible to return. Conditions for readmission may be specified.

j. University Expulsion: Permanent separation of the student from the University.

k. Revocation of Admission and/or Degree: Admission to or a degree awarded from the University may be revoked for fraud, misrepresentation, or other violation of University standards in obtaining the admission or degree, or for other serious violations committed by a student prior to graduation.

l. Withholding Degree: The University may withhold awarding a degree otherwise earned until the completion of the process set forth in this Student Conduct Code, including the completion of all sanctions imposed, if any.

m. The Grade of Unforgivable Failure (UF).

2. More than one of the sanctions listed above may be imposed for any single violation.

3. Other than University expulsion, revocation or withholding of a degree, or the grade of unforgivable failure, disciplinary sanctions imposed hereunder shall not be made part of the student's permanent academic record, but shall become part of the student's disciplinary record. Upon graduation, the student's disciplinary record may be expunged of disciplinary actions other than residence hall expulsion, University suspension, University expulsion, revocation or withholding of a degree, or the grade of unforgivable failure, upon application to the Student Code Administrator. Cases involving the imposition of sanctions other than residence hall expulsion, University suspension, University expulsion, revocation or withholding of a degree, or the grade of unforgivable failure shall be expunged from the student's confidential record seven (7) years after final disposition of the case.

4. The following sanctions may be imposed upon team, group, or student organization:

a. Those sanctions listed above in Section B.,1., a through f.

b. Loss of selected rights and privileges for a specified period of time.

c. Deactivation. Loss of all privileges, including University recognition, for a specified period of time.

5. The role of the Student Conduct Board will be to determine whether or not a student has violated the Student Code of Conduct and to impose sanctions as set forth in this Code. The Chair of the Student Conduct Board shall advise the accused in writing of its determination and the sanction(s) imposed, if any.

C. Interim Suspension

In certain circumstances, the Vice President of Student Affairs or his/her designee may impose a University or residence-hall suspension prior to the hearing before a Student Conduct Board.

1. Interim suspension may be imposed only: a) to ensure the safety and well-being of members of the University community or preservation of University property;

b) to ensure the student's own physical or emotional safety and well-being; or

c) if the student poses a definite threat of disruption of or interference with the normal operations of the University.

2. During the interim suspension, students shall be denied access to the residence halls and/or to the campus (including classes) and/or all other University activities or privileges for which the student might otherwise be eligible, as the Vice President of Student Affairs or his/her designee may determine to be appropriate.

3. The interim suspension does not replace the regular process, which shall proceed on the normal schedule, up to and through a Student Conduct Board Hearing, if required.

Residence Hall Standards of Conduct (2010) [Distributed to students living in residence halls from Office of Residential Education]

The residential student conduct process has jurisdiction over all residence halls and its surrounding properties. In addition to its contribution to the academic mission of the University, the student conduct process is also designed to support community standards while allowing students to make decisions in line with their individual lifestyles and value systems. Policies have been established in accordance with other University regulations, local, state, and federal laws, and input from previous residents.

Violations of any rule or regulation will lead to disciplinary action. Where such action is necessary, residence hall students may also face civil liability or criminal prosecution. Students are responsible for becoming familiar with and acting upon their rights and responsibilities.

Matters of safety and security are of primary importance to the residence hall community. Students who are careless may jeopardize the welfare of the larger community. As such, safety violations will be addressed with serious sanctions, including termination of a student's housing contract. Students are expected to forego personal convenience in the interest of community safety. This means that behaviors like propping doors, using alarmed doors, and not locking room doors, etc., are considered serious infractions. Residential Education reserves the right to initiate administrative moves made in the best interest of the residential community. Also, roommates who cannot resolve issues or come to a mutual understanding may be administratively moved to different rooms, floors and/or residence halls. In accordance with the housing contract, Residential Education reserves the right to inspect all areas of a student's room if there is information that indicates University policies are being violated or if the condition of the room is thought to present a health and safety concern.

Process. All student conduct procedures are designed to minimize disruption to the residential learning communities. The disciplinary action timeline outlines the student conduct process from the time the policy violation is reported, its student conduct meeting held and appeals filed, until its conclusion with the final decision.

- A formal complaint (usually through an information report) is submitted.
- A disciplinary body (person or person(s) assigned to resolve a student conduct matter) is assigned to consider charges against a student. Disciplinary bodies will be assigned according to the severity of the situation, previous student conduct history, and the appropriateness of the disciplinary body.
- A notice of charges and a notice of the time, date, and location of the student conduct meeting generally will be sent at least two days prior to a student conduct meeting.
- An outcome letter including sanctions will be sent after the student conduct meeting.

Sanctions. When determining appropriate sanctions, the disciplinary body will consider the following: willingness to accept responsibility for one's behavior, previous student conduct history, severity of the incident, and any recommendations made by the complainant or victim.

Decisions of this nature may be shared directly with parents through a letter or telephone call in compliance with the Family Educational Rights and Privacy Act (FERPA).

Recommendation for Other University Sanctions

Resident students who commit serious and/or chronic violations of the residence hall policies will be referred to the University Student Conduct Office for further disciplinary action.

The sanctions listed below represent the sanctions typically imposed if a student is found responsible for violating a particular residential policy as defined below.

Alcohol Possession/Use. Alcohol is not allowed on any residence hall property even if student is 21 years of age or older. The physical presence of alcoholic beverages in assigned residence hall rooms, or other property (or adjacent properties) constitutes possession and/or use under this definition. It is expected that a student immediately separate him or herself from policy violations of this nature, and report violations to appropriate staff members.

Minimum sanctions include:

- First violation: Residence hall probation; parental notification; 10–15 hours community service; Student Assistance Program Alcohol Innerview; reflection exercise.
- Second violation: Deferred removal; parental notification; 15–20 hours community service hours; Student Assistance Program Assessment and AlcoholEdu® for sanctions; reflection exercise.
- Third violation: Residence hall removal.

Alcohol Containers and Paraphernalia. Empty alcohol containers including, but not limited to: beer cans, liquor and/or wine bottles are not permitted on residence hall property. Paraphernalia used to consume or store alcohol including, but not limited to, beer bongs, shot glasses, empty kegs, etc., are also prohibited.

Minimum sanctions include:

- First violation: Notice of policy violation; 5–10 hours community service.
- Second violation: Residence hall probation; 10–15 hours community service; Student Assistance Program educational session; reflection exercise.
- Third violation: Deferred removal; 15–20 hours community service; Student Assistance Program Assessment and AlcoholEdu® for sanctions; reflection exercise.
- Fourth violation: Residence hall removal.

Alcohol or Drug-Related Behavior. Residents and their guests may be held responsible for behaviors related to the consumption of alcohol or illicit drug use regardless of where the alcohol or drugs are consumed. This includes, but is not limited to, underage consumption of alcohol, public intoxication, and any behaviors that disrupt the residential community.

Minimum sanctions include:

- First violation: Residence hall probation; parental notification; 10–15 hours of community service; Student Assistance Program Alcohol Innerview; reflection exercise.
- Second violation: Deferred removal; parental notification; 15–20 hours of community service; Student Assistance Program Assessment and AlcoholEdu® for sanctions; reflection exercise.
- Third violation: Residence hall removal.

Drugs (Controlled Substances). Students may not possess, use or distribute controlled substances on residence hall property. Students may not use any prescribed drug in a manner inconsistent with the prescription, nor may a student distribute prescribed drugs to others.

Minimum sanctions include:

- First violation: Deferred removal; parental notification; Student Assistance Program drug referral (assessment and two counseling sessions); reflection exercise; 10–15 hours of community service.
- Second violation: Residence hall removal. Distribution or intent to distribute controlled substances will result in removal from University housing. Possession of 15 grams or more of cannabis products (i.e., marijuana) may result in removal from residence halls on first offense and the student will be referred to the University Student Conduct Office for additional disciplinary action.

Drug Paraphernalia. Possession of drug paraphernalia is prohibited on residence hall property. This includes, but is not limited to, bongs, pipes, hookahs, water pipes, or any items modified or adapted so that they can be used to consume illegal substances. Minimum sanctions include:

- First violation: Residence hall probation; 5–10 hours community service; reflection exercise.
- Second violation: Deferred removal; 10–15 hours community service; reflection exercise; Student Assistance Program drug referral.
- Third violation: Residence hall removal.

Harassment/Threats/Physical Assault or Abuse. Conduct that intimidates, threatens, or endangers the health or safety of any person is not permitted whether communicated in writing, orally, electronically (e.g., Facebook, text messaging, e-mail, etc.), etc. This includes but is not limited to:
- Physical abuse of any person (e.g., battery and fighting).
- Retaliation for physical assault or abuse to one's self or on behalf of another.
- Threatening violence.
- Behavior that intentionally or recklessly causes physical, financial, or emotional harm to any person including intimidating behavior and behaviors that are deliberately intended to cause emotional distress to a group or person.
- Intimidating, threatening, or other endangering behavior against a person or persons because of race, sex, age, disability, veteran status, religion, sexual orientation, color or national origin.
- Behavior that is construed as a nuisance, including prank phone calls, and thereby disrupts the residence hall community.

Sexual Offenses. Any sexual activity with a person who does not consent or is unable to consent is prohibited. This includes, but is not limited to, sexual intercourse with, and/or sexual intrusion against (including sexually based touching), a person capable of giving consent, without such person's consent, or a person incapable of giving consent. Sexually based gestures and non-consensual sexually based communication, whether communicated in writing, orally, electronically (e.g., Facebook, text messaging, e-mail, etc.), are also prohibited. Violations of this policy typically result in removal from University Housing and are referred to the University Student Conduct Office for disciplinary action.

Theft. Theft of any nature is not permitted in the residence halls. This includes but is not limited to attempted or actual theft or possession of stolen goods, borrowing items without permission and unauthorized use of residence hall television cable system. Violations of this policy may result in removal from University housing and a referral to the University Student Conduct Office.

Vandalism. Vandalism includes, but is not limited to, public urination, willful, wanton, or reckless damage to University premises or property, or the property of a member or guest of the University community. Defacing of bulletin boards, posted materials, or any other University property is also prohibited and will be treated as vandalism.

Drug-Free Schools and Communities Act [Disseminated to students, faculty, and staff from Offices of Student Affairs and Human Resources.]

General Requirements of the Drug-Free Schools and Communities Act:

Amendments of 1989. Purpose: To comply with the Drug-Free Schools and Communities Act Amendments of 1989 (Pub.L.No.101–226, 103 Stat. 1928).

Coverage: All University employees, including faculty, classified and non-classified staff, administrators, and students.

The Drug-Free Schools and Communities Act Amendments of 1989 requires an institution of higher education, as a condition of receiving funds or any other form of financial assistance under any federal program, to certify that it has adopted and implemented a program to prevent the unlawful possession, use, or distribution of illicit drugs and alcohol by students and employees. As part of its drug prevention program for students and employees, PU annually distributes in writing to each student and employee the following information:

- Standards of conduct that clearly prohibit the unlawful possession, use or distribution of illicit drugs and alcohol by students and employees on its property or as a part of any of its activities.
- A description of applicable local, state, and federal legal sanctions pertaining to the unlawful possession, use, or distribution of illicit drugs and the abuse of alcohol.
- A description of health risks associated with the use of illicit drugs and the abuse of alcohol.
- A description of available drug and alcohol counseling, treatment, rehabilitation, and re-entry programs.
- A clear statement of the disciplinary sanctions that the University will impose upon students and employees who violate the standards of conduct.

A. Standards of Conduct. The unlawful possession, use, or distribution of illicit drugs and alcohol by students or employees on University property or as part of any other University regulated activities is prohibited.

B. Disciplinary Sanctions. The University will impose disciplinary sanctions on students and employees (faculty, classified and non-classified staff) who violate the above standards of conduct. Students should recognize the fact that for violation of these standards they will be subject to disciplinary sanctions up to and including suspension or expulsion from the University and referral for prosecution. Employees should be aware of the fact that violation of these standards of conduct will subject them to sanctions up to and including immediate dismissal and referral for prosecution. You should consult your student handbook, classified employee's handbook, or faculty handbook for review of the specific sanctions which may apply.

State Laws Regarding the Unlawful Possession, Use, or Distribution of Illicit Drugs and Alcohol

A. Alcohol Violations
Violation and Penalty. Misrepresentation of age for the purpose of purchasing or drinking beer or liquor or gaining admittance to any establishment from which he or she would otherwise be barred by age. Penalty: Imprisonment in county jail for up to 72 hours and fine up to $50.

Furnishing alcohol to a minor under 21 years of age by person not related by blood or marriage. Penalty: Imprisonment in a county jail not to exceed ten days or a fine in an amount not to exceed one hundred dollars.

Alcohol in Public Places:
1. Public intoxication
2. Drinking alcohol in a public place
3. Tendering a drink of alcoholic liquor to another person
4. Possessing alcoholic liquor in an amount in excess of one gallon
   First Offense: A fine of not less than $5 or no more than $100.

Second offense: A fine of not less than $5 nor more than 60 days in the county or regional jail or completion of not less than 5 hours of alcohol counseling at the nearest community mental health center.

B. Controlled Substances Violations
Except as authorized by law, it is unlawful for any person to manufacture, deliver, or possess with intent to deliver controlled substances. (See below for definitions of drug schedules.)

Violation and Penalty
1. Offense involving Schedule I or Schedule II substance which is a narcotic.
   Penalty: Imprisonment in the state controlled correctional facility for 1–15 years and a fine of $25,000
2. Offense involving any other controlled substance which is not a narcotic above in Schedules I, II, III.
   Penalty: Imprisonment in the state controlled correctional facility for 1–5 years and a fine of $15,000
3. Offense involving a Schedule IV substance.
   Penalty: Imprisonment in the state controlled correctional facility for 1–3 years and a fine of $10,000
4. Offense involving a Schedule V substance.
   Penalty: Confinement in a county jail not less than 90 days, not more than 6 months and a fine of $1,000
5. Offense involving possession of a controlled substance without a valid prescription.

Penalty: Confinement in a county jail not less than 90 days, not more than 6 months and a fine of $1,000

6. Offense involving an imitation controlled substance.
Penalty: Confinement in a county jail for 6 months to a year and a fine of $5,000

Definitions of Drug Schedules.[1] Schedule I drugs are defined as drugs with no currently accepted medical use and a high potential for abuse. Schedule I drugs are the most dangerous drugs of all the drug schedules with potentially severe psychological or physical dependence. Some examples of Schedule I drugs are: heroin, lysergic acid diethylamide (LSD), marijuana (cannabis), methylenedioxymethamphetamine (ecstasy), methaqualone, and peyote.

Schedule II drugs, substances, or chemicals are defined as drugs with a high potential for abuse, but less abuse potential than Schedule I drugs, with use potentially leading to severe psychological or physical dependence. These drugs are also considered dangerous. Some examples of Schedule II drugs are: cocaine, methamphetamine, methadone, hydromorphone (Dilaudid), meperidine (Demerol), oxycodone (OxyContin), fentanyl, Dexedrine, Adderall, and Ritalin.

Schedule III drugs, substances, or chemicals are defined as drugs with a moderate to low potential for physical and psychological dependence. Some examples of Schedule III drugs are: Combination products with less than 15 milligrams of hydrocodone per dosage unit (Vicodin), Products containing less than 90 milligrams of codeine per dosage unit (Tylenol with codeine), ketamine, anabolic steroids, testosterone.

Schedule IV drugs, substances, or chemicals are defined as drugs with a low potential for abuse and low risk of dependence. Some examples of Schedule IV drugs are: Xanax, Soma, Darvon, Darvocet, Valium, Activan, Talwin, Ambien.

Schedule V drugs, substances, or chemicals are defined as drugs with lower potential for abuse than Schedule IV and consist of preparations containing limited quantities of certain narcotics. Some examples of Schedule V drugs are: cough preparations with less than 200 milligrams of codeine or per 100 milliliters (Robitussin AC), Lomotil, Motofen, Lyrica, Parepectolin.

Anti-Hazing Laws [Available online, as part of State's Criminal Codes]

The state's Anti-hazing Law defines hazing as: "any action or situation which recklessly or intentionally endangers the mental or physical health or safety of another person or persons or causes another person or persons to destroy or remove public or private property for the purpose of initiation or admission into or affiliation with, or as a condition for continued membership in, any organization operating under the sanction of or recognized as an organization by an institution of higher education."

Such activities and situations include, but are not limited to:

Any brutality of a physical nature, such as whipping, beating, branding, forced consumption of any food, liquor, drug or other substance, or any other forced physical activity which could adversely affect the physical health and safety of the individual or individuals, and includes any activity which would subject the individual or individuals to extreme mental stress, such as sleep deprivation, forced exclusion from social contact, forced conduct which could result in extreme embarrassment or any other forced activity which could adversely affect the mental health or dignity of the individual or individuals, or any willful destruction or removal of public or private property.

Any person who is involved in acts of hazing is guilty of a misdemeanor, and, upon conviction "shall be fined no less than one hundred dollars nor more than one thousand dollars, or confined in a county or regional jail, not more than nine months, or both fined and imprisoned."

Appendix D

OFFICIAL CRIME STATISTICS
FOR PARTY UNIVERSITY AND PTOWN

Table 1. Crime at Party University (Based on Clery statistics, 2009, 2010)

	2009	2010
Murder	0	0
Forcible sexual offenses	4	7
Robbery	5	5
Aggravated assault	9	2
Burglary	21	20
Motor vehicle theft	3	1
Arson	2	3
Overall crime rate[a]	15.28	12.16
Arrests		
Liquor law arrests	428	551
Drug law arrests	121	205
Disciplinary actions		
Liquor law violations	1231	1501
Drug law violations[b]	98	104

Source: U.S. Department of Education, Office of Postsecondary Education website: ope.ed.gov.

[a] Note: crime rates based on enrollments (undergraduate and graduate). 2009 enrollment: 28,800; 2010 enrollment: 31,247. Using these enrollment numbers as denominators to calculate rates is only an estimate, as crimes on campus can include faculty, staff or visitors.

[b] The 2009 number comes from the PU police website rather than ope.edu.gov, to correct for a problem with the data recorded in the OPE website.

Table 2. Crime in Ptown (Based on Uniform Crime Reports, 2009, 2010)

	2009	2010
Murder	1	1
Rape	10	9
Robbery	23	22
Aggravated assaults	96	68
Burglary	196	187
Larceny theft[b]	604	N/A
Motor vehicle theft	18	22
Arson	5	3
Overall crime rate[a]	211.70	N/A
Violent crime rate	43.35	32.00
Property crime rate	274.43	N/A

Source: Uniform Crime Reports, FBI.gov.

[a] Note: crime rates based on 2009 population: 29,989; 2010 population: 31,247. Using these z population numbers as denominators to calculate rates is only an estimate, as population numbers do not include part-time students living in Ptown during the academic year.

[b] The FBI determined that Ptown's data for larceny theft in 2010 were underreported. Consequently, those data are not included in this table.

Table 3. **Crime (selected) at Party University from Crime Logs (April 2010)**

Time reported	Nature and brief description
2:43 PM	Theft: report of cash and a gold money clip stolen from residence hall. Value: $221.
5:14 PM	Theft (building): report of a stolen cell phone, back pack, and T-shirt.
8:33 PM	Drug offense: report of a smell of a controlled substance.
10:42 PM	Drug offense: a citation was issued for possession of marijuana less than 15 grams at [resident hall].
10:56 PM	Indecent exposure: report of naked male subject. Area checked and the male subject could not be found.
12:33 AM	Liquor law: a citation was issued for underage consumption at the lobby of [residence hall]. Subject was transported by EMS to hospital.
1:01 AM	Battery (physical): report of a battery on [street].
1:17 PM	Breaking and entering (vehicle): report of a vehicle that had the window broken out and a Sony laptop stolen. Value $1,350.00
1:45 AM	Liquor law: citations were issued for underage consumption and public intoxication.
2:11 AM	Liquor law: a female subject was arrested for public intoxication and disorderly conduct at the intersection of [Main Street] and [Campus Drive].
2:18 AM	Destruction of property: complainant reported his room being trashed, but nothing was missing.
2:22 AM	Destruction of property: report of the rear window broken out of a vehicle. Value: $200.
3:19 AM	DUI offense

Source: PU Police department website.

Notes

Chapter 1. Situating the Party School (pp. 3–13)

1. Enrollment numbers are based on schools that participated in Title IV federal student financial aid programs in 2010–11. According to the U.S. Department of Education, there were 7,178 Title IV institutions with just under 3,000 schools classified as four-year colleges, just over 2,000 two-year colleges, and another 2,000 less-than-two-year colleges (See Knapp, Kelly-Reid, and Ginder 2011).

2. Though only 23 percent of four-year universities and colleges are public or state institutions, they enroll approximately 58 percent of students overall and close to 61 percent of undergraduates (Knapp et al. 2011).

3. According to Gumprecht, there was an intentional effort to establish many public universities in quiet rural settings away from the "evils of city life" (Gumprecht 2008: 17).

4. With less money coming from the state, public universities and colleges have increased tuition costs substantially. Between 1999 and 2009, tuition increases nationwide have been approximately 37 percent after adjustment for inflation (from http://nces.edu.gov/programs/digest/).

5. According to articles in the *Chronicle of Higher Education* and *USA Today*, college athletics programs that participate in the NCAA Division I conferences can pull in from $10 to $60 million or more in revenues annually. Yet, after expenditures, only 22 percent of football programs in the Division I operate in the black (Wieberg, Upton, and Berkowitz 2012).

6. In addition to enforcing laws and providing protection to students, faculty, and employees who work on campus, university police departments offer other services that can include conducting criminal background checks for employees, initiating campus emergency alerts, patrolling special events, traffic enforcement, and providing crime awareness and safety prevention education (Flowers 2009; Reaves 2008).

7. Many large campuses also employ student patrols or cadets, especially within the residence halls, trained to identify potential threats and report criminal offenses but who have no arrest authority (Bromley and Territo 1990).

8. Gumprecht (2008: 23–24) suggests that there are at least two categories of college towns best distinguished by the type of school located there—flagship or land-grant university. He claims that the land-grant university, founded to provide aid for agricultural education, retains a more rural orientation, and is less urbane, more conventional, and not as heterogeneous as flagship towns. Moreover, towns

that host land-grant institutions (e.g., Pullman, home of Washington State, and Morgantown, home of West Virginia University) are not nearly as affluent as towns with flagship research universities (e.g., Ann Arbor, home to University of Michigan, and Bloomington, home of Indiana University).

9. One reason for the enrollment increases at public universities during the previous recession is that as high tuition costs at private schools soar, more students (or their parents) are taking advantage of lower tuition costs at state schools, although these costs, too, are creeping up.

10. Redevelopment and renewal plans in some college towns have begun to replace old houses with newer high-rise apartments equipped with game rooms and high-speed Internet access (Gumprecht 2008, p. 95).

11. At Virginia Polytechnic Institute and State University (Virginia Tech) (2007), an undergraduate killed thirty students and two professors, and wounded twenty-four others in a rampage that began in a dorm and ended in a classroom, before taking his own life; At Northern Illinois University (2008), a graduate student opened fire in a lecture hall; At Kent State University (1971), National Guard troops opened fire on antiwar demonstrators, killing four students and wounding nine. (See Karmen 2010, p. 307, for more information on these cases and other violent shootings at American universities and colleges.)

12. Clery statistics are available to the public on the website sponsored by the Office of Postsecondary Education of the U.S. Department of Education (ope.ed.gov /security/).

13. In 2008 Congress amended the Clery Act to require schools to implement campus emergency response plans that would notify students as soon as an emergency is confirmed.

14. The Clery Act also requires colleges to report incidents believed to be hate crimes.

15. In addition to collecting crime numbers from campus police, Clery requires a "reasonable good faith effort" in obtaining statistics from local law enforcement agencies (U.S. Dept. of Education 2011, p. 82).

16. Clery numbers may also be misleading due to manipulation by institutions in an attempt to make their campuses appear safer than they are. For example, burglary can be downgraded to larceny, a crime not required in Clery reports (Seward 2006).

Chapter 2. Contextualizing the Party Lifestyle (pp. 14–23)

1. In an effort to reduce underage drinking and the negative consequences associated with it (e.g., drunk driving), the National Minimum Drinking Age Act was signed into law in 1984, raising the minimum age for the purchase or public possession of alcoholic beverages to twenty-one. States that did not comply faced a reduction in highway funds under the Federal Aid Highway Act. The act led to compliance in every state (Flowers 2009, p. 3)

2. Gumprecht points out that fraternity houses are not always regulated by the

university. In fact, most Greek organizations voluntarily submit to regulations by the university even though their houses are privately owned and are often located off-campus (Gumprecht 2008).

3. According to Gumprecht (2008) a disproportionate number of alumni-donors are fraternity men.

4. Research findings regarding differences in drug use by race, class rank, and age are inconsistent (see Mustaine and Tewksbury 2004).

5. According to a recent news story, a student drug ring at Texas Christian University that included four football players was busted for selling marijuana, cocaine, ecstasy, and prescription drugs (Brown 2012).

6. Many college administrators agree that alcohol abuse contributes to student attrition. But retention numbers are not typically released to the public (Sullivan and Risler 2002; Thompson 2007). Therefore, linking alcohol consumption to retention is mostly speculative.

7. One example of an alcohol-related tragedy is an incident that took place at Ohio University (a designated party school according to the Princeton Review). In 2009, an intoxicated student died from a fall off a second story balcony while attending a party. This tragedy followed within a few months of another deadly fall by a student at the same university who was found to have had drugs in his system at the time of the accident (10TV News 2009).

8. For a comprehensive list of alcohol-related student fatalities at college, see compelledtoact.com, a website that compiles media reports on student deaths where alcohol was a cause or contributing factor.

9. Liquor law violations include prohibited manufacture, sale, or possession of liquor but exclude public drunkenness offenses and DUI/DWI. Drug law violations include production, distribution, and/or use of certain controlled substances (U.S. Department of Education 2011, pp. 68–70).

10. According to the Clery Handbook, *arrest* is defined as persons processed by formal arrest, citation, or summons. *Disciplinary action* is defined as the referral of a person to any official who initiates a disciplinary action by which a record is kept and may result in the imposition of a sanction (U.S. Dept. of Education 2011, pp. 65–67).

Chapter 3. Introducing Party University (pp. 27–37)

1. The collection year for "official data" is 2009 to be consistent with the year in which survey data were collected for the Campus Crime Victimization Survey.

2. The PU Student Conduct Code further states that the university "will not request special consideration for students charged with violations of a city, county, or state law on the basis of their status as students, nor will prosecution by federal, state, or local authorities necessarily preclude disciplinary action by the university."

3. Beyond the jurisdiction of residence halls, possession and distribution of drugs are prohibited by state and federal law, as specified in the Uniform Controlled Substances Act, and the Drug-Free Schools and Communities Act and Amendments

of 1989. These acts delineate very clearly the laws and sanctions for drug possession and sales at schools and elsewhere (See appendix C). As mandated by the Drug-Free Schools and Communities Act, PU annually distributes to every student and employee information on the laws that prohibit possession and distribution of illicit drugs and alcohol on its property.

4. As a comparison, Ann Arbor, home of University of Michigan has a median household income (2006–2010) of $52,625, and 20 percent of its population is under the poverty level. In contrast, Pullman, home of Washington State University, is similar to Ptown with a median household income of $25,609 and poverty level at 39 percent (see U.S. Bureau of the Census. 2012).

5. An important exception to the general lack of businesses in Ptown is its very vibrant alcohol industry. There are almost fifty bars, clubs, and liquor stores in Ptown. With little else for students or residents to do, these businesses stay very much in the black.

6. As a comparison to PU, the crime rate at Penn State in 2009 was 19.92, at University of Delaware it was 18.45, at University of Florida it was 15.46, and at Indiana University in Bloomington it was 15.35 (see Office of Postsecondary Education of the U.S. Department of Education, ope.ed.gov, for Clery reports).

7. As a comparison to major cities, and based on 2009 UCR crime rates, Los Angeles had a violent crime rate of 62.5 per 10,000 and property rate of 245 per 10,000; Boston's crime rate was 98 per 10,000 and property rate was 332; San Francisco's violent crime rate was 74 per 10,000 and property rate was 426. As a comparison to other college towns for 2009, Newark, Delaware, had a violent crime rate of 42 per 10,000, and property crime rate of 320; Athens, Ohio's violent crime rate was 15 per 10,000 and property rate was 207; and Bloomington, Indiana's violent crime rate was 51 per 10,000 and property rate was 447.

8. An example of a non-sports event that recently inspired a celebratory burning at PU occurred in May 2011, when hundreds of students poured into the streets to watch a couch set on fire in celebration of the death of Osama bin Laden (Ryan and Terry 2011).

Chapter 4. Playing Hard: Students' Drinking and Drug Routines (pp. 38–53)

1. GPAs may be skewed based on three possibilities. First, students with higher GPAs may be more willing to take voluntary research surveys. Second, students with the lowest GPAs may have flunked out prior to the distribution of the survey in late spring. Finally, these high GPAs may reflect a school-wide grade inflation where the majority of students really do earn As and Bs.

2. Although the conventional measure of binge drinking is five or more drinks in one sitting for men and four or more for women (see Wechsler and Nelson 2008), the same standard for both men and women is used in this book based on discussions with students who overwhelmingly agreed that the four-drink criteria for women is too low

to be considered "bingeing" or excessive. In fact, students also consider five drinks for men as rather "lightweight," and certainly not excessive.

3. The original CCVS used a combined two-to-three-days response category that conflated the weekend drinker (i.e., Friday and Saturday) with persons who extend their weekend to include a third night). The revised survey (CCVSr) corrects this, showing that 47 percent of students drink once a week, 26 percent drink two days, 17 percent drink three days, and 10 percent drink four or more days. Based on this data, drinking alcohol is much more than a weekend activity for one in four PU students.

4. The terms "freshman" and "freshmen," rather than the more gender-neutral "first-year student" or students, are used in this book to be consistent with students' own self-identification as freshmen.

5. It is important to note that 50 percent of students who work more than twenty hours a week still party rather regularly (i.e., as heavy partiers). This may be explained by the money involved in partying. Even as *not* working may provide time to party, it does not provide the resources necessary. As one student from the revised CCVS says "I don't consider myself a partier; I don't have the time or money."

6. Note that 40 percent of students involved in academic clubs, 50 percent in student government, 50 percent in ROTC and 21 percent in religious groups are heavy partiers. These large numbers of students involved in conventional organizations and activities who still manage to party extensively may be explained by the normativity of heavy partying at the party school. In other words, no matter what one's activities, most students still find time to party at levels considered "normal," which is apparently quite heavily.

7. The contradiction between upperclassmen's assessment of partying less and their drinking and drug routines indicating that they actually party more during their junior and senior years may be explained by social learning. As students get acclimated to the dual roles of partying and studying, they may see themselves as partying less because they put forth less effort in maintaining good grades while still partying. In this manner, partying becomes so normal that students' may underestimate the amount of time they actually spend doing so.

8. Although students do not specifically mention it in the CCVS, it is also possible that partying slows down once students turn twenty-one and their drinking routines shift from house parties to bars. It is at house parties where students engage in the most extreme partying rituals with the least amount of supervision.

Chapter 5. Getting Wasted: Extreme Party Rituals and Risks (pp. 54–72)

1. A traditional definition of *ritual* in anthropology suggests that rituals are an important part of the culture of a group of people, used to mark important occasions and transitions, and to express group identity. But rituals can also be informal, everyday shared experiences (Barnard and Spencer 2012). This second definition is most appropriate to the concept of party rituals used in this book.

2. It may not be a coincidence that it is a female student who refers only to mixed drinks and not beer. Anecdotally, women at college tend to drink less beer than men, often choosing mixed and sweetened alcoholic beverages instead.

3. The reference to bonging refers to the act of using a bong or funnel-like mechanism to drink large quantities of alcohol (usually beer) very rapidly. Alcohol is filled to the top of a bong or funnel and suspended above the drinker for gravitational pull. According to PU students, using this method makes it possible for someone to consume up to sixty ounces of beer or liquor in fifteen seconds.

4. "Taking a bottle to the face" means to consume alcohol very fast usually straight from the bottle.

5. It is important to note that women may not be as concerned about costs of drinks at bars or clubs due to the custom that men will purchase at least some drinks for women at these establishments.

6. Flip cup is a drinking game played in teams where drinkers compete to see who can drink their beer more quickly and then flip their cups over to win.

7. House parties generally collect a small cover charge in exchange for entrance and access to alcohol, although females often get in for free.

8. Cornhole is similar to horseshoes except bean bags are tossed at wooden platforms for points.

Chapter 6. Flirting with Danger: Criminal Consequences of the Party Subculture (pp. 73–98)

1. Another important contrast between the CCVS and Clery statistics is that CCVS includes incidents "while at PU," and not necessarily that happen only on campus and during one specific year. (See chapter 1 for more detail on the Clery Act, and appendix A for more detail on CCVS methodology.)

2. Burglary is defined as unlawful entry to commit theft; vandalism is defined as willful destruction or defacement of property; larceny theft is defined as the unlawful taking of property. The CCVS used simpler language that asked about property broken into, damaged, or stolen.

3. Since few victims of property crime ever see their offenders, questions pertaining to offender characteristics were not asked for these crimes.

4. Faculty who live near these downtown "hot spots" can also be victims. Two of my colleagues who live downtown have recently had their cars burglarized while parked overnight in their own driveways.

5. Burglary may be an exception to the linkages between crime and partying, as risks for this crime are more likely to be associated with general student routines, such as living in "student ghettos" and frequent traveling out of town, rather than how much students party.

6. Intimates, friends, and neighbors/roommates may or may not also be students. CCVS response categories did not allow for multiple responses, so the "students" category is most likely comprised of non-intimate acquaintances from PU.

7. Ironically, men's sense of obligation to fight is contrary to the ethic of nonintervention described in chapter 5, and where students are expected to mind their own business.

8. Survey question reads: Did offender appear to be drunk or high on drugs?

9. It should also be noted that men are twice as likely to be injured from fights while intoxicated (see appendix B, table 10). For men, 27 percent of extreme partiers, 11 percent of heavy partiers and 5 percent of light partiers experience injury from fights. For women, 11 percent of extreme partiers, 5 percent of heavy partiers and 1 percent of light parties experience injury from fights.

10. In a poll of my criminology students last year, the majority of the class agreed that it was not unusual to see women at PU fighting while out at night, and one student responded that "it shows she can take care of herself." Of course, the acceptance of women fighting may be less about diminishing gender stereotypes than about the circumstances under which these fights commonly occur, namely while intoxicated and at bars, clubs, and parties.

11. Yet when respondents were asked if they had ever experienced sexual assault while intoxicated or as a result of intoxication, only 5 percent of respondents (7 percent of women, 2 percent of men) attributed sexual assault to intoxication.

12. Another shared narrative among many students at PU is the exaggerated danger of being "roofied" at parties or bars (i.e., having rohypnol or some other drug surreptitiously dropped into a drink in order to incapacitate someone as a potential victim). For instance, more than a third of PU students believe that someone they know (including themselves) has been roofied while at PU. Despite research that contradicts the prevalence of such crimes, students still believe that this crime is quite common at college (See Weiss and Colyer 2010).

13. Educational programs such as Green Dot's violence prevention and bystander intervention program now operate in many schools to educate students how to recognize crime and intervene in effective manners (Casey and Ohler 2012; McMahon and Banyard 2012).

14. Even "hooking up" can be coercive. Although the process seems mutual, Kimmel (2008) suggests that it is men who are usually in control during this ritual, and women are expected to play along. For instance, it is men who are more likely to initiate the hook up; and hook ups most often take place at his place, meaning that women are the ones who must find their way home in the morning, and take the so-called walk of shame after "regrettable" sex, often having used no protection (Wechsler and Wuethrich 2002).

15. An unintended fallout of some rape prevention programs is that women may blame themselves when they are sexually assaulted because they feel as if they should have known better. In other words, when women fail to assess a situation as dangerous, or get too drunk at a party, they may see themselves as responsible for failing to see the warning signs or for drinking too much.

16. Considering the large numbers of PU students who drive drunk, and so few traffic accidents, PU students appear to be rather "competent" drunk drivers.

17. Only students who drink alcohol while at PU were asked about arrests and disciplinary actions for alcohol violations; only students who use drugs at PU were asked about arrests and disciplinary actions for drug violations.

18. CCVS defines legal sanctions separately, following Clery definitions. Recall (see chapter 2, note 10) that *arrest* is defined as being processed by formal arrest, citation, or summons. *Disciplinary action* is defined as the referral of a person to any official who initiates a disciplinary action by which a record is kept and may result in the imposition of a sanction. Disciplinary actions at PU are most commonly implemented in residence halls and the student activities center.

19. In addition to paying fines ($235 for each citation) this student claims to have attended Alcoholics Anonymous (AA) meetings as part of his penalties for underage drinking. If true, I question whether this is an appropriate sanction, as these students are probably not alcoholics. Having nonalcoholics sit through meetings without a commitment to being sober can undermine the seriousness of the program and is disrespectful to actual alcoholics trying to stay sober.

20. For an extraordinarily vivid (and sometimes entertaining) visual of student-police conflict, tune in to Campus PD on the cable network G4. Similar to the long running television show COPS, Campus PD is filmed exclusively on college campuses.

21. These responses come from a survey question that reads: What is your opinion of the jobs that University and local police do to control crime, noise and other disturbances that occur on campus or in your neighborhood?

Chapter 7. Party Disturbances:
Secondhand Harms to Campus and Community (pp. 99–114)

1. The conceptualization of secondhand harms used in this chapter is similar to the concept of secondary harms used in victimology to distinguish between a direct (or primary) victim who experiences crime and its consequences firsthand, and secondary (or indirect) victims (e.g., friends, family, witnesses, neighbors, first responders) who are not immediately involved in the crime but are nonetheless impacted indirectly. Secondary harms can be far reaching, and can include entire neighborhoods, states, and countries (see Karmen 2010, p. 2).

2. It is not just students who are targets of verbal harassment. For instance, I have been screamed at (incoherently) by young men driving by in cars while simply walking near my office at night. And a couple of my male colleagues tell me that they have had slurs such as "faggot" screamed at them on more than one occasion, underscoring a possible problem with bias at PU.

3. Survey question reads: Please feel free to add any additional comments that you would like to share regarding your experiences at [PU], including perceptions of safety, and police response to crime and disturbances on or near campus.

4. These interviews were conducted for a secondary project that examines in more detail the disorder and conflict in college towns from the perspective of nonstudents.

5. The assertion of a hands-off-approach by police is based on a discussion with a student who "shadowed" campus police at a football game last year. During his four hour assignment, he did not observe even one arrest, despite witnessing many clearly intoxicated students. When the student asked the officer what his stipulations were for arresting someone on a game day, the officer's response was "as long as they're not driving drunk or killing someone, we usually don't bother with them."

Conclusion: Sobering Reflections of the Party School (pp. 132–47)

1. The tougher policies and penalties for malicious burning have not yet had much of an effect at PU. But changing a tradition can be a very slow process.

2. When party house ordinances are discussed in my criminology course, students unanimously agree that in Ptown, a sticker that labels a dwelling as a "party house" would merely elevate both the house in question and its residents to the ultimate partier status.

3. One of the proponents of social norm programs is the University of Virginia (UV). Two years after an intoxicated student fell down a stairway to her death (the fifth Virginia college student to die of alcohol-related causes that autumn and the eighteenth student since 1990), UV launched an educational campaign that emphasizes moderation over abstinence, with funding, ironically, from Anheuser-Busch Co., the nation's largest brewer (Murray and Gruley 2000). The company's wholesalers are required to contribute a penny from each case of beer sold to alcohol education efforts.

Appendix A. Research Methods (pp. 151–60)

1. Asking about crime "while at PU" meant that seniors would have had a greater chance of experiencing crime during their years at college than other students, making comparisons of crime by age and class rank impossible.

2. Data regarding four other crimes—motor vehicle theft, robbery, stalking, and sexual harassment—were also collected, but results are not included in this book for various reasons. For instance, only two traditional students at PU had experienced a car theft (0.3 percent), and only thirteen students (less than 2 percent) were robbed. Stalking and sexual harassment were omitted due to the contexts of these offenses that differ from the focus of this book—party-related crime and victimization. These incidents will be discussed in future projects.

Appendix C. Student Conduct Code and Regulations (pp. 181–94)

1. Source: "Drug Schedules." U.S. Drug Enforcement Administration, U.S. Department of Justice. www. Justice.gov/dea/druginfo/ds.shtml.

Works Cited

Armstrong, Elizabeth A., Laura Hamilton, and Brian Sweeney. 2006. Sexual assault on campus: A multilevel, integrative approach to party rape. *Social Problems* 53(4): 483–99.

Associated Press. 2011. Reward offered in attack of [football] fans at [PU] game. *Charleston Daily Mail*, September 30. Retrieved from http://dailymail.com.

Barnard, Alan, and Jonathan Spencer (eds.). 2012. Ritual. In *The Routledge encyclopedia of social and cultural anthropology*, 2nd ed., p. 617. New York: Routledge.

Barkan, Steven E. 2012. *Criminology: A Sociological Understanding*, 5th ed. Upper Saddle River, NJ: Prentice Hall.

Baum, Katrina, and Patsy Klaus. 2005. *Violent victimization of college students, 1995–2002.* Bureau of Justice Statistics special report. Washington, DC: U.S. Department of Justice.

Best, Joel. 1990. *Threatened children: Rhetoric and concern about child-victims.* Chicago: University of Chicago Press.

———. 1999. *Random violence: How we talk about new crimes and new victims.* Berkeley: University of California Press.

Blumer, H. (1969). *Symbolic interactionism: Perspective and method.* Englewood Cliffs, NJ: Prentice Hall.

Boswell, A. Ayres, and Joan Z. Spade. 1996. Fraternities and collegiate rape culture: Why are some fraternities more dangerous places for women? *Gender & Society* 10(2): 133–47.

Brenner, James W., Stacie M. Metz, and Christina J. Brenner. 2009. Campus involvement, perceived campus connection and alcohol use in college athletes. *Journal of Drug Education* 39(3): 303–20.

Bromley, Max. L. 2007. The evolution of campus policing: Different models for different eras. In *Campus Crime: Legal, social and policy perspectives*, edited by Bonnie S. Fisher and John J. Sloan, 280–303. Springfield, IL: Charles C. Thomas.

Bromley, Max L., and Leonard Territo. 1990. *College crime prevention and personal safety awareness.* Springfield, IL: Charles C. Thomas Publishers.

Brower, Aaron M., and Lisa Carroll. 2007. Spatial and temporal aspects of alcohol-related crime in a college town. *Journal of American College Health* 55(5): 267–75.

Brown, Caitlin. 2012. Texas Christian University drug case: Students arrested on felony charges. *Huffington Post*, February 15. Retrieved from www.huffingtonpost.com.

Buddie, Amy M., and Kathleen A. Parks. 2003. The role of the bar context and social behaviors on women's risk for aggression. *Journal of Interpersonal Violence* 18: 1378–93.

Burgess, Robert L., and Ronald L. Akers. 1966. A differential association-reinforcement theory of criminal behavior. *Social Problems* 14: 128–47.

Burn, Shawn Meghan. 2009. A situational model of sexual assault prevention through bystander intervention. *Sex Roles* 60: 779–92.

Bynum, Jack, and William E. Thompson. 2005. *Juvenile delinquency: A sociological approach.* New York: Pearson.

Carlson, Melanie. 2008. I'd rather go along and be considered a man: Masculinity and bystander intervention. *Journal of Men's Studies* 16(1): 3–17.

Casey, Erin A., and Kristin Ohler. 2012. Being a positive bystander: Male antiviolence allies' experiences of "stepping up." *Journal of Interpersonal Violence* 27(1): 62–83.

Centers for Disease Control and Prevention. 1997. Fact sheet: National college health risk behavior survey, 1995. Retrieved from www.popcenter.org.

Chen, Chiung M., Mary C. Dufour, and Hsiao-Ye Yi. 2004. *Alcohol consumption among young adults ages 18–24 in the United States: Results from the 2001–2003 NESARC Survey.* National Institute on Alcohol Abuse and Alcoholism. Retrieved from www .niaaa.nih.gov/Publications.

Clark, Burton, and Martin Trow. 1966. The organizational context. In *College peer groups: Problems and prospects for research,* edited by Theodore Newcomb and Everette K. Wilson, 17–70. Chicago: Aldine.

Cohen, Lawrence E., and Marcus Felson. 1979. Social change and crime rate trends: A routine activity approach. *American Sociological Review* 44: 588–607.

Coker, Ann L., Patricia G. Cook-Craig, Corrine M. Williams, Bonnie S. Fisher, Emily R. Clear, Lisandra S. Garcia, and Lea M. Hegge. 2011. Evaluation of green dot: An active bystander intervention to reduce sexual violence on college campuses. *Violence against Women* 17(6): 777–96.

Cook, Colleen, Fred Heath, and Russell L. Thompson. 2000. A meta-analysis of response rates in Web- or Internet-based surveys. *Educational and Psychological Measurement* 60(6): 821–36.

Cooper, Josh. 2010. Portable toilet fire cause still unknown. *Daily Athenaeum,* September 30. Retrieved from www.thedaonline.com/news.

Core Institute. 2010. *Executive summary of the Core Drug and Alcohol Survey, 2008.* Carbondale: Core Institute, University of Southern Illinois.

Crum, Travis. 2011. One charged after fight in 'Lair Garage. *Daily Athenaeum,* January 30. Retrieved from www.thedaonline.com.

DA Staff. 2009. Bad week for college campus safety. *Daily Athenaeum* October 19. www.thedaonline.com.

Dowdall, George, W. 2007. The role of alcohol abuse in college student victimization. In *Campus crime: Legal, social and policy perspectives,* edited by Fisher, Bonnie and John J. Sloan III, 2nd ed., 167–87. Springfield, IL: Charles C. Thomas.

Durkin, Keith F., Timothy W. Wolfe, and Gregory A. Clark. 2005. College students and binge drinking: An evaluation of social learning theory. *Sociological Spectrum* 25: 255–72.

Durkin, Keith F., Scott E. Wolfe, and Ross W. May. 2007. Social bond theory and drunk driving in a sample of college students. *College Student Journal* 41(3): 734–44.

Fabian, Lindsey E. A., Traci L. Tommey, Kathleen M. Lenk, and Darin J. Erickson. 2008. Where do underage college students get alcohol? *Journal of Drug Education*, 38(1): 15–26.

Felson, R. B., S. F. Messner, A. W. Hoskin, and G. Deanne. 2002. Reasons for reporting and not reporting domestic violence to the police. *Criminology*, 40: 617–47.

Felson, Richard B., and Keri B. Burchfield. 2004. Alcohol and the risk of physical and sexual assault victimization. *Criminology*, 42(4): 837–59.

Fisher, B. S., L. E. Daigle, F. T Cullen, and M. G. Turner. 2003. Reporting sexual victimization to the police and others: Results from a national-level study of college women. *Criminal Justice and Behavior*, 30: 6–38.

Fisher, Bonnie S., Leah E. Daigle, and Francis T. Cullen. 2010. *Unsafe in the ivory tower: The sexual victimization of college women.* Thousand Oaks, CA: Sage.

Fisher, Bonnie S., and Andrew R. P. Wilkes. 2003. A tale of two ivory towers: A comparative analysis of victimization rates and risks between university students in the US and England. *British Journal of Criminology* 43(3): 526–44.

Fisher, Bonnie S., John J. Sloan, Francis T. Cullen, and Chunmeng Lu. 1998. Crime in the ivory tower: The level and sources of student victimization. *Criminology* 36(3): 671–710.

Flowers, R. Barri. 2009. *College Crime: A statistical study of offense on American campuses.* Jefferson, NC: McFarland & Company.

Fox, Kathryn J. 2003. Real punks and pretenders: The social organization of a counterculture. In *Constructions of deviance: Social power, context and interaction*, edited by Patricia Adler and Peter Adler, 4th ed., 337–52. Belmont, CA: Wadsworth.

Glass, Ira, and WBEZ Chicago. 2009. #1 party school. *This American Life*, 396, December 18. www.thisamericanlife.org.

Graham, Kathryn, Samantha Wells, Sharon Bernards, and Susan Dennison. 2010. "Yes, I do but not with you": Qualitative analysis of sexual/romantic overture-related aggression in bars and clubs. *Contemporary Drug Problems* 37: 197–240.

Greenberg, M. S., and R. B. Ruback. 1992. *After the crime: Victim decision making.* New York: Plenum Press.

Grossbard, Joel, Justin Hummer, Joseph LaBried, Eric Pederson, and Clayton Neighbors. 2009. Is substance use a team sport? Attraction to team, perceived norms, and alcohol and marijuana use among male and female intercollegiate athletes. *Journal of Applied Sport Psychology* 21: 247–61.

Gruley, Bryan. 2003. Watered down: How one university stumbled in its attack on alcohol abuse; as industry resisted change, Florida State's president focused on campus image; beer pong and phony IDs. *Wall Street Journal*, October 14: A1.

Gumprecht, Blake. 2008. *The American college town.* Amherst: University of Massachusetts Press.

Harford, Thomas C., Henry Wechsler, and Bengt O. Muthen. 2003. Alcohol-related aggression and drinking at off-campus parties and bars: A national study of current drinkers in college. *Journal of Studies in Alcohol* 64: 704–11.

Harford, Thomas C., Henry Wechsler, and Mark Seibring. 2002. Attendance and alcohol use at parties and bars in college: A national study of current drinkers. *Journal of Studies in Alcohol* 63: 726–33.

Harki, Gary. 2010. Ryan Diviney: Tragedy of a night in Morgantown. *WV Gazette*, December 2. Retrieved from www.wvgazette.com.

Hart, Timothy C., and Callie Rennison. 2003. *Reporting crime to the police, 1992–2000*. NCJ 195710. Washington, DC: U.S. Department of Justice, Office of Justice Programs.

Hashima, P. Y., and D. Finkelhor. 1999. Violent victimization of youth versus adults in the national crime victimization survey. *Journal of Interpersonal Violence* 14: 799–820.

Heckert, Alex, and Druann Maria Heckert. 2002. A new typology of deviance: Integrating normative and reactivist definitions of deviance. *Deviant Behavior* 23: 449–79.

Hewitt, John P. 1988. *Self and society: A symbolic interactionist social psychology*, 4th ed. Boston: Allyn and Bacon.

Hickson, Mark III, and Julian B. Roebuck. 2009. *Deviance and crime in colleges and universities: What goes on in the hall of Ivy*. Springfield, IL: Charles C. Thomas.

Hingson, Ralph, Timothy Heeren, Michael Winter, Henry Wechsler. 2005. Magnitude of alcohol-related mortality and morbidity among US college students ages 18–24: Changes from 1998 to 2001. *Annual Review of Public Health* 26: 259–79.

Hirschi, Travis. 1969. *Causes of delinquency*. Berkeley: University of California Press.

Hoover, Eric. 2002. Reading and rioting. *Chronicle of Higher Education* 49(16): A40–41.

Johnson, L. D., P. M. O'Malley, J. G. Bachman, and J. E. Schulenberg. 2007. *Monitoring the future national survey results on drug use, 1975–2006, Volume II: College students and adults ages 19–45* (NIH pub 07–6206). Bethesda, MD: National Institute on Drug Abuse.

Karmen, Andrew. 2010. Crime victims: An introduction to victimology. Belmont, CA: Wadsworth.

Kimmel, Michael. 2008. *Guyland: The perilous world where boys become men*. New York: Harper.

Knapp, L. G., J. E. Kelly-Reid, and S. A. Ginder. 2011. *Postsecondary institutions and price of attendance in the United States: 2010–11, degrees and other awards conferred: 2009–10, and 12-month enrollments 2009–10*. NCES 2011–250. Washington, DC: U.S. Dept of Education, National Center of Education Statistics. Retrieved from http://NCES.edu.gob/pubsearch.

Kuehnle, Kristen, and Anne Sullivan. 2001. Patterns of anti-gay violence: An analysis of incident characteristics and victim reporting. *Journal of Interpersonal Violence* 16(9): 928–43.

Lanza-Kaduce, Lonn, Michael Capece, and Helena Alden. 2006. Liquor is quicker:

Gender and social learning among college students. *Criminal Justice Policy Review* 17(20): 127–43.

Lerner, Melvin J. 1980. *The belief in a just world: A fundamental delusion*. New York: Plenum.

Lewis, Laurie, Elizabeth Farris, and Bernie Green. 1997. *Campus crime and security at postsecondary education institutions*. National Center for Education Statistics Statistical Analysis Report, NCES 97–402. Washington DC: U.S. Department of Education.

Lowe, Robert D., Mark Levine, Rachel M. Best, and Derek Heim. 2012. Bystander reaction to women fighting: Developing a theory of intervention. *Journal of Interpersonal Violence* 27(9): 1802–26.

McMahon, Sarah, and Victoria L. Banyard. 2012. When can I help? A conceptual framework for the prevention of sexual violence through bystander intervention. *Trauma, Violence and Abuse* 13(1): 3–14.

Meilman, P. W., J. S. Leichliter, and C. A. Presley. 1999. Greeks and athletes: Who drinks more? *Journal of American College Health* 47: 187–90.

Menning, Chadwick L. 2009. Unsafe at any house? Attendees' perceptions of microlevel environmental traits and personal safety at fraternity and nonfraternity parties. *Journal of Interpersonal Violence* 24(10): 1714–34.

Michener, H. Andrew, and John D. DeLamater. 1999. *Social psychology*. 4th ed. New York: Harcourt Brace.

Miethe, Terrance D., and Robert F. Meier. 1990. Opportunity, choice and criminal victimization: A test of a theoretical model. *Journal of Research in Crime and Delinquency* 27(3): 243–66.

Mohler-Kuo, Meichun, George Dowdall, Mary Koss, and Henry Wechsler. 2004. Correlates of rape while intoxicated in a national sample of college women. *Journal of Studies on Alcohol* 65: 37–45.

Mullaney, Jamie L. 2007. Telling it like a man: Masculinities and battering men's accounts of their violence. *Men and Masculinities* 10(2): 222–47.

Murray, Shailagh, and Bryan Gruley. 2000 Anheuser and rivals sponsor programs that encourage drinking in moderation—legacy of a death at U. VA. *Wall Street Journal*, November 2: A1.

Mustaine, Elizabeth Ehrhardt, and Richard Tewksbury. 2004. Profiling the druggie lifestyle: Characteristics related to Southern college students' use of illicit drugs. *Sociological Spectrum* 24: 157–89.

———. 2007. Routine activities and criminal victimization of students: Lifestyle and related factors. In *Campus crime: Legal, social and policy perspectives*, edited by Bonnie Fisher, and John J. Sloan III, 2nd ed., 147–66. Springfield, IL: Charles C. Thomas.

Neal, Dan J., and Kim Fromme. 2007. Hook 'em and heavy drinking: Alcohol use and collegiate sports. *Addictive Behaviors* 32: 2681–93.

Nelson, Toben F., and Henry Wechsler. 2003. School spirits: Alcohol and collegiate sports fans. *Addictive Behavior* 28: 1–11.

NIAAA (National Institute of Alcohol Abuse and Alcoholism) Task Force on College

Drinking. 2002. *A Call to action: Changing the culture of drinking at US colleges.* Washington, DC: National Institutes of Health.

NIAAA (National Institute of Alcohol Abuse and Alcoholism). 2007. *What colleges need to know now: An update on college drinking research.* NIH publication no. 07-5010. Retrieved fromwww.collegedrinkingprevention.gov.

Novik , Melinda G., Donna E. Howard, and Bradley O. Boekeloo. 2011. Drinking motivations and experiences of unwanted sexual advances among undergraduate students. *Journal of Interpersonal Violence* 26(1): 34–49.

Nuzum, Lydia. 2011. Seven fires reported after LSU game. *Daily Athenaeum*, September 26: 1–2.

O'Brien, Jodi. 2006. Symbolic Interactionism: A perspective for understanding self and social interaction. In *The production of reality: Essays and reading on social interaction*, edited by Jodi O'Brien, 4th ed., 44–62. Thousand Oaks, CA: Pine Forge Press.

Offredo, Jon. 2007a. Stabbing death trial begins. *Daily Athenaeum*. October 11. Retrieved from www.thedaonline.com.

———. 2007b. Two tapes, different stories in trial. *Daily Athenaeum* October 17.

O'Grady, Kevin E., Amelia M. Arria, Dawn M. B. Fritzelle, and Eric D. Wish. 2008. Heavy drinking and polydrug use among college students. *Journal of Drug Issues* 38(2): 445–66.

Peterson, Z. D., and C. L. Muehlenhard. 2007. Conceptualizing the "wantedness" of women's consensual and nonconsensual sexual experiences: Implications for how women label their experiences with rape. *Journal of Sex Research* 44: 72–89.

Pezza, Paul E., and Ann Bellotti. 1995. College campus violence: Origins, impacts and responses. *Educational Psychology Review* 7(1): 105–23.

Pitts, V. L., and M. D. Schwartz. (1997). Self-blame in hidden rape cases. In *Researching sexual violence against women*, edited by M. D. Schwartz, 65–70. Thousands Oaks, CA: Sage.

Presley, Cheryl A., and Philip W. Meilman. 1992. *Alcohol and drugs on American college campuses: A report to college presidents.* Carbondale: Southern Illinois University.

———. 1994. Development of the Core alcohol and drug survey, initial finding and future decisions. *Journal of American College Health* 42(6): 248–55.

Princeton Review. n.d. The Princeton Review's college rankings. Retrieved from www.princetonreview.com/college/college-rankings.aspx.

Reaves, Brian A. 2008. *Campus law enforcement, 2004–05.* Washington, DC: US Department of Justice, Bureau of Justice Statistics, Office of Justice Programs.

Reinarman, Craig. 2006. The social construction of drug scares. In *Constructions of deviance: Social power, context and interaction*, edited by Patricia A. Adler and Peter Adler, 5th ed., 139–50. Belmont, CA: Thomson/Wadsworth.

Riemer, Jeffrey W. 1981. Deviance as fun. *Adolescence* 16: 39–43.

Robinson, Mathew B., and Sunghoon Roh. 2007. Crime on campus: Spatial aspects of campus crime at a regional comprehensive university. In *Campus crime: Legal, social and policy perspectives*, edited by Bonnie Fisher and John J. Sloan III, 2nd ed., 231–58. Springfield, IL: Charles C. Thomas.

Rohan, Tim. 2012. Sandusky gets 30 to 60 years for sexual abuse. *New York Times*, October 9. Retrieved from www.nytimes.com.

Ryan, David, and John Terry. 2011. Students head to streets, burn couches in reaction to bin Laden's death. *Daily Athenaeum*. Retrieved from www.thedaonline.com.

Scott, Marvin B., and Stanford M. Lyman. 1968. Accounts. *American Sociological Review* 33 (February): 46–62.

Scott-Cheldon, Lori A. J., Kate B. Carey, and Michael P. Carey. 2008. Health behavior and college students: Does Greek affiliation matter? *Journal of Behavioral Medicine* 31: 61–70.

Seaman, Barrett. 2005. *Binge: What your college student won't tell you. Campus life in an age of disconnection and excess*. Hoboken, NJ: John Wiley and Sons.

Seward, Z. 2006. FBI stats show many colleges understate campus crime. *Wall Street Journal*, October 23: B1, B12.

Shinew, Kimberly J., and Diana C. Parry. 2005. Examining college students' participation in the leisure pursuits of drinking and illegal drug use. *Journal of Leisure Research* 37: 364–86.

Simons, Lori, Stephanie Klichine, Valerie Lantz, Laura Ascolese, Stephanie Deihl, Brian Schatz, and Latoya Wright. 2005. The relationship between social-contextual factors and alcohol and polydrug use among college freshman. *Journal of Psychoactive Drugs* 37(4): 415–24.

Sloan, John J. III, Bonnie S. Fisher, and Francis T. Cullen. 1997. Assessing the student right-to-know and campus security act of 1990: An analysis of the victim reporting practices of college and university students. *Crime and Delinquency* 43(2) 148–68.

Sloan, John J. III, and Bonnie S. Fisher. 2011. *The dark side of the ivory tower: Campus crime as a social problem*. Cambridge: Cambridge University Press.

Sperber, Murray. 2000. *Beer and circus: How big-time college sports is crippling undergraduate education*. New York: Henry Holt and Company.

Sullivan, Michael, and Ed Risler. 2002. Understanding college alcohol abuse and academic performance: Selecting appropriate intervention strategies. *Journal of College Counseling* 5: 114–23.

Sun, Ivan Y., and Jamie G. Longazel. 2008. College students' alcohol-related problems: A test of competing theories. *Journal of Criminal Justice* 36: 554–62.

Sutherland, Edwin H. 1939. *The principles of criminology*. Philadelphia: Lippincott.

Sykes, Gresham M., and David Matza. 1957. Techniques of neutralization: A theory of delinquency. *American Sociological Review* 22 (December): 664–70.

Teed, Kenneth C., Melanie Cook, Ken Tennant, Dana Brooks, Ron Althouse, and Damien Clement. 2010. Investigating ritualized campus and student fan misbehavior. *Journal for the Study of Sports and Athletes in Education* 4(2): 173–90.

10TV News. 2009. OU fights party school image after student's death. July 28. Retrieved from www.10tv.com/content/stories/2009.

Tewksbury, Richard, and Diane Pedro. 2003. The role of alcohol in victimization. In *Controversies in victimology*, edited by Laura Moriarty, 25–42. Cincinnati, OH: Anderson.

Tewksbury, Richard, and Elizabeth Ehrhardt Mustaine. 2003. College students' life-styles and self-protective behaviors: Further considerations of the guardianship concept in routine activity theory. *Criminal Justice and Behavior* 30(3): 302–27.

Tewksbury, Richard, George E. Higgins, and Elizabeth Ehrhardt Mustaine. 2008. Binge drinking among college athletes and non-athletes. *Deviant Behavior* 29: 275–93.

Thompson, Kevin M. 2007. Alcohol-related legal infractions and student retention. *Journal of Studies in Alcohol and Drugs* 68: 689–96.

Thompson, Edward H. Jr., and Elizabeth J. Cracco. 2008. Sexual aggression in bars: What college men can normalize. *Journal of Men's Studies* 16(1): 82–96.

Thompson, William E., and Joseph V. Hickey. 1999. *Society in focus: Introduction to sociology*, 3rd ed. New York: Longman.

Tucker, Eric. 2009. Scarlet letters: RI students, landlords fight police, orange stickers branding party houses. *Star Tribune*, August 4. Retrieved from www.startribune.com.

U.S. Census Bureau. 2012. State and County Quick Facts. Retrieved from http://quickfacts.census.gov/qfd/index.html.

U.S. Department of Education. 2011. *The handbook for campus safety and security reporting*. Washington, DC: U.S. Department of Education, Office of Postsecondary Education.

U.S. Department of Justice, Bureau of Justice Statistics. 2010. *National crime victimization survey*. Including Basic Screen Questionnaire (NCVS-1) and National Crime Victimization Survey Crime Incident Report (NCVS-2). Ann Arbor, MI: Inter-University Consortium for Political and Social Research.

U.S. State News. 2007. Senator Turner bill to extend animal house provisions passes senate panel. News release from NJ state senate. Retrieved from lexisnexis.com.

Vander Ven, Thomas. 2011. *Getting wasted: Why college students drink too much and party so hard*. New York: New York University Press.

WBOY News. 2010. Pittsburgh man dies in Morgantown stabbing. September 12. Retrieved from www.wboy.com.

Wechsler, Henry, and Toben F. Nelson. 2008. What we have learned from the Harvard School of Public Health college alcohol study: Focusing attention on college student alcohol consumption and the environmental conditions that promote it. *Journal of Studies on Alcohol and Drugs* 69: 481–90.

Wechsler, Henry, and Bernice Wuethrich. 2002. *Dying to drink: Confronting binge drinking on College Campuses*. New York: St. Martin's Press.

Wechsler, H., G. W. Dowdall, G. Maenner, J. Gelhill-Hoyt, and H. Lee. 1998. Changes in binge drinking and related problems among American college students between 1993 and 1997. *Journal of American College Health* 47(2): 57–69.

Weiss, Karen G. 2009a. Boys will be boys and other gendered accounts: An exploration of victim excuses and justifications for unwanted sexual contact and coercion. *Violence against Women* 15(7): 810–34.

———. 2009b. Blaming the victims. Rape myths. Victim facilitation. In *The Praeger handbook of victimology*, edited by Janet Wilson. Santa Barbara, CA: Praeger.

———. 2010a. Too ashamed to report: Deconstructing the shame of sexual victimization. *Feminist Criminology* 5(3): 286–310.

———. 2010b. Male sexual victimization: An exploration of men's experiences and perceptions. *Men and Masculinities* 12(3): 275–98.

———. 2011. Neutralizing sexual victimization: A typology of victims' non-reporting accounts. *Theoretical Criminology* 15: 445–67.

Weiss, Karen G., and Corey J. Colyer. 2010. Roofies, mickies and cautionary tales: Examining the persistence of the "date rape drug" crime narrative. *Deviant Behavior* 31: 348–79.

Weitzman, Elissa R., Toben F. Nelson, Hang Lee, and Henry Wechsler. 2004. Reducing drinking and related harms in college: An evaluation of the "A Matter of Degree" program. *American Journal of Preventive Medicine* 27(3): 187–96.

Wieberg, Steven, Jodi Upton, and Steven Berkowitz. 2012. Texas athletics overwhelm rivals in revenue and spending. *USA Today*, May 15.

Wilkins, Emily. 2012. Cities look at Tucson's tags to silence loud parties. New York Times Student Journalism Institute. January 13. Retrieved from tucson12 /nytimes-institute.com.

Wilkinson, Deanna L. 2009. *Event dynamics and the roles of third parties in urban youth violence.* Final report submitted to the National Institute of Justice. Retrieved from www.ncjrs.gov/pdffiles1/nij/grants/227781.pdf.

Wilkinson, Deanna L. 2007. Local social ties and willingness to intervene: Textured views among violent urban youth of neighborhood social control dynamics and situations. *Justice Quarterly* 24: 185–220.

Wilson, Robin. 2008. Despite alcohol crackdown, the party goes on. *Chronicle of Higher Education* 55 (December 5): A1.

Woldoff, Rachael A., and Karen G. Weiss. 2010. Stop snitchin': Exploring definitions of the snitch and implications for urban, black communities. *Journal of Criminal Justice and Popular Culture* 17(1): 184–223.

Zack, Harold. 2011. Pittsburgh man, others attacked in traffic after weekend game. September 30. *Charleston Daily Mail*, September 26. Retrieved from www.dailymail .com/News/201109262726.

Index

academics, xxi

academic student organizations, 45–46, 169, 205n6

Adderall, 42, 193

alcohol, 14–17, 57–61, 92–93, 135, 192–93; and aggression, 81, 91; cost of, 58, 143, 206n5; deaths caused by, 20, 203n7; "drinking until you drop," 55, 56–57, 59–60, 72; and drug use, 19, 41; efforts to curb consumption of, 138, 140–43, 145; frequency of consumption, 40, 43, 164, 205n3; majority of party school students drink, 15, 22, 39, 52, 133, 146; and minimum drinking age laws, 15, 40–41, 44, 48, 142, 202n1, 205n8; and party routines, 11, 55–57, 164; prevalence at party schools of, xv, 36, 39–41, 133, 137–38, 146; and "responsible drinking," 10, 143, 145, 180; and sports, xvi, 17, 46, 134, 137; statistics on consumption of, 15–16, 39–41, 164, 166; student conduct codes on, 30–31, 189. *See also* binge drinking; intoxication; party rituals; underage drinking

Alcoholics Anonymous, 95–96, 208n19

alumni, 17, 136, 137, 203n3

American College Town, The (Gumprecht), 7

Amethyst Initiative, 142

Animal House Laws, 10, 144–45, 209n2

arrests for liquor and drug violations, 21, 36, 94–96, 203n10, 208n18

arson, 34–35, 204n8. *See also* couch burning

athletics. *See* sports

attacks. *See* physical attacks

Becker, Howard, xx

Beer and Circus (Sperber), xvi

beer pong, 58, 59, 61

Binge (Seaman), 20

binge drinking, xiii, 19, 55–57, 142, 143; and college attrition, 19, 203n6; and criminal misconduct, 20–21, 91; criteria for measuring, 204–5n2; getting wasted as goal of, xvii, 16, 56–57, 72, 134, 142; physical harms from, 19–20, 23; profile of participants in, 16–17; socialization in, xix–xx; statistics on, 39–40, 164; and victimization, 20, 23. *See also* alcohol; intoxication; party rituals

blacking out, 65–66, 85, 134, 170

bonding with peers, 19, 38, 63, 64, 136

bonging, 56, 206n3

burglary, 11, 74–75, 80, 115, 206n2, 206n5; statistics on, 33, 74, 173–75, 202n16; in student neighborhoods, 75, 206n3

bystander effect, 70

Campus Crime Victimization Survey (CCVS), xxiv–xxv, 38, 73–74, 151, 206n1; data collection from, 151–56, 209n2

capable guardians, 69, 73, 80; absence of, xviii, 75, 79, 87, 135

class rank, 43–44, 156, 163, 168, 205n7

Clery Act, 12, 36, 202n13

Clery statistics, 12–13, 73, 202nn14–16, 206n1

cocaine, 41, 42, 193

college towns, 7–10, 201–2n8; geographically isolated, xv, 3, 8, 27; housing in, 8–9, 32, 39; income level of, 32, 204n4; party schools and, 9–10, 32, 38; in rural areas, 4, 31–32; as transient places, 7–8, 11. *See also* student neighborhoods

collegiates, xxi

complainers, 127–30, 131

couch burning, 35, 62–63, 136, 144, 209n1

crime, xix, 10–13, 14, 91–93, 101, 115, 173–75; and gender differences, 80, 81, 177; at hot spots, xix, 73, 86, 90–92, 98, 135; off-campus, 12, 78, 84; and partying, 13, 21, 72, 85–88, 89–91, 111, 132, 135, 206n5; statistics on, 11, 12–13, 21, 33–37, 73, 130, 197, 198, 202nn15–16, 206n1; strategies to reduce, 9, 139, 143–45; violent, 11, 33, 80–81, 197, 198. *See also* intoxication crimes; nonreporting of crimes and incidents; victimization

Daily Beast party school list, xv

differential association and reinforcement, xix

disciplinary actions for liquor and drug violations, 12, 21, 35, 94–95; definitions of, 203n10, 208n18; number of cases,

21, 36; student conduct codes on, 29–30, 186–90

drinking age, 15, 40–41, 44, 48, 202n1, 205n8; efforts to lower, 142. *See also* underage drinking

Drug-Free Schools and Communities Act, 191

drug use, 14, 17–19, 23, 41–42, 193; alcohol and, 19, 41; arrests and citations for, 21, 36, 94, 95, 135, 203n10; athletes and, 18–19, 203n5; extreme partiers and, 53, 167; at fraternities and sororities, 18, 46; gender differences in, 42, 165–67; statistics on, 17–18, 22, 42, 52, 165, 166, 167; student conduct codes on, 30, 189

drunk driving, 19–20, 93–94, 100, 104, 135, 170, 207n16

dry events, 141

Dying to Drink (Wechsler and Wuethrich), 9

ecstasy, 42, 69, 71, 193

extreme partying, xix–xx, 53, 94, 133, 146; amount of alcohol consumed in, 55–57, 164; athletics and, 46, 134; and crime, 135, 206n5; drinking until you drop during, 55, 56–57, 59–60, 72; in fraternities and sororities, 46, 134; negative consequences of, 65–66, 114, 147; party subculture and, xxi–xxii, 50–51, 53, 54; profile of participants in, 43–44, 134; risks in, 67–68, 70, 134, 147; and studying, 45, 47, 48, 134, 205n7; and victimization, 79, 98. *See also* binge drinking; party rituals

faculty, 6–7, 28, 29, 139; housing for, 8–9, 206n4

fights, 11, 33–34, 80–84, 115, 134, 173–75;

alcohol and, 81, 82; at bars and sports events, 82–84; injuries from, 34, 80, 83; men and, 81, 82, 83, 120–21, 207n7, 207n9; women and, 82, 121, 207nn9–10

financial obligations of students, xvi, 39, 46, 169

flip cup, 58, 61, 206n6

football games, 6, 34–35, 83–84, 109–14; police at, 6, 28–29, 111–13; post-game rituals, 61–65; pregaming before, 57–60; and tailgating, 28–29, 60–61, 136, 137. *See also* sports

fraternities and sororities, 64, 85–86; alumni from, 17, 203n3; drug use at, 18, 46; and extreme partying, 16–17, 46, 59, 134; at party schools, xvi, 27, 39; regulation of, 17, 202–3n2

Frostburg State University, 10, 143

gender differences: and crime, 80, 81, 177; and drinking, 16, 40, 66, 164, 166, 171–72; and drug use, 42, 95, 165, 166; and fighting, 82, 207n9; and illness, 68; and partier types, 43, 167, 168

getting wasted. *See* intoxication

grade point average (GPA), 19, 39, 45, 163, 204n1

Gumprecht, Blake, 7, 8, 31, 145, 201n8

hazing, 29, 182–83, 193–94

"hooking up," 87, 207n14

hospitalization, 20, 80, 137; from fights, 34, 83; from injuries, 68–69, 71, 80

hot spots, xix, 98, 135; for attacks and fights, 80–81, 83; bars and parties as, 73, 80, 83–84, 90–92; for property crime, 79–80; for sexual crimes, 86, 90–92; student neighborhoods as, 75, 76, 206n3

house parties, 59, 68, 144, 205n8, 207n7; rapes at, 85, 86–87

housing, 48, 75; in college towns, 8–9, 32, 39. *See also* student neighborhoods

illness from alcohol and drugs, 132; from extreme partying, 65, 66–67

injuries, 122, 132; from extreme partying, 65, 67–68; from fighting, 34, 80, 83; hospitalization from, 68–69, 71, 80

intoxication: and aggression, 81, 82, 89, 90, 91; blackouts from, 65–66, 85, 134, 170; consequences of, 36, 67–68, 71–72, 132, 170, 171–72; and crime victimization, xviii, 20, 23, 73, 85, 87, 88, 89, 90; and criminal misconduct, 20–21, 85, 91, 92–93, 135; and drunk driving, 19–20, 93–94, 100, 104, 135, 170, 207n16; as excuse, 87, 88, 121, 126–27; as goal, xvii, 15–16, 56–57, 59–60, 72, 134, 142; lowering of inhibitions by, xvii, 81, 121; management of, xx, 57, 69–70, 124; minimization of harms from, 124, 142; routine activities theory on, xviii–xix. *See also* alcohol; binge drinking

intoxication crimes, xviii, 12, 33–34, 37, 73, 97–98, 130–31; statistics on, 20 21

jobs, students with, xvi, 39, 45, 205n5

land-grant universities, 4, 28, 31–32, 201–2n8

larceny theft, 78–79, 80, 115, 134, 173–75, 206n2

littering, 101–2, 106, 135

LSD, 41, 193

marijuana, 36, 41–42, 57; extreme partiers and, 43, 53, 133; statistics on use of, 18,

22, 166; in student conduct codes, 30, 189

medical amnesty policy, 122–23, 140

murder, 12, 33, 197, 198

National Center for Education Statistics, 11, 21

Newark, Del., 9, 33, 145, 204n7

Newsweek party school list, xv

noise disturbances, 32, 100, 102–3, 106, 135; citations for, 119, 144–45

nonreporting of crimes and incidents, 70–71, 113, 120, 124, 130–31, 136; of burglary, 115, 176; of fights and attacks, 115, 176; of rape, 87, 115, 176; of unwanted sexual contact, 90, 125, 176; of vandalism, 78, 115, 176. *See also* rationalizations of party subculture

normalization of crime, 35, 115, 123–24, 132; condemning complainers, 127–30; making excuses for, 126–27; minimizing harm from, 124–26

nuisance problems and behaviors, xiv, 99–100, 110, 113, 138, 179, 190; labeling party houses for, 10, 144–45; nonreporting of, 116, 119–20, 130; in student neighborhoods, 32, 99, 100–109, 114. *See also* secondhand harms

partier identity, 38, 49–52, 54

partier justice, 81

partier types, 42–48, 82, 167–72, 176–77

partying as a right or entitlement, 41, 96–97, 98, 130, 142, 147

party rituals, 146; couch burning, 35, 62–63, 136, 144, 209n1; crimes during, 79–80, 89–91, 97–98; drinking games, 38, 54, 57, 60, 134, 138; in extreme partying, 60–61, 72, 132, 145, 205n8; fighting and, 82–84; group bonding, 19,

136; party subculture and, 38, 54, 134; post-game, 61–65; pregaming, 57–60; tailgating, 28–29, 60–61, 136, 137

party school characteristics: centrality of alcohol, xv, 36, 39–41, 133, 137–38, 146; centrality of Greek life, xv, xvi, 27; public or state university, xv, 3, 27; residential university in college town, xv, 3, 22–23, 27, 38; sports program, xvi, 27, 29; traditional students, xvi, 15, 38, 39

party school label and image, 63, 68; administrators' approach to, 137, 138; definition, xiv–xvi; efforts to modify image, 139–40; as fun, xvii, 132; as marketing tool, 52, 53, 136, 137; national ranking list, xiii, xiv–xv, 39; positive and negative perceptions of, xv, 49–50, 51, 179

party school strategies and measures, 140, 145–46, 147; for controlling partying on campus, 10, 144–45, 146, 147; for crime control, 9, 139, 143–44; for curbing alcohol consumption, 138, 140–43, 145; for medical amnesty, 122–23, 140; for modifying marketing of school, 139–40

party subculture: centrality at party schools, xiv, xxii; defining, xxi–xxii; drinking rituals, 38, 54, 57, 60, 134, 138; and extreme partying, xxi–xxii, 50–51, 53, 54; harms caused by, 66–68, 72, 78, 98, 99, 106, 124–26, 135; identification with, 46, 49–50, 132–33; nonstudent residents and, 9–10, 107–8, 125–26, 147; normativity of, 124–26, 147; and police, 116–17, 136; pranks in, 63–65; risk in, xxii, 37, 65, 91; socialization into, 44, 56, 69–70, 134; strategies for changing, 145–46; and student neighborhoods, 75, 100–101, 104–5, 108–9, 147; and studying, xv, xxi, xxii, 38, 45, 46, 47, 48, 134; transitory commitment to, 46–48, 47, 52, 109, 134; and victimization, 91, 110–11. *See also* rationalizations of party subculture

peer groups, 13, 17, 18–19, 63, 133; loyalty to, 71, 113, 114, 120, 130, 146; and socialization, xix–xx, 125, 134

Pennsylvania State University, 5, 22, 204n6

pharmaceutical drugs, 42, 166, 193

physical attacks, 80–81, 115, 173–75. *See also* fights

police, 83–84, 139; arrests and citations by, 21, 36, 94, 95, 119, 135, 144–45, 203n10; campus, 6, 29, 36, 201nn6–7; as ineffective, 115–19, 130, 136; non-partiers' view of, 105–6, 117; partiers' view of, 96–97, 116–19; as soft on student misconduct, 112–13, 130, 209n5; at sporting events, 6, 29, 111–13. *See also* nonreporting of crimes and incidents

pranks, 63–65

pregaming, 57–60

Princeton Review party school list, xiii, xv, xvii, 3, 39, 203n7

prohibition of alcohol, 141, 142, 143

property crime: in student neighborhoods, 75, 76, 124; statistics on, 11, 33, 198, 204; victimization, 74–80

property disruption, 21, 101, 114, 115

rape, 72, 84–88, 134; alcohol and drugs and, 11, 85, 87; blaming victims for, 87–88, 129–30, 207n15; nonreporting of, 87, 115; statistics on, 33, 83–84, 173–75

rational choice, xvii, 94, 119

rationalizations of party subculture, xxviii, 133, 147; condemnation of

complainers, 124, 127–30, 131; making excuses, 88, 126–27, 131; minimization of harm, xxiii, xxvii, 68, 70, 114, 123–26, 130, 131, 142; normalization of crime, 115, 123–24; police as ineffective, 115–19, 130, 136; as private matter, 115, 120–22, 136, 137

Revised Campus Crime Victimization Survey (CCVSr), xxv, 156–57

risks, xviii, xx, 79; from extreme partying, 67–68, 70, 134; of illness and injury, 65–72; in party subculture, xxiii, 37, 65, 91, 147. *See also* victimization

Ritalin, 42, 193

rituals, 54, 205n1. *See also* party rituals

rohyphnol, 207n12

routine activities theory, xviii–xix, 79–80, 135

Seaman, Barrett, 20, 58

secondhand harms, 21–22, 99, 114, 115, 116, 131, 135, 208n1; during sporting events, 109–14; in student neighborhoods, 100–109

sexual assault, 11, 20–21, 70, 115, 183, 190. *See also* rape; unwanted sexual contact

situational normativity, xiv, xxii–xxiii, 104, 107; and extreme partying, 136, 145

social bond theory, 17, 45

social learning theory, xix–xx, 142

social norms approach, 145–46, 209n3

Sperber, Murray, 138

sports, 31; and alcohol, xvi, 17, 46, 134, 137; athletes as celebrities, 6, 19; and drug use, 18–19, 203n5; at party schools, xvi, 27, 29; profitability of, 5, 6–7, 201n5. *See also* football games

student conduct codes, 29–31, 35, 140, 144, 181–91, 203–4nn2–3 student neighborhoods, 8–9; crime in, 9, 75; littering in, 101–2; noise disturbances in, 32, 100, 102–3, 106, 119; nonstudents living in, 9–10, 106–8, 125–26, 147; nuisance problems in, 32, 99, 100–109, 114; as party subculture epicenter, 75, 100–101, 104–5, 108–9, 147; verbal harassment in, 100, 103–4. *See also* college towns

studying, 47, 48, 134; partying as detriment to, xxi, 38, 205n7; statistics on, 45, 46

subcultural theory, xx–xxii. *See also* party subculture

tailgating, 28–29, 60–61, 136, 137

This American Life, 22

traditional students, xvi, 15, 38, 44

tuition costs, 5, 201n4, 202n9

underage drinking, xx, 48, 105, 120, 121, 122, 130; police citations for, 36, 94, 95–96, 117–18, 119; prevalence of, 40–41, 121; proposals for changing laws, 123, 135, 142, 143; student conduct codes on, 30–31, 35, 135, 189. *See also* drinking age

universities and colleges, 3–6, 13, 146–47, 201n1; enrollment at, 3–4, 28; geography of, 4, 201n3; marketing and promotion of, 5, 52, 136, 137–38, 139–40; public or state, xv, 4–5, 27, 201n2; residential schools, xv, 11, 14, 22–23, 27; tuition at, 5, 201n4, 202n9. *See also* college towns

University of Arizona, 10, 144

University of Delaware, 9, 10, 143, 145, 204n6

University of Rhode Island, 10, 144

University of Virginia, 209n3

unprotected sex, 71–72

unwanted sexual contact, 88–92, 125, 173–75

urination in public, 9, 22, 99, 190

vandalism, 11, 76–78, 80, 100, 190, 206n2; nonreporting of, 78, 115; statistics on, 76, 173–75

Vander Ven, Thomas, xx, 57

verbal harassment, 125, 135, 208n2; student conduct codes on, 182, 184, 190; in student neighborhoods, 100, 103–4

victimization, 115, 132, 134, 176, 177, 178; binge drinking, 20, 23; blaming victims for, 87–88, 128–30, 207n15; characteristics of victims, 163, 168; extreme partying and, 79, 98; at hot spots, xix, 73, 75, 76, 80, 83, 84, 86, 90–92, 98, 135, 206n3; intoxication and, xviii, 11–12, 20, 23, 73, 85, 87, 88, 89, 90; party subculture and, 91, 110–11; in property crimes, 74–80; in sexual crimes, 84–91; in violent crimes, 80–84. *See also* crime

Virginia Tech, 11, 202n11

vomiting, 66–67, 77, 99, 102, 110

Wechsler, Henry, 9, 17, 143

witnesses, 33, 81, 91–92, 110–11, 120, 130; at bars or parties, 70, 79; and intoxication, xviii–xix. *See also* nonreporting of crimes and incidents

women, 68; and alcohol consumption, 40, 55, 92, 204–5n2, 206n2; and fights, 82, 121, 207n10; and sexual crimes, 84, 87–88, 129–30, 207n15. *See also* gender differences; rape; unwanted sexual contact